REDEMPTION ROAD

REDEMPTION ROAD

A thug's journey towards enlightenment

LUKE KENNEDY

A Gelding Street Press book
An imprint of Rockpool Publishing
PO Box 252
Summer Hill
NSW 2130
Australia

www.geldingstreetpress.com

Originally published in 2014 as *Stabbed Ego* by Daniel Press.

This edition published in 2022 by Rockpool Publishing.

ISBN: 9781922579232

Edited by Lisa Macken
Design by Sara Lindberg, Rockpool Publishing

A catalogue record for this book is available from the National Library of Australia

Printed in Australia by IVE
10 9 8 7 6 5 4 3

PROLOGUE

'I think it's a punctured lung. Who did this to you?'

The paramedic looked hard into my flickering eyes. As I lay dying in the back of a screaming ambulance my main concerns should have been about life and death, but although I did want to live it wasn't because I loved life but because I wanted to be around to hear the story of my survival. Life wasn't as important to me as my ego.

This was all just a popularity contest: the fights, the crews and the graffiti were all just tools to be talked about, to be heard, to be seen – that was my life. To be stabbed and survive in my crazy world was a badge of honour. It was a story that would, of course, be spoken about.

My father had always told me that the smart ones go unheard. I grew up believing that, but the feelings I gained from this popularity contest – a contest I felt I was winning – were unmatched.

The sirens of the ambulance were blaring and its horn beeping, and I was struggling to stay alive with a gaping wound across my back. I desperately wondered how I got to this point. My knife-wielding opponent was not the attacker; it had been an act of self-defence. He'd been defending himself against an ego-driven, menacing thug who was intent on hurting him.

That thug was me.

My breaths were getting shorter from my pierced lung. I closed my eyes . . .

CONTENTS

INTRODUCTION

'Identification with your mind creates an opaque screen of concepts, labels, images, words, judgments, and definitions that block all true relationship.'

– Eckhart Tolle, *The Power of Now*

This is the story of my life, a life that throughout my teenage years and early manhood repeatedly placed me in situations in which my ego got me close to being killed. I was kicked out of school when I was 15, and out of school and with nothing to do I got caught up in the world of graffiti and became a writer. From there I became a fighter, and from there I became a violent thug and alcoholic.

Apart from painting, alcohol, drugs and fighting were the only things that silenced my frantic mind. I had no sense of achievement in life so I searched for outer sources to make me feel good. Those outer sources did make me feel good – for a short time.

My mind was full of incessant worry: about the past and the future, about what people thought of me or would think of me. When your mind is full of thoughts like these it can create a false identity, and this false identity is your ego. It's how you see yourself, and it's attached to all the labels your ego believes are important to your identity. It's that voice in your head, the cause of your pain, and it's in love with the labels you believe to be 'you'.

In my case the labels my ego held most dear were 'fighter' and 'leader'. In honour of these labels I came close to killing many times and was nearly killed by other people, but the labels did nothing more than enhance my fake mind-made self. This mind-made self would even make me speak differently depending on the environment I was in.

There is a second part to my story when, step by step, inch by inch, I learned how to quell those thoughts, release those labels and be (almost) free of my destructive ego and on a journey back to peace.

I searched for a long time and came across many different books that put me on a path away from violence. At the start, when I listened to different audios or watched videos online or read books I'd tend to drift off and doubt it was all worth it. It was. My success is the result of constant improvement via personal development, self-exploration, changing my environments, understanding and feeling past traumas and now having the ability to learn from my mistakes – even though I still make them.

There's an endless amount of modalities for change, some of which worked for me and some of which didn't. If you don't explore any of them, though, you'll remain trapped in circumstance and the past. At the start I did all the feel-good stuff that helped me make some good shifts in my life, but it wasn't until much later in my developmental stage that I stopped looking beyond myself and actually turned back in on myself, and felt the pain and trauma that I had spent many unconscious years trying to avoid. This is what brought the biggest breakthroughs.

The forever crazy and doubtful mind will want to shy away from making changes because they can be hard, extremely hard. Often, as well, when first making changes there are few results and the mind will have you thinking it's a waste of time, but changing your life for the better is a process. In this book you'll get a personal insight into my process.

While reading my story you'll probably notice similarities in your own thinking, and realising your habitual and looping thinking patterns is the first step towards releasing them. I'll also describe and explain many things I'm not proud of to show you that no matter how deep down in a hole you are, like me you too can get out. After all, we all tend to have regrets about the past or anxiety about the future and our minds make matters worse, wanting to feel alive by causing angst, but when we become aware and truly grasp that the present moment is the only thing that's real, anxiety is diminished and all that remains is lightness.

Sit for a moment and look around: is everything okay? Nothing bad is happening. Whenever you feel worried or scared, stop and take a second: is the present moment worthy of such a feeling? Most times it's not – our mind has just made up different scenarios to warrant such fear.

When something negative is happening in the present moment know that it will soon be in the past. Stop your mind for a few minutes and attempt to get a glimpse into this exact moment. Such a glimpse will open doors to pure bliss.

I get my high now by seeing others or myself succeeding at a goal. Striving for a positive victory and hitting the mark gives me 10 times the rush of any alcohol I consumed or trains I painted. I feel happiest when my mind is at ease. Free from heavy thoughts, I catch myself smiling now for nothing other than a clear head space. I'm a man in his mid-30s and the incessant loudness of the past has shifted to keeping things simple. I used to believe that being a tough fighter with a life of drama meant strength but it couldn't have been further from the truth, because real strength comes with calmness, presence and simplicity. My past understanding of simplicity was that it equalled a lack of something, weakness or living in scarcity.

When I used to hear someone say 'I don't want all that, I just want a simple life,' I thought they were copping out and had no drive. I've now experienced the opposite and truly believe in it. Living a simple life comes with an abundance of self-knowledge that allows you to understand where you stand and simply stay strong. It's a bit of a paradox, because it takes a lot of work to live simply. You have to siphon through the bullshit you don't want or deserve and work through past conditioning that confuses what you want out of life. I'll say it again: *there's strength in simplicity.*

It's keeping your circle small but solid. Living simply is throwing away or ceasing the chase of material things that are choking your space. Simplicity is knowing your boundaries and simply releasing people or things that aren't aligned. It's knowing your worth and not accepting anything else. It's being in your body and not your head: grounded, present. It's knowing your purpose and not getting pushed off course by social pressures to be something different. It's narrowing down your life to things that truly matter.

That's strength: simplicity.

Looking back at all these little things that led to the present, it's comforting to know that where I am as a person is where I am meant to be. I was definitely looked after by a higher source, and you'll get the same belief once you read through my story.

In this book I'll show you how I came to be me, free of my destructive ego and free of the labels that limited me. This book alone may not be capable of instantly changing you, but it will help. As someone once said to me, 'Constant dropping wears the stone' or, in other words, 'Many small changes make a big difference.'

CHAPTER 1

BORN PURE

Liverpool Hospital in Sydney's Western Suburbs was the setting for this boy's arrival; 1985 was the year. An extra second had been added to the calendar year, but to Rube and Diane Kennedy the only addition that counted was that of their new boy. I'm the middle child of three. Ruben, my brother, is three years older and my sister Sarah is a year younger. We might have had an older brother, Daniel, but he died just after he was born.

My parents grew up in the western Sydney suburb of Miller. Dad was the youngest of four kids and my mother was one of five. Growing up was tough for Dad. His mother, Wilma, with whom I later became extremely close, was your typical Australian battler: she never had any money but would do anything for her family.

My mum is an incredibly kind lady with a laugh that's recognisable in any crowd, and she's adored by everybody I introduce her to. Mum's parents are two people I cherish spending time with, as they make me smile when I sit and watch them talk. Elderly people tend to appreciate each moment more, and their presence in the moment can be felt by those around them – if those around them are present enough to witness.

Mum and Dad grew up together and soon fell in love. Dad was a champion rugby league player and dreamed of playing professionally. He showed plenty of heart in all of his games, and even made it into reserve grade. Dad was one step away from achieving his lifelong dream when Mum got pregnant with Daniel and life was set. Daniel was born on 6 April 1982 at Liverpool Hospital. From the outset he had to battle for his little life, but at just 10 days old he tragically died from the complications of his birth. Daniel's death left a huge hole in my parents' hearts. Losing their firstborn was a struggle, and 40 years later Mum still gets tearful when speaking about Daniel. Dad gave up football to be there for Mum and never played again.

When I was aged two Mum and Dad moved us into a Housing Commission townhouse in Belmont Street in Alexandria, a 10-minute drive from Sydney's central business district. I'm thankful I lived in Alexandria as a little kid, as I had a heap of friends and Mum and Dad would regularly take us on outings to local restaurants or parks. Even though my parents struggled from time to time for money we never missed out on anything. We loved heading to the neighbouring suburb of Newtown with its long strip of shops and cafes and all kinds of people: artists, Goths, ravers, pub goers and musicians.

I was just six when I found a can of spray paint and wrote some harsh words on a wall near my house. On our way to school in the mornings we'd drive past the wall and I'd look away in shame, hoping my parents wouldn't see it and suspect me. Little did I know that spray painting on walls would later not only become my obsession but would dominate my life, resulting in violence, injury, gaol time, friends' deaths and, very nearly, my own death.

Dad took up boxing training. I was always told by his friends that as he grew up he could really handle himself on the streets and was known to be a good fighter. He was not a bully, but a man who'd stand up for himself and his friends. Dad won his first few amateur bouts, as all those who knew him expected he would – at 30 years of age he was the fittest he'd been in his whole life. Sometimes I'd be allowed to go to his fights to cheer him on. As I watched him fight I could see his confidence. He always held his ground, never stepping back from his opponent and throwing big punches that made him the easy winner. Dad was our hero. We'd go to school and tell all our friends about our warrior father who'd just slaughtered yet another opponent.

When we couldn't attend the fights we'd stay at Grandma's green fibro home back in Miller, where we'd wait impatiently to hear the outcome of the fight. When the phone finally rang we'd listen for Grandma's excited cry of 'You beauty!' Grandma was very proud of Dad and always told us what a great man we had for a father. That I knew.

I loved staying at Grandma's: she and I were really close. When I wasn't with her she'd ring and ask for me and we'd speak for hours. Often she'd call me after she'd had a few drinks, and I'd sit and listen to her cry and talk about the past. Without knowing it for the first 35 years of my life, that relationship with my grandma during my conditioning years from birth to the age of seven, with what I heard, felt and witnessed, impacted me in ways that prevented me from opening my heart to unconditional love.

It must have been hard for Grandma living by herself, sitting with her thoughts and bottles of beer. I still cry now thinking about my poor grandma.

CHAPTER 2

I LOVED THE HYPE

When I was seven years old we moved to Hurstville in Sydney's south, where I started at a new school. Dad's boxing career was progressing and he was being trained by the legendary trainer Johnny Lewis. Dad and Johnny became close, and we'd spend most weekends together.

Johnny was funny and would always crack jokes and make us kids laugh. Dad was training at the Newtown Police Citizens Youth Club, and any chance we got we'd be there watching the Spartan-like men punching the bags or, better yet, each other. The air would be filled with sweaty vapour and the mirrors fogging up as some young hopefuls shadow-sparred their reflections. We'd sit watching, amazed at how strong they were.

'Luke, come on, your turn,' Johnny would call out, snapping me out of my trance.

Reluctantly I'd make my way into the ring. Waiting with a smile on his face, Johnny would then put me through my paces on the pads. I was eight years old and overweight, so I didn't last too long. Johnny would comment on how hard I was punching, but then I'd look up to catch him winking and smiling at my watching father. Those times were incredible. Other kids I knew weren't close with their parents, but Dad took us everywhere and introduced us to some amazing people. I couldn't have asked for a better upbringing.

When I was 10 I travelled to Las Vegas with Dad and my brother Ruben to attend Kostya Tszyu's world title fight. Johnny was Kostya's trainer, and Dad was helping him out in the corner by siphoning water into his fighters' mouths between rounds. A couple of nights before the big fight I told Dad I wanted to be a fighter. At the local fights I'd noticed the reaction of the crowd to each blow and how excited it made them. I'd also seen Kostya's preparation for the fight and the respect people showed him. I loved the hype.

Even at the age of 10 I was interested in being respected. I could picture myself as a fighter and envisioned everybody talking about me. Maybe it wasn't respect I wanted, being a self-conscious overweight kid; it was probably more that I just wanted to be liked. I'd come to believe that fighters were in a different league to everyday civilians and were validated by all those around them, people buying them things, asking for photos and calling them 'Champ' and having beautiful women hanging off them.

I suppose being liked and validated for whatever reason was something I wanted to feel – I wanted to feel good about myself. As a kid and even as an unaware adult the desire for validation from outside sources can become addictive, because for brief moments your internal lack of self-worth is not felt and is forgotten about. However, the external feel-good validation is short lived: it's surface level and results in an addiction to the outside source and an eternal chasing of the validation tail.

The day before the fight our group went for a walk. We stopped to get photos in front of the huge MGM lion that stood at the entrance to the MGM Grand Hotel. As we walked down the strip after taking the photos Dad asked me to repeat to Johnny what I'd told him the night before. I was embarrassed.

I didn't want to tell Johnny. I didn't want to look like an idiot, because the fact was I was obese. I was so ashamed about my stomach and big chest I rarely took off my shirt, which meant missing out on school camps, swimming carnivals and beach trips. Terrified of people seeing my bare body, I couldn't sleep from the worry. Even at that young age I cared deeply about what other people thought: I told myself that if they thought I was a fat loser then I was a fat loser.

As an overweight kid I held in a lot of the worrying emotions. I laughed along with the jokes made about my weight and had begun to take on a role as the 'fat kid', pretending it didn't get to me. But it did get to me and it ended up deeply affecting my confidence, and it still does from time to time.

I guess I was lucky, because despite being overweight I was a popular kid and was always the leader. Even as a young child I could encourage others and persuade them to do things. I can't imagine how bad life must be for those who are overweight and bullied.

Johnny noticed my shyness and reluctance to open my mouth. 'What did you say, Luke?' he asked.

'I want to start boxing. I want to be a fighter,' I shyly whispered, hoping nobody walking past would hear. I knew Johnny was the best trainer, so I thought to myself: *even if I'm no good he'll make me good.*

'Well, mate, you know you've got to be disciplined,' Johnny said. 'You've got to run every day, train. You can't eat all those lollies.' For the entire trip Johnny had seen me eating endless packets of lollies.

'I'll do all of that, I swear!' I said.

Johnny smiled and we kept walking. Kostya won by a knockout and we went back to his room to celebrate. I was just happy to stare at the belt Kostya had won, which was spread across his bed on top of his pillows. I badly wanted that recognition.

I put the idea of becoming a boxer at the back of my mind. I wanted to do it but I was an overweight 10 year old, and there was no way I was running every day or giving up my lollies.

CHAPTER 3

THE SMART ONES GO UNHEARD

I was getting into trouble at school, as a girl had told the teachers that my friends and I were skipping class. After she told on us we never spoke another word to her. Even at the age of 10 I had it firmly in my mind that you don't inform on anyone, which had been directly and indirectly reinforced by my father. Sometimes I'd overhear him commenting on the news: 'Damn give up!' he'd say if someone spoke out about a crime they had nothing to do with. 'Luke,' he would sometimes add, 'in life you keep your mouth shut. The smart ones go unheard. The smart ones shut their mouths.'

The first week of high school was an eye-opener. I was playing football and a kid in Year 10 I hadn't seen before told me to give him the ball. It was our kick-off so I just kicked it instead and watched the ball float towards the other side of the field. Suddenly my body froze with shock: a hand was tightly gripped around my throat.

'I told you to give me the bloody ball,' the guy yelled. 'I can break your neck like a chicken's.'

I wanted to cry but held it in, remembering that I was at big school now. The kid's hands were still wrapped around my neck. 'Do you know who my brother is?' I managed to croak.

The kid let go and laughed like a tough guy. 'Who's your brother?'

'Ruben Kennedy,' I announced with a grin. Ruben was in the tougher kids' group, and judging by the petrified look on the guy's face he now had something to worry about. 'Ah, man, I just wanted to kick! You shouldn't have been a smart-arse. Sorry!'

'You weren't sorry till you knew who my brother was,' I said, walking away. 'You're finished now.'

'We'll go see him at recess,' Ruben said the next day. Ruben's friends nodded their heads.

'Make sure the teachers don't see what you do to him,' I said, a big smile on my face. I couldn't wait for my revenge on the bully.

'What do you mean what we do to him?' Ruben said. 'You're the one who's fighting him.'

That wiped the smile off my face but I hastily replaced it with another, slightly less convincing one. I didn't want the older boys to think I was scared but I hadn't been in a proper fight before, especially against someone older. I was 12 and this guy was 15 so it was only three years' difference, but at my age it was like fighting a man.

We went searching for the guy. 'Make sure you really hurt him' were the only words of inspiration I was offered. Walking to my first fight, I was almost sick with worry. When I was older I loved a street fight but not when it was planned, because my nerves would always eat me up inside and cause extreme anxiety as I contemplated the outcome. I preferred a fight that came from nothing. My mind always started with the doubts: *what if I get beaten? What if I look like I can't fight?* It was never a question of what would happen if I got hurt, because I didn't care about the pain. I cared only about what others thought. In a fight I wanted to win, not to hurt the other guy but for the validation, feelings and accolades a victory would bring.

We looked around the playground but couldn't find my opponent. It was almost time to head back to class and my nerves were fading.

'There he is!'

I squinted to see across the school grounds and there he was indeed, seated underneath a stairwell with a bunch of his friends. When he noticed us walking over I saw the spirit leave his body. He looked like a different person this time around. The day before he could have taken on the world, but today he was a person who lacked heart.

As we drew closer he stood up. I could hear whispers behind me: the boys were pumping me up. I felt alive!

I now know that this feeling was an escape from my mind, which was always arguing with itself. I later became addicted to fighting, but until recently I didn't know why. Now I do: during fights my obnoxiously echoing mind was still. Fighting brought me into the present moment completely free from thought. It was, however, just a cover, and hiding from the mind is not the solution. Releasing it is.

We stood a couple of metres away and I looked at Ruben. 'Well, go on, then,' Ruben said, as if he was disappointed I hadn't already attacked. Thinking my big brother was angry at me was all I needed. I flew at my opponent, throwing a right hand that landed flush on his cheekbone to put him straight on his backside. 'Break my neck like a chicken?' I shouted, standing over him.

The boys were going crazy, teasing my opponent. 'You got buckled! You got dropped by a kid in Year 7!' I looked at him and suddenly felt sorry. His friends didn't say a word; they just sat still with their heads down. I felt bad for them, too. What could they do? But as I walked away I was soon overcome by a feeling of satisfaction. The older boys' arms were around me and I felt like a man.

Ruben's friends ran up to other boys to boast of my win, and thanks to their praise I felt accepted. Now I was a fighter, which made me feel powerful. I justified my actions by thinking about what that kid had done to me the day before and tried to raise my spirits by telling myself that he deserved it, but I felt something deep inside. That feeling was my true soul laughing at me, and I knew I was lying to myself. It was the start of almost 10 years of the soul-ego seesaw, during which I battled between two worlds. What I felt deep down was right, my true self, but I thought I had to keep up with an image and that was my ego talking. I wanted to be liked, to be validated.

Inside my heart and soul I knew I was good enough. I loved myself, but on the outside I was a body-conscious and socially awkward kid and I hated myself. One punch had turned all of that completely around: soft and shy had mutated into arrogant, strong and confident.

Is this all it takes? I wondered.

CHAPTER 4

YOU ARE YOUR ENVIRONMENT

The next two years passed in a blur. What I remember most from that time was meeting my lifelong friend Lucas and playing sports with him on weekends. I was a terrible student, opting for skipping school and hanging out with mates or going to class only to cause trouble and act like a fool. I had terrible eyesight but wouldn't wear glasses because I was worried about what other kids would think of me, so in class I struggled to read anything the teacher wrote on the board and was easily distracted.

Caring what others thought was already badly affecting my life. I was also getting into fights and had even started to enjoy them. Fighting was a way to boost my reputation and win respect from those who didn't have my respect. Why I cared so much I didn't know.

You have to fight him. Everyone knows what he said about you, my bad thoughts would start. *Who cares what people think?* I'd try to reason. *What do you mean? You're the fighter; everybody looks up to you.* My bad thoughts always had a better argument.

I met a new kid, Mark, who had moved from another school close by. He was short and skinny and had a pimply face, and he always wore a distinctive red jacket that he loved. Mark and I hung out and became firm friends. I was in Year 9 and he was one year below me, but I gelled more with him than those my own age.

Mark got into an argument out the front of school and I watched on as he convincingly triumphed over another kid. Though Mark was tiny he would always be willing to have a go and could handle himself well, and we soon had each other's back. Mark was always doing graffiti, tagging the word 'Base' on the toilet walls and all over his books. Now that my mate Base was tagging I attempted to do it too, but I wasn't any good. I did enjoy the thrill of tagging walls, though, so I persisted.

Base and I would go to local stormwater drains to paint, which were easy spots because they were hard to see. Only occasionally would we be chased off by locals.

My tag was 'Punisher'. It was a long word and took too long to write, so Base always encouraged me to adjust it. With graffiti you have to be quick – an extra letter or two in a tag might see you being charged by the police. We were young so getting into trouble with the law meant a phone call to our parents, which for us would be worse than death but it didn't stop us. We were looking for something to do.

The 2000 Sydney Olympics were due to start in a few months, and large Olympic flags were flying high on the power poles that ran along busy roads.

'How much do you think they're worth?' I asked Base one day.

'Nothing now, but in the future: heaps!'

We decided there and then to abduct some flags for future profit. That night during a break in the traffic Base stood on my shoulders to carry out the flag nabbing. Happy with two flags, we headed home to safety. Not long after we were walking across a park when we were approached by a tall, skinny, Indian-looking man in his early 20s.

'Hey, Charlie,' Base said, walking over to shake his hand. 'This is Luke.'

'I've been seeing your tags down the drain canals. You're getting better,' Charlie said to Base. He turned back to me. 'Is this Punisher?'

I smiled. I was happy to hear that this guy knew my tag, as graffiti is all about being seen. In your mind a tag is a part of yourself. If people notice your tag you're someone of notoriety, and every time you're noticed the illusion grows. Tagging also happens when you're somewhere with a friend or family member and you engrave your names on a tree. You want to leave a mark for the future; you want something of you to last beyond you. It was all we had.

'Your tag's too long. You need to practise more before painting everywhere. It's toy.' He was right: I was a terrible tagger. I felt like an idiot and was jealous of Base because he'd just been told his tag was looking good. Mine wasn't. 'If you want to be a writer,' Charlie went on, 'show respect by not crossing out other writers. You're going to cause beef before you've even started.'

Charlie was talking about writing over other people's tags. If I saw a good spot that had been taken and I wanted to get up in the same position I'd paint over the other work. A good spot was one that could be seen by a lot of people or wouldn't get painted over for a while, so the effort was worth it. I had no idea about the rules of all this graffiti stuff but I didn't want to start off on the wrong foot.

'You want to buy an Olympic flag?' Base asked Charlie. I guess future profit would have to wait.

'Was that you little pricks on top of the pole the other night? You woke me up!'

Little pricks? I thought. I was six years younger than Charlie but 30 kilos heavier and the same height. We were young, though: I'd be 15 in a few months and Base was nearly 14.

'Who does that skinny arsehole think he is?' I said to Base as we walked away.

'That's Snap, man! He's in RM crew.'

Charlie was an established writer. I'd seen his tag, 'Snap', more than the inside of my eyelids. When I caught the train to the city I'd be amazed to see his tag in what seemed to be impossible to get to places. I thought it was so ballsy, all the spots I'd see them up. *He had to go on the train tracks to do those tags*, I thought.

'I don't care who he is,' I replied, thinking it was now even worse being called a toy since Snap knew what he was talking about.

For the next week I practised relentlessly, and my bedroom was covered in scraps of paper full of different tags and pieces. A piece is different to just a tag: it's your word in a mural form, outlined and filled in with full colour. Writers with special artistic ability would occasionally paint a character of some sort beside their work but a piece was meant to look like real art.

Mine just looked like rubbish, but the practice started to pay off. I was getting better, and on Snap's advice I decided to find a shorter word. I didn't want to put the last few months of obsessed drawing down the drain, so I looked for a word with similar lettering. While drawing outlines I searched for a new word. *Pun* . . . No, don't like it. *Punish* . . . Not a fan of the letter 'S'. *PUNCH!* I loved it. It was me, dead on. I loved to fight and the letters were perfect.

I spoke to Base about my new tag, and after he told Snap we agreed it was a good one. We were set to launch our new careers as writers.

I know how ludicrous the thought of graffiti may seem, but there's a lot more to it than some people think. Sure the main plan is to get your tag far and wide, defacing property in the process; however, to kids who think they have no hope or any form of talent to shine the politics and the adrenaline involved bring a whole new meaning to life. The sense of achievement becomes addictive, because for the first time ever you're praised by your peers. Even though most of your new-found associates are criminals, their praise feeds a mind yearning for attention.

Base and I wanted some of that attention, but if we were to succeed in our chosen field we'd need tools: paint, and lots of it. Just how we were going to get our hands on it we still didn't know.

CHAPTER 5

PICKING UP ENERGY

Base and I started hanging around the streets, hoping we'd run into Snap. One day we went into a store to buy some spray paint and there he was, standing in front of a shelf shaking cans.

'Hey, boys, you getting paint too?' he asked.

'Yeah, we're going bombing tonight,' Base said proudly.

As we picked up the different cans Snap commented on each one. 'You don't want to get that one: it doesn't cover the best. You can use these to fill your piece in,' he said, pointing to a couple of chrome colour cans. 'This one's for your background.' He was holding a nice light blue. 'I've got some Belton at home. You can use those for your outline.'

The cheaper paint was terrible to use, although the odd colour would be okay. You could get away with using crappy paint to colour in your piece or for a large background, but for the touch-up parts such as the final outline you needed a good paint brand like Belton, which was top of the range so it wouldn't drip through your piece, fail to cover properly or make uneven lines.

'You can come piece with us tomorrow night,' Snap said. 'I'm painting the wall.'

The wall was on the train lines 30 metres north of the station; years later across from it I started my first business. Two passions: one from the wrong side of the tracks and the other my ultimate quest – to help people.

Snap walked out of the store and left us with a few cans to buy. With the money we were given for lunch we could only afford one can, so we had to put the other cans back on the shelf.

'That's the sickest! We're going to piece the wall!' I said with excitement as we left the store. I'd travelled past the wall most days and now I was going to paint it.

'With what paint? We only have one can.' Base was right: we didn't have enough paint, but if we pulled out of painting the wall it would look like we were afraid.

'Should we steal it?' I said.

'Yeah, we have to!'

I hadn't expected that response. I'd never stolen anything from a shop before; to go into a store and swipe something then walk past the victim was something I didn't want to do. Growing up, I'd hear my parents' comments about thieving: they were strongly against it like any normal people would be. I recall an occasion when I was 10 and Dad and I were watching television. On a news report someone asked what you would do if you knew you were going to die in a week, and Dad turned and asked me what I would do.

I sat and thought. 'I'd rob a bank with a gun! I'd give all the money to you guys when I died. Even if I got caught, I'd only be in gaol for a little bit before I died.' I thought Dad would appreciate the fact I wanted to supply them with the earnings from my deathbed robbery.

'Yeah? What if someone else died!' Dad yelled.

I didn't know how to take that. 'What do you mean, Dad? I was the one with the week to live.'

'In the robbery! What if something went wrong with the gun and you hurt someone?'

I just sat there and kept watching the television. *What did I do wrong?* I thought. I could tell there was some other meaning behind his reaction, and I later found out that someone close to my dad had shot a man dead in a botched armed robbery.

We weren't told that story until we were almost adults. Now, standing with Base outside the store all I could think was I really want to paint, so we went back in. While I made my way back to the spray paint Base distracted the shopkeeper with a fictitious question. I stashed some cans down my shorts then, unable to breathe, I tried to casually walk past the shopkeeper. In a stupid attempt to prevent suspicion I feigned talking on my phone. I didn't want to look the woman in the eyes.

At home that night I felt ashamed of myself. I imagined the shopkeeper's disappointed look as she watched the security video and saw the polite boys who regularly greeted her in the street now stealing from her. I envisaged her sadness. I'd crossed a line I hadn't wanted to cross and saw myself as a criminal. It was a minor event with major outcomes: if I hadn't stolen that paint would I have progressed to other criminal activities? I'd been trying to impress Snap, so if I hadn't met Snap the week before would I have stolen the paint? If I hadn't met Snap would you be reading this book?

CHAPTER 6

THE GATEWAY CRIME

The next day I was charged with energy. As I sat in class I kept my head down and practised my tags on paper while the teacher talked on. *I'm painting the wall!* I thought.

Around 9 pm I snuck out through my bedroom window and met up with Base, then together we headed to Snap's house to plan the night ahead. When we knocked on the door Snap's mum yelled out in Italian (so Snap wasn't Indian after all); no doubt she was telling him to get rid of the boys on her front step.

Snap's room had three couches, a big-screen television and his bed. He was sitting on his bed preparing his bong. Two other writers I hadn't met before were there, chopping their mix up and also preparing to smoke. Between bongs they all had their heads down doing outlines on pieces of paper.

Someone handed the bong to me. 'No thanks, I don't smoke,' I said. Base said the same.

After a few hours of sitting around I began to feel pretty foggy from the fumes.

'Ah, I forgot! I gotta show you boys something!' Snap jumped up and motioned for us to follow. He opened a door to another room, inside which we were met with a painter's dream: the whole floor was covered in boxes of spray paint, the lids of the cans revealing the colours inside.

'The boys broke into a hardware store and got all this paint. Twenty dollars a box for you boys.'

We had no money, so Snap gave us a box each and told us to pay him back when we got it.

Back in Snap's room I could tell he didn't really like me. He'd cut me off with smart remarks and pay little attention to me when I spoke. He'd only known me for a couple of days so I thought it was fair enough to be treated like an outsider.

'Doin', lad?' A guy wearing shorts that looked a size too small came in, walked straight past me and shook everyone else's hand except mine.

'This is Luke,' Snap said. 'What's your tag again? Ah, that's right, Punch. This is Kon.'

Kon barely looked up. He shook my hand with a couple of fingers as though implying I wasn't worth a proper handshake. I didn't like him. He sat and spoke to Snap with attitude two words at a time in a deep voice.

'Yeah, probably.'

'Don't know.'

'Fuck it.'

'Yeah, sweet.'

Kon loosened up after half an hour. I watched countless times as he put on this same front every time he met someone new, but after a while he'd crack jokes and we'd all have a laugh.

'Boys, tonight I'll sketch up your outlines.' Snap wanted to draw up our first outline on the wall. He knew we weren't any good so he wanted to help out, or he didn't want his piece next to a couple of useless ones. Reputation was everything in this game. With Snap sketching up the outline all Base and I had to do was stick to painting inside the lines, then finish with the dark touch-up outline to give the piece its letters.

A piece is made by first drafting up the letters, and this is where you're allowed to make mistakes because you're just going to fill in over the stuff-ups anyway. You colour it in with different patterns and colours, then you take the outline can and spray the letters over all the different colours before adding the 3D shadow on your word, which produces a life-like piece of art on the wall. To finish a full-colour background is painted before the final touch-ups of your outline, when you get rid of any drips that may slide down and ruin it.

'Yeah, sweet,' we responded.

I wanted to do my own but I knew it would be good if Snap did it. I was ecstatic at having the chance to see a quality Punch on the wall. I'd be able to lie and tell everyone at school that I did it all!

'All right, I'm going.' Kon got up and shook hands, mine included.

We packed our bags tightly so the cans didn't shake and walked out of Snap's house into a warm, cloudless night full of stars – I was seeing stars anyway from sitting in that room full of fumes. It was great to be out in the fresh air, walking through a park with the smell of freshly cut grass. I looked at the others as they stared ahead, the moonlight reflecting on their glassy eyes. Not a word was spoken as we walked together. I don't know if they were nervous or just smashed from the infinite bongs their skinny bodies had inhaled.

Base and I walked with big grins on our faces from the excitement. When we reached the other side of the park we took the back streets to avoid the police. If you were a police officer and spotted five guys walking along the road with backpacks on at midnight it would be worth pulling them over. I held my breath with every car that approached, hoping it would be a civilian. Those driving at this time of night were either taxi drivers, drug dealers, drunk drivers or the people we were trying to avoid: the police.

In one of the back streets I saw a couple of old Snap tags and noticed that he didn't even take a second look at them. The presence he had as a writer was such that it was an everyday occurrence to walk past his handiwork. I knew that if my tag went unnoticed I'd probably make a comment like 'Damn, should have used a different colour!' or something lame like that to draw attention to it.

A large row of bushes and a fence stood guard in front of our target. We scratched our way through the thick shrubs and reached the steel gates that separated the real world from a graffiti writer's home – the train tracks. Snap lifted the bottom of the fence to reveal a gap he'd prepared earlier, and two of the boys crawled through.

'Your turn,' Snap whispered.

I bent down but got stuck as I attempted to push my way through.

I could hear muffled giggles coming from above; my fellow graffiti buddies thought it was hilarious. I felt like a fool. Base and Snap helped me by making the hole bigger.

The sharp rocks crunched together under my feet, the noise breaking through the still night like a brick through a clean window. *Surely people will hear us*, I thought. I started walking on my tippy toes but Snap and the two older boys cruised past me casually, not fussed by the loud crunching. They'd been on the tracks countless times.

I relaxed a little and released my breath for the first time in what felt like an hour. Base and I persisted in our stumbling and tripping, as the land's foreign surface gave way and rocks slid from under our feet. Like first timers on an ice rink, we grabbed at each other in an attempt to stay upright; it would take numerous times before we were comfortable on the surface.

As we peered north towards the next station we could see the train tracks sparkling in the limited light. Scared as I was, it was impossible to miss its beauty. Two lines of glistening silver ran for 50 metres through a man-made rock face before disappearing into the mouth of a gaping dark tunnel in the distance.

'Train!' I heard in whispered urgency.

We ran up a grassed slope towards the base of the wall. We crouched down to wait for the train to pass, and my heart was thumping and my breathing heavy. Hearing a slight hissing noise as the train made its way closer, I put my head down between my knees to lessen my chances of being spotted. The train roared past, and a huge gust of wind swept across my body.

I glanced between a gap in my arms and found the others watching it pass. The regulars to this environment were relaxed but hypnotised by and in awe of the menacing machine. As the train's back lights disappeared into the distance Snap wasted no time and stood up to begin sketching up our pieces.

Base and I stood back, mesmerised. Snap was confident and accurate with each spray. With his back to his audience and his arms moving in all directions, he composed his symphony. The can moved with his body as though he'd been born with an extra limb attached, and he turned the light, pasty blue wall into a piece of art. When he ended the draft this felonious Picasso took a few steps to his left without taking his eyes off the artwork. He then introduced Base's letters to the wall.

I placed my bag at my feet and unzipped it slowly, scanning the wall. Contemplating my colour scheme, I picked up the terracotta orange and with a pop forced its lid off, pushing out a couple of paint sprays into the air like I had noticed Snap doing earlier.

'Train!' I heard from my left.

I crouched down again but this time I kept my head up to watch the almost empty train go past; the only occupants were Chubb Security guards dressed in their conspicuous blue vests. It was an older-style train with ridges all along the side, and we writers dubbed these trains 'ridgies'.

When it was gone I started to wildly fill in my piece. Snap noticed my failing attempt and stopped his attack on the wall to casually walk over to assist me. He asked for my can and gave a step-by-step demonstration of how to vandalise. I think it's the only time I've heard a presentation that was whispered, his gentle voice contrasting with his usual hard attitude. As I heard his whisper, though, I felt that he genuinely cared.

He watched on as I attempted again. 'That's it, man! Perfect.' He smiled like a proud father watching his kid ride a bike for the first time. I'd been pretty uptight, but seeing Snap's composed manner settled me down. Snap suddenly appeared to be at peace – his face had relaxed and his shoulders had dropped as though an evil spirit had left his body, leaving behind his true self. This was the nicest he'd been to me.

Adrenaline-fuelled activities bring on camaraderie with your fellow daredevil hombres. Experiencing fear or utter elation with another person brings you together and makes you appreciative of each other. It forces you into the present moment, and you have no thoughts about the past or the future. Other people played team sports or went skydiving or paragliding to get this rush and togetherness, but we'd paint, fight and break the law to get ours.

Now it was time for the outline and I finished the 'P', then suddenly the importance of letters on the wall disappeared: I heard a branch breaking near the hole in the fence. We all looked at each other, bending our knees slowly to crouch as we turned to see what it was. My heart was actively attempting to burst out of my fat chest. *What if I get caught? Which way am I going to run?* I looked around for possible escape routes.

'All sweet,' Snap said, going back to painting. 'Must have been a possum or something.'

It's amazing to think that one moment, terrified I'd be caught, my body had seized up, my breathing became instantly shorter and my pulse suddenly started pounding, then the next second I was back to painting away in a relaxed state. Nothing in the situation had changed besides my thought process, yet my body's reactions couldn't have been more different. My two physical reactions were created by the way my mind perceived the situation. Becoming aware of how your mind controls things opens up eternal possibilities.

I finished my outline. Glad it was over, I went over to Base's to compare and was happy to see mine edged out the favourite. We were the closest of friends, but being new to the game meant there was a little competition between us. 'Good work, boys,' Snap said as he shook our hands. He grabbed my can to show us where the shadows of each letter should go.

Afterwards, mission accomplished, we walked home. I felt giddy from the adrenaline and possibly the paint fumes. I climbed back through my window to the safety of my bed and realised my clothes had prickly little things all over them from plants on the tracks. After picking them off I thought I'd be able to get some sleep, but I kept reliving the night that had been full of trepidation and other stimulating emotions. I couldn't sleep because I so badly wanted to see my piece in daylight.

Base and I skipped school the next day and met up with Snap. We shook hands, paint still on our fingertips. I could see they were as tired as me but they had a buzz to them. Once more we battled and crawled through the thick shrubs, this time to get a view of the wall. We stared, bent necked like tourists getting their first glimpse of the Sistine Chapel. I was speechless, seeing myself as a 21st-century Michelangelo, but straight away I heard a little voice in my head. *You didn't even do it! People will laugh when they find out that all you had to do was fill in between the lines.*

That voice would always creep in to cut me down to size. Even when I was happy I could feel my mind searching desperately to find something to worry about. It was as though it felt more alive when it was worried: like a ravenous stray dog creeping through a dark alley, my mind would sniff out any worry to feed on.

Snap broke the silence. 'Come back to mine, boys.' I sensed I'd passed the test and had now been accepted.

CHAPTER 7

MY FIRST BIT OF RESPECT

Base and I now spent most of our time at Snap's house, as Snap didn't work and I was rarely at school. One day Snap was all excited. 'Adrian says that if we go up to the hardware store just after his shift starts at nine we could be sweet to rack heaps of paint.'

I hated stealing; I got a sickening, nervous energy just thinking about it. As we arrived at the hardware store and headed straight for the paint section I imagined what the shopkeepers were thinking: *those dirty peasants coming into my store to steal. Do they think I'm stupid?*

At the front counter, Adrian had a worried look on his face. He glanced around the shop and signalled for us to keep our eyes out. As we walked down an aisle lined with full-length mirrors I noticed Adrian's worried look had rubbed off on me. I nodded at my reflection, wishing him luck. I hoped our impersonation of valuable customers was believable.

An older man in a store uniform watched us sceptically, but we played it cool and continued to look at hammers and screwdrivers while waiting for him to drift away. Finally, assuming our laughable parody of customers looking for a product had worked, we headed for the paint section.

'Get the fuck out.' The older employee had snuck up behind us. 'I'm sick of you bastards coming in here thinking you're clever. Piss off.'

With our miserable masquerade blown out the door, I was more than happy to leave the store. Snap, however, stood and argued with the guy.

I felt awkward and wanted to crawl into one of the toilet bowls that were on sale and die. I grabbed a swearing Snap and dragged him out.

At the front counter the worried look on Adrian's face had turned into a tremble. We headed for Kon's as fast as we could, hoping the store hadn't called the police. Not trusting many, we'd decided Adrian had set us up and were ready to hang him. We got to Kon's as he pulled up in a car.

'Hey, what's doing?' Snap asked as Kon closed the car door.

'How you doing, boys? I went up to the hardware store before. I got three cans but on my way out Adrian's boss saw me and was about to say something so I took off running.'

It turned out Adrian hadn't set us up at all. A paint store that was easy to steal from had to be kept on the hush, otherwise every writer would go there and security would be on high alert.

One afternoon I took a friend from school over to Snap's. Kon walked in and was instantly rude to the kid, just like he was to me the first time we met. Kon had a reputation to be feared; you understood that in any little argument he could stab you. He was someone you had to be careful around, as a wrong sentence or action with no harsh intention would be interpreted the wrong way and start World War III.

Kon's notoriety was compounded by the fact that his older brother Billz was the leader of their graffiti crew, RM, a crew that didn't put up with any shit. They had the unequivocal fame of being at the top of Sydney's graffiti crews and were known for fighting. Billz had hunted someone down and beaten him to near death with a crowbar. RM also had some talented writers, stretching from Sydney's inner-city suburbs to the south-west right out to the Western Suburbs. I would have done anything to be in that crew!

As we sat in Snap's room some boxing came on the television and I made a comment about one of the fighters. 'You think you can fight?' Kon asked in response to my comment.

'I go all right,' I said as I shrugged my shoulders.

'You think you can beat me?' he fired back.

Everyone stopped what they were doing to stare, anticipating my reply. Even the cloudy smoke, it seemed, stopped floating through the air to see what was about to go down. I didn't know how to respond: I didn't want to say 'Yes' and end up with a knife in me but I also didn't want to back down. The room of boys watched on.

'Don't know, I haven't seen you fight,' I said, hoping my neutral response wouldn't raise a temper. I wasn't scared of Kon; I was just trying to avoid an argument. I was hoping to be in their crew and didn't want my chances sabotaged by a meaningless altercation.

Kon sat and stared at me, the only movement in the room his fingers slowly tapping the couch's armrest.

'What about you get some boxing gloves and go across the road to the park!' one of the boys said, his words cutting through the tension and bringing some life back into the place.

'I've got gloves at home. I'll bring them tomorrow,' I said, knowing I had a good chance of beating Kon.

'Aw, it's on!' There was a buzz of energy in the room. They couldn't believe that this young kid had not only taken up the offer but enforced it. Kon giggled. I sensed he was nervous and it gave me confidence.

At home that night I practised throwing punches in front of the mirror.

Base rang. 'Lad, are you really going to fight Kon?'

'Yeah,' I laughed.

'Man, just be careful. If you bash him he might stab you.'

'I've already said I'm bringing the gloves. You coming to watch?' I asked.

'For sure, you know I'll be in your corner.'

I had to fight Kon, because in this new world I was in status was everything. To fight one of the older boys and win would boost my credibility and, hopefully, get me closer to being in the crew – depending on how Kon took the beating.

The next day I arrived at Snap's house with two sets of gloves stuffed in my backpack and was met at the door by the boys.

'Ah, he's seriously got them! He's got the gloves!'

I suppose they thought I wouldn't come, but I cared so much about other people's opinions I was prepared to once more get myself into a sticky situation.

Snap's neighbour Paps pulled me aside and congratulated me. 'Even if you get beat you're a champion for showing up.' None of them had ever spoken to me like that before.

We all walked across the road towards the park. Snap set up two milk crates for corner stools and we were ready to go. Base was behind me in my corner, and Kon was opposite with six supporters behind him.

Snap mimicked a boxing announcer and introduced the fighters. 'Standing to my right a newcomer to the game, zero fights with zero wins. In the blue corner – Punch Kennedy!' Base clapped. 'And to my left –' the other corner began cheering loudly '– with an unblemished record and would stab you anyway if he lost, in the red corner, Don't Mess With Me Kon!'

The cheering was deafening and it excited me. There's no way I would let him win.

'Just watch out, bro,' Base said.

'Ding!' Snap mimicked a bell sound to indicate the fight had started.

I walked slowly to the middle of the ring. Kon flew at me throwing big hits but I kept my cool. I threw a single straight right that had him instantly backed up. With a couple more solid shots to his head I could hear Base screaming out, ecstatic with my efforts. I couldn't hear anything coming from the other corner. I had him: I was hammering him.

At the end of the round I went back to my corner totally exhausted. I was terribly unfit and was close to spewing. After a couple of minutes' rest we were back into it, and I replicated the first round and annihilated Kon again.

The fight was over and I'd won – convincingly. I went back to my corner and Base took off my gloves. I wasn't celebrating but Base couldn't control his happiness.

I looked over at Kon seated on the milk crate. He was breathing heavily, his arms resting on his knees and his face blood red. I'd just beaten him badly as plenty watched on, and now I didn't know whether he'd accept the defeat or seek instant retribution. I waited for him to jump up and ferociously attack, pulling out a blade to get his revenge.

I walked over to him hesitantly, knelt down and attempted to make him feel better. 'Man, my head hurts. You got me with some good shots!' I said.

'Fuck, bro,' he replied. 'You flogged me.' He put his hand out and I shook it.

From that day forward I had more respect for him than I'd ever had before, and now it was my time to step up even further.

CHAPTER 8

THE LADDER

As Snap had explained when we met him there were rules in the graffiti world, rules that were enforced by fighting. Opposing crews of writers would battle it out over who got up the most on what train line and who crossed who out. Crossing someone out showed disrespect and more often than not led to a fight.

Different spots for painting trains were like the battle plans of an army general: they had to be kept secret. In some cases a certain crew would claim a train yard, and if another person or crew was found at that yard a brawl would break out.

After the fight with Kon there was a big change in the way I was treated. I'd taken a step up the ladder and the older boys now greeted me enthusiastically, but I believed I deserved more recognition. I'd overtaken a couple of guys older than me who'd become complacent towards progressing in status. I was hungry for more and wouldn't be stopped, and soon the conflict and fighting were what I relished most. Other people would solely paint and do it for fun, but for me graffiti was war.

The attitude among the older boys that I hung around with was that if you couldn't defend yourself you were less of a person. It was an attitude I'd grown up with. As a little kid I'd put on the gloves and fight Ruben or my cousins in the backyard at family barbecues while the men watched on.

After the fighting I'd overhear them talking: 'Mate, Luke goes well with the gloves on. He's tough.' It made me feel good hearing them speak like that, and their tone gave the impression they were very much impressed.

I'd soak it up. These little things, these minor spoken words, had a lasting effect on me. I wanted that adulation.

On New Year's Eve in 2000 Base's older brother Shawn convinced our parents to let us go into the city with him. Our idea was to ditch Shawn once we were out and meet up with Snap and the RM boys.

The city was loaded with drunken people everywhere, fights breaking out every 20 minutes. I was still aged just 15 and totally out of my comfort zone. Sure, I'd fought at school and in the backyard and now I'd fought and beaten Kon, but out in this real world I felt incredibly vulnerable – a slightly confident sheep among other sheep who now found himself in a pack of wolves. The violence, the heavy energy of screaming and swearing and of big grown men with half-ripped shirts and blood-grazed faces shredded away any confidence I had.

'Let's go meet the boys,' Base said, as we marched through the city. We were alone, searching for our heroes, then we spotted Snap with 20 other writers.

You could tell writers from a mile away. They were dressed in Nautica, Polo, Lacoste and Gant, short shorts, baseball caps and Nikes on their feet and arrogantly strutting. Writers like this were known as 'lads'. They weren't so common in the early 2000s, when they opted to keep a low profile so they could quietly steal and commit other crimes. Like most subcultures it later got thrashed, and pretty soon the whole of Sydney was full of so-called lads. Anything that's led by ego eventually self-destructs.

I only knew a few of the boys Snap was with. He was acting a little differently, sweating heaps and seemingly agitated. I noticed him walk off with another boy then put something into his mouth, followed by a swig of water. It was one of the first times I'd seen someone take hard drugs. Snap introduced us to the others and we were soon just kicking back on George Street.

A big guy with 'Bad attitude' spelt across his face started talking to Snap about painting trains. 'Yeah, we're going to paint it tomorrow night,' the large man said.

'You serious, Stevie? If you do, give us a call.' Snap grabbed my arm. 'Hey, Punch, this is Stevie.'

I could see sweat dripping off the big guy's eyelid. He too was off his head.

'Hi, mate.' I put out my hand. The guy just turned and walked away. I looked at Snap. I still had my lonesome hand out like a stood-up date sitting at a candlelit table waiting for company, but none was to come so I lowered my arm.

'Don't worry, Punch. He's just off his head,' Snap said, trying to make me feel better.

I kept close to Snap after that. Although I'd gained a little respect from the boys I could see it going bad at any moment. These boys were all in the same crew but Base and I weren't, so they would back each other up against us. It was good to know that Snap was there; there was no way I'd be there if he hadn't been.

I turned to my left just in time to see Snap punch another writer flush on the cheek. The guy ran off to the safety of a police officer, Snap on his heels.

'You bitch!' the RM boys screamed.

'He crossed me out, now he wants to run away?' Snap said as he ran back. He was greeted by the other boys, who congratulated him for whacking someone. They all stood more closely as if wanting to be seen in his company.

Is this all it takes? I thought as I watched on. All that had happened was that Snap's fist had met another human's face, but it had boosted his image and he stood taller. More importantly, it seemed to make other people think he was different. Of course, it depended on who you were as to whether being different was positive or negative. The crew we were in loved a fight, so they thought Snap deserved recognition. On the other hand, those walking by would have been disgusted by the violence.

In either case being different made you special, which sounded good to me.

CHAPTER 9

SMASHED

'Luke, you better not be doing that graffiti bullshit!' Dad said one morning. 'It's a dog's act to paint on someone's house in the dark while they sleep. What have they done to you?'

The word 'dog' had a strong meaning among my family and friends, as it was used to describe someone who would snitch, dob or give someone up. It was a word that wasn't thrown around lightly.

It intrigues me now that one little word – a noise that comes out of the mouth – came to be the cause of countless fights in my world back then. Like the labels we place on ourselves and others we attach different emotions to words, so describing a four-legged animal, for example, holds no evil but once your mind uses the exact same word in a new situation and gives it a new meaning then rational thinking is destroyed.

What I didn't know back then was that words can be extremely powerful; they can make a life or break one. Words we use against each other can be hugely impactful, but more so the ones we use in our day-to-day lives that go against ourselves. Each word carries a specific frequency and emotion, and if we're constantly using a specific word that emotion gets solidified in our bodies even if we think we're playing around.

If you took notice of your language and that of other people for a few days you'd be surprised by the amount of negative and limiting words we use on ourselves and those around us. They may seem innocent or funny, but they're actually casting spells.

For Dad to say he thought graffiti was a dog's act meant he really didn't like it. Dad was old school and understandably old school didn't understand or appreciate painting a word on a wall, especially if it meant coming to the attention of the law.

Dad was usually jovial, mucking around and having a laugh, but when he was serious about something you knew you'd better pull yourself into line because Dad had a bad temper. He could lose his cool at the littlest thing, turning his whole being into a wrecking ball. Dad never hit us, but just his presence and knowing what he was capable of made us not want to get on his bad side.

I'd never seen him back down from anyone. Even though he was aged almost 40 he was still ready to take on the world when his temper got the better of him. His true self would be possessed by a hungry mind that needed feeding, and that clouded his judgement. This time, I knew Dad was referring to all the scribbles in my room. Wanting to put the fire out quickly, I lied.

'No, I'm not doing graffiti, I just do outlines on paper. I like writing on paper.'

'Make us proud, Luke,' Dad said. 'Before you do anything wrong, think of your mother and me.'

In fact, I was painting every couple of nights. It was usually only Snap, Base and me but sometimes we'd have other people tag along. I was in a smaller crew with Base, Kon's cousin Dean and a few other kids. We'd hang out and paint, all striving to move up and be in RM. On our nights off we'd sit around at Snap's, and one night Base had an idea.

'Let's have a smoke,' he said, excitedly. Base had smoked weed a couple of times before but I'd never tried it, although I didn't let on. I just nodded my head in agreement.

Snap handed me the bong. Luckily I'd seen him do it before so I knew how to smoke it, but my body froze the moment the smoke went down my throat.

'Ah, Punch punched a cone!' Snap laughed. Snap's voice echoed inside my skull. I tried to play it cool and laugh it off, but I was ruined. My mind couldn't handle it: *they're all laughing at me*, I thought.

Along with Snap's, other voices started to bounce around in my head, crazy voices I hadn't heard before. I jumped up off the couch. 'Let's go!'

I said. I looked down at Base, who was as smashed as me and no doubt going through the same mind-junk I was.

Base slowly got up, and soon we were walking across the park in the pitch black. I had tunnel vision, as though I was moving through a dark, enclosed waterslide.

'Let's paint,' Base slurred, pulling a can out of his bag. I agreed, as it would be a welcome distraction from my fidgeting, loopy mind.

The next morning I looked over at Base, who was asleep on a mattress on the floor. He opened his eyes and we both laughed.

'That shit was crazy, brother!'

We walked up the street to get some breakfast and saw all of our tags from the night before. To our surprise and amusement I'd left the letter 'c' out of all of them, writing 'punh' everywhere. I'd been so far from reality I couldn't even spell my own name.

A few months had passed since Base and I had got into graffiti, and I was failing miserably at school. I had too much fun away from it. Base and I had become extremely comfortable on the train tracks and spent most nights painting and causing havoc. We'd travel the line and had it covered from Cronulla to Bondi: we were obsessed!

Any time I saw another crew's tags along our line I'd get a sick feeling low in my stomach. *They've done it to piss me off*, I'd think. This is our line. I took everything personally. It was a stretch of train tracks that ran for over 30 kilometres but I believed this was my line, and if someone else tagged it I felt as though it was done as an attack on myself.

My main man, Eckhart Tolle, explained the idea of ownership incredibly well in his book *A New Earth*:

> To 'own' something – what does it really mean? What does it mean to make something 'mine'? If you stand on a street in New York, point to a huge skyscraper and say, 'That building is mine. I own it,' you are either very wealthy or you are delusional or a liar. In any case, you are telling a story in which the thought form 'I' and the thought form 'building' merge into one. That's how the mental concept of ownership works. If everybody agrees with your story, there will be signed pieces of paper

to certify their agreement with it. You are wealthy. If nobody agrees with the story, they will send you to a psychiatrist. You are delusional, or a compulsive liar.

It is important to recognize here that the story and the thought forms that make up the story, whether people agree with it or not, have absolutely nothing to do with who you are. Even if people agree with it, it is ultimately a fiction. Many people don't realize until they are on their deathbed and everything external falls away that no thing ever had anything to do with who they are. In the proximity of death, the whole concept of ownership stands revealed as ultimately meaningless. In the last moments of their life, they then also realize that while they were looking throughout their lives for a more complete sense of self, what they were really looking for, their Being, had actually always already been there, but had been largely obscured by their identification with things, which ultimately means identification with their mind.

As I grew up I'd never had a passion worthy of my effort and had nothing I saw as my own, which I thought was a negative. Now I'd found a hobby I was desperate to excel in and I was eager to attach myself to this new way of life. I started to believe that if I got my tag everywhere I was more of a person. When I saw other writers' tags on our line it was as though they were trying to take away a part of me.

One night we broke into a factory that backed on to the train lines and stole a couple of fire extinguishers, then we stood on a bridge that crossed a road and waited for a car to come. We couldn't believe our luck: a convertible with its top down cruised to a stop at the traffic lights directly beneath us. We let rip with the extinguishers, laughing uncontrollably. Base almost dropped his. We watched as the desperate driver scrambled to get out of the way of the foam, driving forwards then backwards as his roof slowly closed, but it was already too late.

We left the bridge and went down to the tracks, giggling like a bunch of twelve year olds when suddenly Base screamed: 'Train!'

I looked to my left, where a speeding train loomed out of the darkness. It was so close I could make out the terrified look on the driver's face.

He wore glasses that sat on lonesome ears on his bald head. I wondered whether seconds before he'd had a head full of hair but lost it all as a result of this terrifying experience. A speeding train smashes most of your senses into overdrive. The flashing spotlights light up the black night just as a fresh sunrise turns night into day and the beeping horn punches you in the face. I could almost feel the blood dripping out of my ears.

I jumped off the tracks and onto a ledge, as did the others except Snap, who'd been slow to react.

Time stood still.

The bellow of the train's horn seemed to stop as I was now deaf, but my mind felt clear and I was immersed in the moment. Nothing entered my head; near death creates stillness.

Snap's skinny body was lit like a nervous performer under a spotlight. He stood static, stunned into submission. Within a split second the performer's life could have ended but luckily Base, who had a front-row seat, grabbed Snap and pulled him up to safety. The train flew past within millimetres, the force of the wind almost blowing us off the ledge. I crouched, waiting for the pressure to drop. Why did I feel so at peace as this speeding coffin approached? What had just happened?

I heard screams of elation as the sound of metal on metal faded. We all began hugging each other. Snap, close to tears, hugged Base, who had just saved his life. It had been a close call. To see someone hit by a train would have been a life-altering experience. What I didn't know then was that it would be an experience I'd eventually go through.

CHAPTER 10

WHY WAS HE SO SCARED?

Thanks to all the paint in my room Mum and Dad knew I was right into graffiti. I lied and told them I painted legally in places where we were allowed to, but they didn't believe me.

'Don't bullshit me, mate,' Dad said. 'You better not get caught doing it.'

Ruben got a full-time job in rubbish removal and moved out of home. I moved into the granny flat out the back, which meant I could sneak out more easily.

I was struggling to stay in school to get my Year 10 certificate. I'd been warned by the principal that my attendance and lack of participation were going to get me expelled, leaving me without any educational qualification. I didn't want that to happen but I didn't want to miss out on going for a paint with the boys, and the fact was that painting was a full-time, graveyard-shift job that couldn't be done unless we'd stolen our materials during the day.

Base and I caught the train to a hardware store that stocked some good-quality paints. I stood in the paint aisle with a can in my hand and glanced around; hopefully no one would notice the fat kid stick the can down the front of his pants. I still didn't like stealing as I hated the thought of being caught, not because I might get into trouble but because the staff and other witnesses would see me as a scummy little thief. I knew if I got caught stealing, especially paint, there'd be extreme consequences at home.

I was breaking the law to break the law more. While I was waiting for the right moment a huge fat guy walked over, grabbed 10 cans and walked to the next aisle. He came back in a couple of seconds empty-handed. I was still standing there holding one can as the big guy winked at me and walked away.

I finally stuffed the can down my pants, and again thinking I had a bulletproof plan by pretending to be on my phone, I made my way out of the store. Base met me halfway back to the station. The big man who'd just stuck a shelf's worth of paints down his pants approached us.

'You're Base and Punch, aren't you?'

'Who are you?' I said. We were always suspicious of any adults, suspecting them of being an undercover police officer or security guard.

'I'm Media,' he said, as he put out his hand.

Media, a grown man in his late 20s, was a big-time writer who had tags all over Sydney from his 10-year career. His reputation was strong, not only for writing but also for his unmatched ability to steal. Rumour had it that paint stores across Sydney kept his photo, hoping one day to catch him. He could steal over 10 cans at a time because his large stomach concealed them.

Media was a man we looked up to, but how did he know who we were? It was the first time I'd been recognised on the streets by another writer. I was excited to meet Media, and he seemed excited to meet us.

'I heard what happened with you and Marnz,' he said, smiling. So, that's how he knew us.

* * *

A month earlier Base and I had been on the train coming back from Cronulla when we saw a bunch of writers painting a legal wall. They would have been given permission to paint the wall either from the council or a friendly shop owner. I rarely painted legal walls: why waste the paint when doing something illegal added all that adrenaline? Such was my thought process.

We jumped off the train at the next stop and ran back to watch them painting; they were doing some really nice pieces. The writers took no notice of us. One, who wrote 'Marnz', finally noticed us and asked if we wrote. When we told him our tags he pulled a face that implied he'd never heard of us. He was about to.

'We write with Snap and Kon,' I said, name dropping.

'Kon's toy,' he said.

I was stunned: Kon and Snap were our heroes and I'd never imagined one of them being spoken about like this. I immediately called Kon, hoping he was in the area with people to help us take on these guys.

'There's someone here painting who says you're toy.'

'Well, fuckin' whack him!' Kon responded.

I was a 15-year-old kid with my 14-year-old friend. There were eight writers there in their 20s, all friends with the guy Kon was telling me to hit.

'If he touches you I'll hunt the dog down,' Kon said, as if he sensed my hesitance.

I hung up, looked at Base and shrugged my shoulders. *Here we go,* I thought. I looked back at the group, psyching myself up.

'Hey, come here!' I yelled in a threatening tone. I walked towards them, Base behind me. I wasn't confident but I was ready to take a bashing from these guys if it meant Kon knew I'd tried to back him up. It would be worth it.

Marnz turned around and must have seen death in my eyes, as he took off running. *Thank God,* I thought, as I reluctantly ran after him. I chased him towards the tracks but he ran down a steep slope and made an easy escape. I didn't really want to catch him anyway.

All his friends stood and watched. I walked over and picked up the bag of paint he'd left behind, now confident they weren't going to attack us. I felt as though I was 10 feet tall.

I rang Kon straight back. 'Hey, the bitch took off!'

'Hey, Punch got Marnz!' I heard Kon say to someone. 'So you hit him and he took off?' he asked.

'Yeah, I hit him and he ran away,' I lied, not wanting to disappoint him.

* * *

Media had obviously heard the story. 'Yeah, I heard you pulled a knife on him,' he said.

That wiped the excited look off my face. 'What do you mean: I've never pulled a knife on anybody. He just took off.'

'Well, he said you pulled a knife out. I suppose you would say something like that, though, if you took off from kids. Who cares, mate? Heaps of people have been talking about it.'

We walked off to get our train. 'Marnz is kidding, saying I pulled a knife out on him. I hate that shit,' I complained to Base, who didn't say anything. He just kept walking with a little grin on his face. 'What's up with you?' I said, intrigued.

He laughed. 'When you were about to hit him I could see his mates were gonna back him up, so I grabbed my bag and pretended I was about to pull something out.'

'You prick!' I said. 'I thought he was just scared of me!' We both laughed. We'd been severely outnumbered so it was a good result.

I thought about it on the ride home. Media was a well-known writer who'd been excited to meet us all because of the drama with Marnz. This whole graffiti thing was about fame, about being noticed. I'd been tagging for months and hadn't had a stranger approach me to ask if I was Punch. Now after one small altercation one of Sydney's best writers wanted to meet me.

It was another step up the ladder.

CHAPTER 11

MY FIRST PANEL

As usual we were sitting around in Snap's room. Kon walked in with a tall, olive-skinned man with a trim but strong build and they sat down. The new guy was clutching his right hand with his left. 'Man, it's buckled. Have to go to the hospital,' he said, without looking up. His hand looked broken. It was shaking and had bumps that weren't supposed to be there.

The guy gave off the energy of intimidation, and Kon and Snap showed him the same respect I showed them. 'Let's get you to the hospital. I'll organise a taxi, or who can we call to pick you up?' Their concern about the guy's welfare suggested this guy was pretty important to them.

I sat there silently, not knowing what to say. The usual jovial atmosphere of the room had been king hit. We heard a car horn and the guy was gone as quick as he'd arrived. 'That was Billz,' Snap said.

Billz was Kon's older brother and the leader of RM, Sydney's most notorious graffiti crew not so much for painting but for their ability to fight. *So that's how he broke his hand*, I thought, he'd just been in a fight. Judging by the way the other boys treated him, they knew what he was capable of. I always believed in first impressions, and my initial feeling about Billz was that he was a mean character.

Snap called me excitedly one day. 'Have you got paint?'

'A couple of cans, not that many.' Even though we were stealing paint we were still only getting one can at a time.

'Have you got cash?'

'Yeah, two hundred dollars I got for my birthday.'

'Sweet. We're going to Paddington to get some good paint.'

'Where are we painting?' I asked, because I was dying to know.

'There's trackwork on our line and one of the boys thinks there'll be a lay-up.'

When there was trackwork trains would be laid up for the night in different spots along the lines away from the yards. Occasionally these trains had no security because they'd only be there a couple of nights at most, and the authorities would take a punt we wouldn't find out they were there.

This was what it was all about: I was going to paint my first train! We'd spent countless nights travelling all over Sydney in the hope of finding these trains, and it looked like we'd finally found one. It would be the apex of my life to date. I'd fallen in love with trains and the violent, unrelenting manner with which they moved. Tangara trains were the newest, and their shells were sexy in their smoothness.

Writers saw trains as blank canvases. Like a ravishingly gorgeous model strutting down a catwalk a painted train strutted its stuff, to be viewed and hunted down for photos. As a train pulled into a station, like eager paparazzi outside a night club as a celebrity arrived writers would scamper around attempting to get the best shot. A piece on a train is known as a 'panel', and it was the pinnacle of a writer's efforts because it travelled so it could be seen by many. It also required courage and research to paint a train, so writers saw it as a ballsy statement.

Writers might spend many nights scoping out train yards, sometimes for no result. Eventually, they might learn the security's movements, which gave them the upper hand the next time they tried to panel. However, one successful panel would put security on high alert and prevent future visits. The disheartening feeling of being chased away halfway through a panel would be compounded by the knowledge that another crew had painted it the night before. The addiction to put paint on steel causes endless chaos – and enjoyment.

'How long do you think we'll get to paint the train?' I asked Snap. We were on the train to the city to buy paint. 'I'm going to use blue, no, orange to fill in,' I said before he could answer.

Snap laughed. 'Settle down, Punchy.'

On the way into the city we passed our tags and pieces. Each wall had its own name – the Guitar Factory, Butcher Wall – and walls that had been named after their area: Arncliffe Wall and Sydenham Wall. Writers travelled in the train's back carriage, where we'd scrawl our tags across the walls and seats. After bombing the back car we'd move to the next carriage so we were removed from the evidence.

In the city Snap and I took a short bus ride to what was a writer's utopia: a hardware store that stocked the best paint made. The store also sold a range of nibs for paint cans that created different effects. One nib would spray the paint out fast and fat, which was perfect for filling in your piece when you didn't have much time like when painting a train. Another nib would spray out thin, which we used for the outline and touch-ups. You could test each can and nib against a wall downstairs to find out how the nib worked on the can or how well it covered and/or worked with another colour. The store knew what writers wanted and every writer across Sydney wanted to buy their tools there.

Snap explained each nib to me like a tradesman tutoring his apprentice. I could barely control my nerves: this was what I'd been waiting for since I'd started writing.

That night Base, Kon, two other boys and I decided to get into position early. To get onto the tracks we jumped a brick wall and then a barbed wire fence, and to our surprise the train was already there. We ducked down and scanned the area for any orange vests. There were none, which meant the train was unmanned.

With its lights standing out against the black night, the monstrous machine appeared weightless as though it was floating on air. I was eager to rush at the angelic beast and commence my first panel, but Snap hadn't yet turned up and there was no way I'd paint without him. Anyway, it wasn't late enough. Trains were still running, so passing drivers would be able to witness our barrage.

The crunching sound of footsteps on the tracks snapped us out of our mesmerised state. We ducked down to avoid a possible sniper. *Damn, security!* I thought. We raised our heads slowly: three guys with backpacks were walking down the tracks.

'Other writers!'

The five of us crept over, keeping our heads down the whole way. My back ached from the full bag of paint I was carrying. The others watched us approach then we faced each other in a circle like businessmen in a boardroom about to start a meeting. Moments like these were dramatic. We never knew if those standing before us were friend or enemy, and it was only when we heard what they wrote that we would know whether we were in for a handshake or an explosive attack.

'What do you boys write?' Kon said in an arrogant tone, trying to sound bigger than he was.

One man spoke confidently in a deep voice that wasn't fake then, like a rehearsed choir, each member of the group spoke one after the other to inform us of their tags: Bunk, Mone and Pins. These three men were big-time quality writers I'd respected since I started, genius painters I'd followed by searching for their pieces on walls and in magazines.

I'm about to do a panel with legends, I thought. I smiled and was about to shake their hands when I noticed Kon hadn't responded. Instead, he slowly reached into his backpack and pulled out a pair of scissors. 'Do you know my brother Billz?' he shouted.

Like a sprinter hearing the starter's gun, one of the other men leapt towards him. These writers had a beef with Billz, and the scene instantly switched from a quiet little huddle to a thunderous mêlée. As the man rushed at Kon one of our boys met him mid-air with a rock to the face, deflecting his surge. Kon attacked another, holding him in a headlock and stabbing him repeatedly in the head with the scissors.

That was the thing about Kon: mostly he was a cool, jovial guy, but on occasions such as this there was no way to talk him round. He'd want blood, and most times he got it. When his temper cracked all sensible thought processes vanished and he had no regard for human life. His ego's hold on him was stronger than that of anyone I knew, and it often forced him to do unforgivable things.

He was notorious for stabbing people. I guess he had attached this label to himself and it had become a part of him. If he didn't live up to the expectations of who he was then what was he? The truth was that until he could break free of such labels he would never be at peace.

Track rocks, fists and scissors were flying everywhere.

'This is the wrong place for this,' I heard one of the other guys yell, and he was right. Backing up the boys was our first priority, and that's what made us different from other crews. There was an unmanned train there for the taking, but so was the fight. The other writers were outnumbered and soon retreated. After giving them a short chase we decided to leave as well, as the noise from the brawl would have raised the alarm.

We were pumped up when we got back to Kon's house, reliving what had just happened. Though we didn't get to paint the story was worth a thousand panels, I figured.

My phone rang; it was Snap.

'Where are you? I'm at the train,' he whispered.

I told him about the fight and he sounded disappointed. 'Stay there, we're coming,' I said.

CHAPTER 12

HOOKED

Only Base and I went back to meet with Snap. Neither of us was going to let a brawl, the possible return of our enemy or the arrival of police officers ruin our chances of our first panel. I didn't want to let Snap down either, as he'd been looking after Base and me. We were his boys and I wanted to paint that train with him.

Snap was there, accompanied by a few other boys from RM. We gave them a quick rundown on what had happened, which made them suspicious of the lack of activity around the helplessly innocent train. We watched it for another 20 minutes, looking for any movement, but it was dead still.

'It's sweet,' one of the RM boys finally announced. He stood and walked confidently towards the train. He was a veteran train painter and he told us what to do. 'Stick to the first three cars. The rest of the train has too much light on it.'

We all moved into position. I was used to standing on a platform next to a train but here I was standing on the track, and the train towered over me. I leaned on it to get my footing. Its massive steel shell was as cold as ice and it sat awaiting its blanket of paint.

The night was still and silent, the air crisp and fresh. There was the sound of hissing snakes as the chemical-smelling paint fumes filled our surroundings. My hands were shaking. I looked to my left to see all the boys working intently on their showpiece. To a writer the sensation of seeing your boys panelling was unmatched, and afterwards we would have discussions about panelling being better than sex. I'd only had sex once and it hadn't been a memorable experience, so I had to agree that train painting was better.

My first spray onto a train was thick and green. It covered the Tangara's silver section like a long-lost child reunited with its parents. The paint held on to the steel, hugging it as though it knew that this was where it was meant to be. With every spray I moved closer towards completion of my first panel, and I suddenly realised what all the hype was about. Painting gave me a sense of stillness, a quiet mind. The world could have been ending around me and I wouldn't have had a clue. I wasn't thinking about anything besides that particular moment.

'Hzzzzzz.' The train's brakes let out a sudden rush of air. I freaked out and jumped back a few metres.

Snap giggled. 'Don't worry, it happened to me the first few times. You'll get used to it.'

Get used to it? *This I could definitely get used to!* I thought. We finished two panels each then stood back to marvel at our work.

'Damn, that's nice, Snap. It's a burner!' Snap was a great painter who was constantly improving. Mine on the other hand was terrible, but I didn't care. It was my first, and I was glad to have been a part of this monumental experience.

I slept deeply that night even though adrenaline had been pouring through my veins. The previous eight hours had teemed with tension, excitement and fear and they'd finished with an overwhelming sense of achievement.

The team assembled at Kon's the next day to mull over the previous night's events. The story had already been going around Sydney's graffiti world and overnight we younger boys, who had been completely unknown, had become household names to any writer.

'What: you still pulled off panels?' Kon asked, with a hint of excitement and a touch of jealousy.

'Yeah, two each,' we said, as though it was an everyday thing.

'Two: what?' Kon shook our hands and thanked us for backing him up, then his phone rang. 'Billz, what's doing?' he said, as he walked out of the room to chat in private.

I was eager to hear what Billz had to say. We'd backed Kon up, which was as good as fighting for Billz. Fighting for the leader of the crew would be sure to win us respect; maybe we'd be allowed into RM.

'Billz said to put you boys in RM.' I looked at Base: I couldn't believe what I'd just heard. I wanted to go out there now and put my tag everywhere with an 'RM' next to it. 'I told him you weren't ready yet, though,' Kon said. He saw the disappointment on our faces. 'You're close, but it was only once. You still have to prove yourself a couple more times and improve your painting skills.'

I was disappointed, but I saw it as a challenge. It was time to turn the heat up.

We went to see our work in daylight: the train's carriages were covered from end to end and it looked as though it had been in a paintball fight. Paint was in places it wasn't supposed to be, the wounds of our panels bleeding colours of pinks, greens, blues and whites. We thought it was beautiful and stood silently, enchanted, taking it all in and admiring the detail of our own work. We each turned to applaud our fellow painters after examining theirs.

'Let's try it again tonight,' Kon said.

It burned him that he'd missed out, especially after seeing our production. We'd have been happy to leave it at that but peer pressure is a bitch. To do more carriages would be more of a risk, as the next four cars were better lit. It was also 50 metres from a police station, and as the train had been hammered the night before it was sure to attract some attention. Still, we went back. I painted slowly this time, taking everything in and savouring the experience. For a while I just sat to watch the boys as they painted away. The lights of the train illuminated the paint mist, sparkling as it rested on their faces.

We were close to finishing when we spotted a man in an orange vest 3 metres behind us, and we knew from his uniform that he was a train driver. He knew we were there but he didn't want to look – he was severely outnumbered, and a wrong move from him meant we would have attacked. He passed us as though he was passing a pride of lions. Not wanting to disturb us, look us in the eye or show fear he simply stared straight ahead, stiff-necked, as he walked by.

'Good morning, mate,' Snap said.

'Morning,' the train driver responded, without turning his head. We hurried to finish off our panels.

'Honnnk!' We looked to our right: spotlights from the train were flashing on and off. The driver was trying to alert the police so we frantically stuffed our bags, scaled the barbed-wire fence to the road and ran to the safety of the cars. Once we were far enough away we celebrated. It was 4.30 am and I felt alive!

I was hooked.

The train we painted ran the lines for three days, which was unheard of as usually a train with even a single tagged panel would be taken out of operation to be cleaned. This train, covered end to end, curved along the tracks for all the graffiti culture to see and talk about.

We rode that train on a few occasions. I loved seeing people heading to work and being woken up from their dull morning by a brightly coloured train. It was also good to see other writers getting photos of it, and we imagined everyone talking about us. The train felt as though it was ours, and we became arrogant towards other writers. We believed what we wanted to believe, and with all the talk of these new writers taking the world by storm, fighting and painting their way to the top, our feelings of supremacy grew.

Through all of this I still I hated the thought of my family finding out. Society viewed our behaviour as wrong and rightly so, but in my new world I wouldn't be accepted unless I went against society's rules. My moral compass was starting to spin out of control. I was being pulled by the magnetic forces of my ego and I'd soon be lost.

CHAPTER 13

EXPELLED

Every day a writer would approach to say they were excited to meet us, and I came to the realisation that painting was just one aspect of the game. Nobody had heard of me before the fight with the other writers. A panel would last just one or maybe two days and half a dozen writers might see it. Before the internet if your panel wasn't seen running it was more than likely never seen, but to fight another writer and win, well, that didn't go unnoticed. The story would last a lifetime, as well as those of their crews and friends. They'd tell the story and soon it would spread.

In the past, when Base and I had met other writers on a train they'd pick on us. 'Base and Punch: bitch toys,' they'd say under their breaths. We took their abuse and didn't say anything. I used to look up to these writers, but they had the same insecurities as me. They looked for advantages through picking on younger kids and acting tough, and they got away with it for a while.

Now we were fighting back. We'd take on anybody and would back each other up regardless of the opposition. I didn't know it at the time, but fighting had become my way of silencing my mind. For me, brawling was a paradox: during fights I had no mental chatter, just a contented relaxedness that I relished, then after the fights my ego would be enhanced and I would feel strong and confident.

Unfortunately, my new arrogance was affecting the rest of my life, especially school. Time and again I was warned for being rude and argumentative. One lunch break at school I got high on weed for the second time in my life then later, as I sat in class, it felt as though the voices of my classmates and teacher were piercing my brain from every direction, spinning me out. *Jump on the table*, my mind was telling me. When I was stoned it was as though a devil-like gremlin in my head tempted me to commit destructive actions. When I was affected by weed I was completely bonkers. I'd often argue with myself, usually losing because of the state I was in. When I was straight my mind chatter would annoy me, but when I was high it dominated me.

What I didn't know was that the mind shouldn't be a battle between good and evil but a slow dance between mind and stillness.

'Pull yourself together,' I mumbled to myself, my head in my hands.

'Luke!' I heard the teacher say.

You're tripping, I thought. *Just keep your head down*.

'Luke!' the teacher said again, more loudly. I slowly raised my head, which felt unusually heavy. The teacher was standing in the doorway with her hands on her hips. Beside her was a student holding a piece of paper. 'Mr Marsh wants to see you.' *No way!* I thought.

I was being called up to the headmaster Mr Marsh every couple of weeks to be told what I was doing wrong and that I'd better pull myself into line or I was out. I'd argue my defence, being rude and leaving him angrier than when I arrived. *How can I face him in this state?*

I walked slowly, dragging my stoned feet down the stairs. Finally reaching the bottom, I turned in the opposite direction to his office: no way was I going to let him see me like this. I would rather cop the consequences of not attending.

'Mister Kennedy?' It was the principal's mature, clever voice. We stood face to face and he began talking.

Act straight.

Stand tall.

Keep your eyes open.

Nod your head.

Act straight.

Stand tall.

Keep your eyes open.

Nod your head.

I repeated the words over and over to myself as Mr Marsh seemed to speak forever! My legs were starting to feel shaky. I was stuck in my head, kicking back and hoping that if I kept my mouth shut I wouldn't raise suspicion.

Act straight.

Stand tall.

Keep your eyes open.

Nod your head.

After 15 minutes the principal tapped me on the shoulder, snapping me out of my affirmations. 'Thank you for listening and not arguing, Mr Kennedy. I've noticed a change in you today. It's exciting to see.' To this day I couldn't tell you a word he had said, and his good opinion of me didn't last. Soon after, when I was about halfway through Year 10 and aged 15, I was kicked out of school due to poor attendance and fighting.

Out of school and with no other commitments besides painting, I started to cement my position on the train lines. Even though I wasn't as good as those I was painting with I was still everywhere to be seen. Base, Snap and I would be on trains every day; they were our playground. We would hold the side doors open and hang out of the train with the wind in our faces and not a worry in the world as we watched the city fly by.

Snap showed us how to break into the vacant guard's compartment to put our tags on the back of the train, so when heading in the other direction it would be at the front of the train. To have a 'front runner' was something worth risking your life for, and climbing the back of the train as it sped along was another thrill. Adrenaline mixed with the fear of death equalled pure excitement, and the truth was that taking a risk such as scaling a moving train erased my anxieties about other issues such as fighting or pressure from Mum and Dad to get a job. When I was in the middle of it all I thought about was that specific moment, a moment I hadn't experienced before with all my mental chatter getting in the way.

One day I was on the train with a couple of friends. We had our heads against the windows and were looking at all the different tags.

'Open your bags. Where're your tickets?' A rounded man with a moustache pulled a badge out of his pocket: he was an undercover transit cop. His colleague did the same to the others behind me. They'd noticed us looking at the graffiti. I didn't have a train ticket but I did have a fat marker in my bag. 'Okay, implement to deface property,' the man barked when he found the marker.

'I'm in school,' I lied, 'of course I have markers in my bag!'

'Don't treat me like a fucking idiot. I saw you looking at the tags. This thing isn't for school,' he said. I shut my mouth. 'No train ticket two hundred dollars, and four hundred dollars for carrying an implement to deface property. Where's your identification?'

'I don't have any.'

'What's your address and home phone number?' *Shit, I hope Dad isn't home,* I thought. I gave the man my details and he called my house on the spot to verify them.

After they left I called Mum and pleaded my innocence. She wasn't happy but she was always forgiving of me. She didn't tell Dad, so I avoided a harsh punishment. It was my first fine. It was also my first contact with transit police, but it didn't stop me. Mum paid the fine behind Dad's back, not the last time she hid my run-ins with the law.

As well as getting my tag up everywhere I could I started fighting more. I'd listen to the RM boys talking about how they got into an argument or a fight with another writer, and I'd take a mental note. I started defending anyone I knew, turning their dramas into mine.

Snap, who'd become a good friend, tried to tell me to pull back. 'You and Base have been getting up heaps, which is good. I'm proud of your efforts. I just want you boys to be careful, though. You're starting to get carried away with all this fighting. I know you look up to us RM boys, but you don't need to fight for us all.'

I knew what Snap was saying was true, but anything I did I wanted to do well. I decided to show the others that I could take it to a new level, that this was only the beginning, so when Base and I overheard that one of the RM boys had been jumped by another crew we made up our minds to get the other crew back. We searched for them on a train line they were known to travel on. Sure enough we found two of them and attacked, hurting them more than they did our boys. After that Billz and Kon decided that I was finally ready: I was in RM.

CHAPTER 14

UPPING THE ANTE

I was excited: from now on any panels I painted would have 'RM' next to them.

My first panel as a fully fledged member of RM would be in a train yard. It was a bigger gamble than doing a trackwork lay-up because there was more security and more chances of a brawl.

Someone had stolen the master key for the train yards from a guard's compartment, but getting in wasn't the hard part. What had me anxious was completing the panel without a raid by police or a punch to the back of the head by other crews. The plan was to creep up to the gates and search for our sleeping beauty then, with a nervous turn of the key, we'd enter the palace. The sleeping beauty's dream-like state would be broken by a kiss of colour, and we'd be enchanted by its spell.

Everybody acted differently, but once the can started it was game on. Lips rested lightly against each other on a relaxed face as eyes scanned up and down, following the can with each spray. Everyone felt they were where they were meant to be, but the second the painting stopped either from hearing a noise or having to change cans, people's expressions returned to their original state – a smile or a tense screwed-up face would appear depending on who the person was. Painting the same art piece created oneness with each other, so much so that even without looking I could sense what the others were up to.

The next day I checked out graffiti forums but was disappointed to see no talk of our efforts from the night before. My ego was taking over and I'd stop at nothing to feed it, so I ended up impersonating two people having a fake conversation about seeing our panels running because I didn't want to go unnoticed.

We were now doing panels every couple of nights but good paint was expensive and I had no job. Lucky for me, I was now a seasoned thief. Base, Snap and I would hit the large stores and just casually fill our bags with cans. Once a store employee bailed me up as I was walking out. 'Sir, could I just have a quick look in your bag?' she said.

I hadn't planned how I'd respond to such a request, so I just turned my head to stare into her eyes, smiled and kept walking. The look on her face showed that my arrogant smile had ripped clear her ability to speak: her mouth was open but no words came out. 'Hey!' A bunch of store employees chased me as I walked out into the car park, but I got away.

We'd see big Media on our adventures and he'd give us paint spots that he kept secret from others. His spots were the best: they were all over Sydney and we'd travel by bus and train or walk for hours just to get there.

I felt like my luck would never run out even though I heard harrowing stories from every writer about being chased by security guards and police, but painting city trains was always a big gamble and eventually it happened to us. One night we crouched in the dark watching a lit-up train that was sitting idle. Two security guards walked past our intended target just 50 metres from where we were hiding. I glanced at my watch; it read 2.08 am. The guards headed towards the opposite side of the yard to check on other trains, their orange vests reflecting the yard's big spotlights.

We sat and waited.

'Let's hit it now,' a newcomer to the group suggested.

'No, just wait,' I whispered back, a little annoyed. I looked over to Base. He was staring intently at the train, so I picked up a twig and tossed it at his face. He looked at me, grinned, and shook his head.

The security guards came back and walked past our train again. The time now read 2.24 am, meaning we had 16 minutes to paint – the perfect amount of time – but I wanted to be sure. The boys readied their bags.

'Just wait. Wait for one more run.'

Around the same amount of time passed until the guards returned.

'Cool. Boys, we have roughly sixteen minutes to paint. Let's do this shit.'

When the guards were far enough away I stood up, ran over to the train and threw down my bag. As I pulled on the zipper I heard a roar: the security guards were running in our direction. They'd done a dummy run, not taking their usual route in the hope of throwing off guys like us who were counting on them to stick to their routine.

I was fat, but I could run fast for about 100 metres. That's all I had in me, and luckily this time that 100 metres was enough to discourage our hunters.

We'd painted country trains a few times and had never seen a security guard, let alone be chased by one. Country trains were fun to paint but there was less excitement because it was so easy, which was why Snap got the idea to whole car it. A whole car is when you do a piece that covers the whole carriage from top to bottom and end to end. If a panel was the pinnacle of a painter's efforts, a whole car was the stars that shone brightly above. You couldn't get any bigger. It had been years since anyone had managed to do a whole car in the Sydney graffiti scene, as the authorities' increased awareness meant we had less and less time to paint before we'd be spotted.

Whole cars were something of an urban myth: only writers who had been painting for more than 10 years could claim to have seen one. I never thought I'd ever get the chance to do one. It made me both nervous and excited listening to the older boys speak about the whole car. I felt I was in a room of hunters who were planning on killing Big Foot. A country train carriage was longer than a suburban one, so it would be a near-impossible effort to pull it off. This was going to be massive!

We travelled by train to our destination, carrying ladders and bags full of paint. It could be risky travelling to panel spots by train, because not only did police carry out random searches on late-night trains, but if we were chased we'd have a hard time getting home. This time we had no other option, as none of us had a driver's licence.

Chubb Security was the trains' first line of defence at the time, but their powers were miserable – they couldn't even ask if we had a train ticket. Transit cops were more of a worry. Travelling as much as we did meant we knew most of the guards and would often have a chat.

'What are the ladders for, boys?' one asked.

'Just doing some renovations,' we said, cheekily.

The guard grinned and kept walking. Given it was past midnight, I was pretty sure he hadn't fallen for our little story. When we finally reached our station we headed for the train yard. Reaching the base of the mammoth beast, we started to fill in the whole carriage even before Snap had put up the outline. Up and down ladders we climbed. My fat legs ached and my muscle-free arms throbbed from holding the can up and spraying continuously for almost 45 minutes. My finger became so numb from holding the nib down I had to swap fingers.

There's a moment during painting when you feel like you're finished and home free, and it usually occurs when you're doing your final touch-ups. Your mind returns to action as you imagine what everyone is going to say about your accomplishment. The time spent painting is for stillness; the outcome is for the ego.

The sun was rising, its light shimmering on the freshly painted silver mountain. My mouth was dry and my nose filled with paint. I felt someone softly tap me on the shoulder: the other boys were signalling for me to stop. Like a new parent following a marathon labour we sat, completely wrecked, to marvel at our creation.

We'd done a whole car, but because it was a country train I knew it wouldn't be viewed in the same light as a suburban whole car. The country whole car had taken us 55 minutes to complete. Besides the lay-up we'd never been able to spend more than 20 minutes on a suburban train, so I couldn't fathom the possibility of pulling off a suburban whole car.

With such an active mind, no matter what goals I achieved I was never content and was always thinking of what would be next. And, never content, I was always bored with anything I was doing at any time. I was continually searching for happiness somewhere else. I decided I'd be fulfilled after we'd completed a suburban train whole car. It was an impossible idea so I left it for a while, but I knew that eventually I'd make it happen.

CHAPTER 15

THE RETURN OF THE TASK FORCE

We had a panel spot west of Sydney with a paintable train on its station. There was another one on a bridge nearby and a third further down the line. You were lucky to paint one panel and get away with it so to attempt three all within 200 metres of each other was being cocky if not stupid, but we'd been getting away with doing some risky spots and our confidence was high.

Base's birthday was coming up. 'Let's do all three spots for his birthday!' I said to Snap.

Snap and I went out in his mum's car to get paint the day before Base's birthday. Snap didn't have a licence, but that didn't hinder us. We surprised Base with all the paint we'd stolen and let him in on our idea of painting all three spots. He hesitated before agreeing.

We had a friend who didn't paint but liked to come and watch. It was great having a spotter with us as I felt more relaxed when we had one. Often, though, with my controlling nature I'd keep an eye on the spotter to make sure he was spotting right, which defeated the purpose.

We caught the last train of the night out to our spot, and when we arrived I handed out gloves to everybody. Normally we'd leave with our hands covered in paint, but this time we were planning to stay to destroy another train. If we had paint on our hands after our first spot security would notice, the police would be called and, if they found us, they'd know we were the culprits.

We jumped a little gate and crept along the fence line. The train was at the bottom of a slope. My heart raced as we moved towards the top of the slope to begin our descent then we heard a clank of metal. The gate we'd just scaled rattled, almost halting my beating heart. Three people were creeping up to the edge and also looking down at the train. They were only 30 metres away, but it was so dark they hadn't noticed us. We ducked down.

'It's Media!' Base whispered, recognising the big man's frame. We were used to coming across Media while stealing paint but we'd never seen him out painting. My fellow cronies stood up; we knew we didn't have to hide from another writer. As we walked over to greet Media and the boys he was with their eyes were glued to the train. They still hadn't looked our way. We sneaked up behind them and I put my finger up to my mouth to signal to the others to be quiet. Media was good for a practical joke, and I was about to scare the fatness out of him.

Within an arm's length our cover was blown. They turned and jumped back, caught off guard. I raised my hand to shake Media's.

Base yelled out, 'Shit, that's not Media!' Either Media, the best thief in Sydney, had joined the police force overnight or we were about to be blasted into a raid.

'Get on the floor!' the fat man screamed, pulling out his badge. We turned and scattered in all directions. Snap took the plunge and headed straight down the huge slope while I ran up a grass patch with Base beside me. The cops were behind us, closing in on their prey. Their footsteps were thumping on the grass, the steps so loud I could hear them over their shouts for us to stop. I jumped a fence. When I reached the top of the gate I braced myself, envisaging a horror movie in which the devil grabs a fleeing victim's leg to pull him down. The devil wasn't fast enough, and soon I was running along a road.

Red and blue lights were flashing all around me, screeching tyres disturbing the silent neighbourhood. I looked to my right and saw our spotter being tackled to the ground. He screamed in anguish. Like a pro golfer taking a swing down the gallery, everything opened up for me. Cars squealed to a halt just in time for a passage to clear and a little ledge was in place for me to jump a fence. I landed softly on the only patch of grass in the yard of a unit block.

I skipped through another block of units and kept running and jumping fences. I was close to crumbling with fatigue. Finally, I stood alone in a building site, scanning my surroundings for an escape. I spotted a portable toilet and hid inside, sitting in the filth while trying to control my breathing.

Sirens and hollering in the distance seemed to be approaching. Voices were getting louder and I could hear nearby fences rattling and feet hitting pavement. I gave up trying to come up with a story that would excuse me for being in a portable toilet at 2 o'clock in the morning so I sat, waiting to be busted. As footsteps drew closer I held my breath.

My dad! I thought. *I'm finished!* I imagined Dad's fuming red face as he claimed me from the police station. Everything went silent. *Do they know I'm in here? Are they about to bust open the door?*

It was dawn when I finally left the toilet and a beautiful morning. On the nearby bay birds skimmed the surface of the water, which glistened in the sunlight. Early joggers were already out. An elderly couple walked past and wished me a good morning. I smiled and nodded my head. These people had no idea of the commotion that had occurred only a few hours earlier. The tweeting birds had replaced the deafening sounds of sirens and shouting.

I made my way to the train station and got on the next train, wondering all the while what had happened to the others. At the second stop I saw our spotter waiting to get on. He saw me through the windows and raised his hands, showing me a bunch of papers. The look on his face was all I needed to know: he'd been charged.

'Man!' he said, as he sat down beside me.

'I saw you get tackled,' I said, checking out his torn clothes and bloody knee.

'They were the graffiti task force.'

Task Force Graffiti was something of legend, although they hadn't been around when I'd started writing. They were known for being ruthless in their pursuit of writers, often bashing and robbing them. They were vigilante types, but they had authority. Because they hadn't been around for long Sydney's graffiti crews had developed a false sense of security, but complacency can be the death of you.

Task Force Graffiti raided three other spots that night and busted plenty of established writers. The word spread quickly: the task force was back! It was a huge smack in the face, and not a day went by that we didn't hear of a yard getting raided. The task force meant business.

CHAPTER 16

IN DEEP AND CLIMBING HIGHER

On my 16th birthday we were hanging out having a couple of drinks when one of the boys pulled out a bag of pills. I'd never touched ecstasy and was scared of the thought.

'You want one, Punch?' he asked. I looked at Base. We were always on the same path with everything: if I would he would, and vice versa.

'Half each?' Base smiled, and we broke the pill into halves and swallowed them.

That small decision had monumental consequences that affected my physical and mental health, memory, relationships and life forever. I sat nervously waiting, regretting what I'd just done, but a sudden rush of ecstatic emotion erased any regrets. With my eyes half-closed I was floating, my body and, more importantly, my mind weightless. Heavy thoughts had drifted away.

I looked over at Base and we both smiled, acknowledging what we were going through. 'We've been missing out,' I slurred, curling up into a ball to get more of a hug from the drug.

We'd been offered pills for years but had always refused – until that night. It was the beginning of years of fruitless searching for happiness through drugs, and from then on I'd consume some form of hard drug every single week. The happiness would last for a few hours but the misery lasted for years, compounding a deepening depression.

It was New Year's Eve and we hit the city. The year before I'd watched our idols from the sideline; now I was a part of the team. I knew that

Stevie, the guy who'd totally brushed me after I tried to shake his hand, was going to be there. He'd always showed a little attitude towards me but now I'd become an important figure in the crew who would back anyone up and he didn't like that. He was known as one of the big guys and he saw me as a threat to his position, which I was.

I sensed that the tension between us would detonate that night, clearing a destructive path for me to step up. I was right.

We ripped through the city drinking and tagging, and soon we were in an argument with a bunch of people that was split up by the police. Snap, his next-door neighbour Paps and Kon's cousin Dean and I were sitting in Hyde Park when someone called out in a voice I recognised. I looked over. Stevie was heading our way.

'Hey, boys,' he said, as he shook everyone's hand except mine. He sat down next to Snap.

'Where've you been?' Snap asked.

'Just with a few boys from my area,' Stevie replied.

I looked over at him and he noticed the attention I was giving him. He stared at me and I stared back. The crowd of people we were with were chatting away, unaware of our stand-off.

'What?' he said to break the silent stare.

I stood up. 'What the fuck do you mean, "What?"' Everyone jumped from their seated position and stood between us.

'Come on, boys, we're all friends here!' Paps said. I agreed and settled down.

'We sweet?' I asked him, as I put my hand out to call a ceasefire. He turned away without shaking it and sat down. My blood boiled. *He made me look like a bitch,* I thought. *Motherfucker, to do that to me again. Who do you think you are? I'm going to crush you.*

In reality the only thing happening was that he had sat down and I had stood up: was that reason enough to want to crush him? In my mind I believed a fight was necessary. I thought I was being tested, and that those around me would mark it as a failure if I backed down.

Over the preceding few months I'd proven myself as a kid who wouldn't take crap, although at 16 I was still an RM apprentice. I thought I had proved myself enough, but being so young meant the boys still had doubts. Stevie definitely doubted me but I was climbing the ladder, and now I had a chance to really cement myself as a force in the crew. I made up my mind there and then that the night would end with one of us getting hurt.

I waited for the right moment. Stevie was still talking to Snap and I looked at him and laughed, hoping for a reaction.

'What the fuck are you laughing at?' he shouted.

It was exactly what I had been looking for. 'All right, bitch, let's do this!' I said, confidently shaping up to fight.

Stevie was shocked and remained sitting for a moment, then he stood up. 'Is this guy serious?' he said, walking over to me. He couldn't believe that the new kid was about to take on one of the main men. His burly frame looked menacing as he drew closer, but my utter hatred for him wouldn't allow for defeat.

He stood within striking distance. 'Are you serious?' he asked again. Was he looking for an out?

'Sure am. I'm sick of you trying to stand over me!'

With those words he attacked. I flinched a little before throwing a single right punch. It connected, and I felt his tooth pierce my knuckle as my clenched fist slammed into his mouth. His pounce forward meant the force of my punch was doubled, and he dropped straight on his arse.

When I was growing up Dad had always taught me to be first. 'If it looks like it's going to be on with some prick make sure you throw the first punch. You don't want to end up knocked out, so make sure you're first every time,' he would say.

Stevie crawled over and tackled me to the ground. He was strong, and his flabby stomach rubbed against mine as he wrapped his bear-like arms around me.

'That's it, Stevie, get on top of him!' I heard one of his supporters yell.

With a cheer from the audience, I managed to headbutt the strength out of him. I was surprised to hear I had more people shouting for me, which gave me greater power, and soon I was on top of him. I'd wanted to do this to him since the first time I'd thought he'd made me look like a fool, and now my frustrations left my body with each blow I landed.

As with a panel, there's a moment in a fight when you know you've won. 'You think you're a tough guy? Look at you now!' I hollered. The boys lugged me off him: they'd seen enough.

Stumbling away happy with my efforts, I celebrated and re-enacted the fight through shadow-boxing but my celebration was cut short. Stevie was back, this time with 10 outraged men backing him up. There was smoke coming out of their ears like an out of control steam train. I stood my ground: I'd just won a fight and thought I could take on these characters, but I was wrong. Paps grabbed my shirt and begged me to run.

'What: you can't take getting bashed by a kid?' I yelled at Stevie as they came closer.

There were only four boys with me now. We were outnumbered, but I wasn't going to run from him. The mob came within punching distance and again I threw the first punch, putting the leading guy out cold, but my world was soon rocked by a barrage of trauma from every angle. I broke free and threw a few more shots. I weighed more than 100 kilos and knew how to use my weight. We were brawling in every direction, and soon we were fighting on a main road. Cars swerved to miss us.

Then my luck ran out when I tripped and a boot kissed my cheek. Within a split second I felt another six feet stomping down on me. I went from protecting my head to pushing on the ground, trying to get up, but that left my head an open target. They were scoring points with my skull as it bounced from foot to foot like a ball in a pinball machine.

It's a surreal feeling being on the receiving end of a bashing from numerous people. So many uncommon sensations: my soft cheeks grinding against an unforgiving concrete surface, the taste of blood mixing with dirt filled my mouth, the city lights getting more blurry with each booted attack. Like a soccer team warming up for practice, they took their turn at attempting a shot at goal.

After relentless boots to the face I was battling to stay conscious. I heard police sirens, and the kicks became fewer as one by one they ran off. Dean raised me to my feet and walked me off the road, carrying me with his head under my arms. He too was suffering as a result of the fight. I looked at Dean. 'Is it bad?' I watched as his eyes scanned my face.

'Let's get a taxi.' He turned and waved down a passing cab.

The next morning my face was itching with pain. I stumbled into the bathroom and looked in the mirror: every part of my face had either a bump, bruise or gaping wound. My phone rang.

'Punch, it's Billz.'

I was worried about the call because I didn't know how Billz would react after hearing the news that two of his soldiers had clashed. 'Hey, don't worry about Stevie. He's finished, barred from the crew. He's been getting disrespectful to everyone but you're the first to take him on. I'm going to come pick you up.'

It was a bootload off my mind, and having Billz back me up relieved some pain. If he hadn't it would have felt like another blow to my already bleeding face.

Billz turned up in his car. 'Fuck it, not a scratch on you! No effect, mate!' He shook my hand and reached out with his other arm to hug me. His casual approach relaxed me and I felt safe in his company.

'I spoke to a few of Stevie's mates and they said you were dropping them like a bag of shit,' Billz said. He was excited, as though he was a boxing manager who'd just come across a hot young prospect. He was glad to have me on his side. Until then Billz and I had rarely hung out – he was much older, and the stories we heard about him made us young guys wary – but after the fight Billz and I became very close. He introduced me to the older boys in his area and followed it up with a couple of stories about recent fights, showing off his new fighter. Being able to handle myself put me at the top of the food chain.

I was hanging out with the older boys, fighting and partying, and my ego soon got out of control.

CHAPTER 17

THE BOYS FROM THE SOUTH-WEST

Base and I started getting on the pills, coke and speed. It became a regular thing, and we added to the mayhem when we started going to raves. We'd go nearly every weekend, finishing days later after consuming a massive cocktail of drugs and alcohol. We never missed one and were soon travelling all over Sydney to attend raves. We'd meet other writers and fight them to increase our stronghold on the scene, and we built up a strong reputation for never backing down. We were creating a new rave scene that was dominated by lads, violence, chaos and thieving.

Other writers would be excited when they met us and we felt like celebrities. We'd rave the night away then continue the party at Hyde Park in the morning while we waited for the bottle shop to open.

One night I looked over and saw a young writer with half-closed eyes: he was completely off his face. He came over and said: 'You're Punchy, hey?' He put out his hand. 'Nice to meet you. I'm Fund.' I shook his child-like grip as he stood there smiling. I liked him immediately. He stood by my side for the remainder of the night.

Fund was from the south-west of Sydney. Meeting him that night was my introduction to another world of writers who became lifelong friends and soldiers by my side in every battle.

Fund introduced us to a couple of his friends. Mick was a lean, short-haired redhead, Rod had a chunky build and, like me, shaved his head bald and Vert was one of the tallest people I've ever seen. Even at his young age he towered over most men, and he had a tattoo beneath his eye of a knife cutting into his skin.

A friend got into an argument with a man who had pushed him, and when the guy also pushed me I gave him a little jab to the nose, not wanting to attract the attention of security. He walked off but was soon back, this time with a rather large man who pushed dancing ravers out of the way to get to me more quickly.

Be first, my mind told me, but I decided against it, reasoning that a fight would cause a huge brawl and effectively end my drug-fuelled fun.

'Why'd you hit my friend?' the man growled, his smelly, wet breath in my face. He was a fully grown man who, with the hairs on his back visible above the neck of his shirt, resembled a silver-backed gorilla. Security wandered over and the big guy walked off, smirking. That smirk told me it wasn't going to be the last I saw of him.

'We got your back, Punchy,' Fund's boys said. I'd known these boys for less than a couple of hours and they were going to defend me. I liked them already. Still, I was edgy for the remainder of the night. The drugs had already made me a little anxious to begin with. Throw a fight into the mix and I was close to being crippled by nerves.

The sun was coming up, spelling the end of the rave. I watched as the reality of daylight sank in, disappointing those around me who were in another world and bringing to light their frowning, drug-abused, purple faces. We walked out into a street of factories. It was a bleak sight: grey concrete, clouded skies and a bunch of drug-affected zombies. I felt a tense energy and took my watch off as I didn't want to break it in the impending battle. I handed it to Skye, a girl who hung out with us.

'Why am I holding this?' she asked.

'Just hold it.'

I spotted my gorilla. He carefully manoeuvred around people this time as though he didn't want to raise suspicion. He was accompanied by a troop of more gorillas that gracefully swung through the trees, making their way towards me. We made eye contact.

Here we go, I thought, holding my breath. *This is going to be a tough one.*

He was clutching a metal pole. Our meeting eyes stopped the world around us. He stared in contemplation then looked away and walked straight past me, speeding towards a small kid, then with a thrust of his arm he landed the pole over the back of the kid's head. The metal bar echoed like a church bell. The kid had nothing to do with this and now he lay motionless on the ground for his trouble. 'You want to hit my friend?' the gorilla screamed.

Game on!

The pole slipped out of his hand as he disappeared into the crowd. One of our boys grabbed it and dropped one of the enemy, and a brawl broke out. Punches, kicks and head stomps were flying everywhere, as well as the occasional dinging noise of the pole meeting a skull. The boys from the south-west stuck to their word and backed me straight up by jumping head-on into the battle.

I went looking for the gorilla and found him at the back of the crowd. We made eye contact again.

'Let's do this,' I said as I took my jacket off.

The crowd of ravers stopped to watch. I was still a kid, but my build made me look a lot older so I was fair game. Another lesson from Dad came into my mind: never let a big guy get hold of you. A larger opponent could grab and manhandle you into a headlock before slamming you to the ground while landing punches and headbutts. 'Keep them long, mate,' Dad would say. 'If they grab you, that's the end of it.'

I got in first, landing a solid jab on his face that backed him up. He threw a big haymaker that missed by a few inches but the punch's wake of wind felt like a blow in itself, its power forceful. Its lack of grace gave me confidence – although it had been a big shot it had no style and I could see it coming from a mile away. If it had landed it would have knocked a bull out.

He came back at me and I threw a straight left-right that rocked him again and put him on his back foot. Not wanting to go for a knockout punch and risk missing, I stayed with the safety of straight shots. If he dodged one of my punches it would give him the opportunity to get over me while I was caught off guard. After landing the one-two he walked back towards me, a little hesitantly this time. His nose was bleeding so he wiped it then looked at me again.

'I can do this all day, brother,' I said confidently.

He ran at me and threw a big, frustrated kick. I moved out of the way and punched him in the back of the head as he flew past. He kept moving, not wanting to look back and concede defeat. *Thank God for that,* I thought.

No matter how many fights someone gets in there's always the risk of getting caught by an unlucky shot and ending up being knocked out. After every fight I'd look to the sky and let out a sigh of relief, thanking God.

For me the intriguing thing about fights was that I was able to feel and predict when they were about to happen: there was an energy in the air I'd pick up.

We were all psyched up, and as we walked to the station the crowd of ravers congratulated us on our victory. The boys I'd just met from the south-west had stayed loyal to their word and fought for me. It was like coming across long-lost brothers; those who risked their own lives for you were family.

Among my associates, trustworthiness was the most valued trait. It was imperative to be able to trust that those standing next to you would splatter as much blood for you as you would for them, but if you were only feigning an allegiance to the crew it wouldn't be long before you were found out. Word would get around about anyone who didn't jump in to help in a battle and those people would be left out in the cold, lonesome. We couldn't risk hanging around with dead weight – it was the difference between walking away smiling and ending up on your back with an opponent's foot in your mouth.

The south-west boys later ended up very close friends, and throughout our late teens and well into our 20s we ran amok. Stabbings, brawls, robberies and plenty of fun is what these allies brought to the table. They had grown up around the same area and now they joined forces with us.

CHAPTER 18

DROPOUT

Base and I were now doing panels by ourselves, but since the raid on Base's birthday we'd mainly stuck to terminators.

A 'terminator' was when a train terminated at a station before heading back the way it had come. Some would stay put for a few minutes, while others stopped for 10 to 15 minutes. We'd be on the other side of the platform painting while unsuspecting passengers sat waiting, reading papers and looking forward to getting home after a busy day. The nice thing about terminators was that unless you thrashed the same spot time after time they were rarely raided by the authorities.

We decided to do another yard paint but I was nervous, afraid that Task Force Graffiti would attack again. Base asked a kid from school to be a spotter for us. Stintz carried a skateboard. He was 15 years old but didn't look a day over 12. He was extremely excited to be there with us, so much so his body shook in anticipation.

The train yard would be hard to paint as security did constant dummy runs and cameras were pointed in every direction. We'd heard rumours that some of the cameras were fake but, as with any rumour, how could you be sure?

The encasing metal-bar fence had endless rows of 3-metre high steel posts that were sharp at the top and impossible to climb over, so our only chance of getting in was to cut through unscrewable steel bolts that attached each post to its solid base. We used a hacksaw, but security would walk within half a metre of the fence and we only had a 10- to 15-minute window for cutting.

It took us over an hour to get through the first few bolts as we had to be patient and do it slowly to keep the noise to a minimum. I lived on a staple diet of hot chips and gravy and was incredibly obese, which caused another problem: we'd need to cut two posts out to fit my fat arse through. It took over two sweating hours to get through all of the bolts.

Like criminals in a movie we had little mirrors we held through the metal bars that gave us a great visual on security's movements. When we spotted them walking in our direction we'd quickly retreat and hide in nearby bushes. On occasion the security guard would walk along and tap each post to listen for any loose bolts, but we managed to cut through the bolts without being discovered. We slipped cautiously through the fence, moving from absolute darkness into bright light, and slowly got into position.

My mind was still at last as I embraced the train with my first spray. Stintz watched on, swinging his head in every direction, although I kept a good eye out myself. Every couple of minutes I'd stop and survey the yard to look for anything out of the ordinary.

Base finished first, and he joined Stintz behind me as I completed my final touch-ups. I put a Stintz tag up next to my panel. His baby face smiled as though it was Christmas. Afterwards we hid out for a few hours then headed home on the night-ride bus. On the way the bus stopped for a road worker holding a stop sign. It was 3 am, and we all commented on how terrible it would be to have to work in the middle of night.

'That'll be you, Punchy, you dropout,' Base said. We all laughed.

The road worker turned the sign and the bus slowly rolled past. I sat quietly, and for the first time in my life thought about my employment future. I'd never had or even attempted to get a job. I was only 17, but lots of kids my age had part-time positions even while they were still at school. I was neither at school nor had a job, and Base's comment perched in my mind like a little bird.

He was right: I was facing a poor future. The thought wouldn't let up, tapping away inside my head like a bird tapping away with its beak. That night I made up my mind to go back to study, not only to get my Year 10 certificate but also my Higher School Certificate. The next day I enrolled at Gymea TAFE, south of Sydney.

'Mate, good to hear,' Dad said when I told him. Both he and Mum had noticed a change in me. I occasionally came home with a black eye or a busted hand and would tell them some bullshit story about how I'd gotten it, but Dad knew the truth. Mum and Dad both hoped that studying would put me back on track.

I was excited because I'd have to get the train daily, which would give me the opportunity to tag on the way. As usual graffiti dictated my decisions one way or another, and most of those decisions were poor ones.

CHAPTER 19

SCAT DAY

After a rave we would either head straight to Hyde Park for scat day, as we called the day after, or if it was too cold we'd go back to my granny flat at the back of my parents' home. Dad worked on a Sunday, so when I'd arrive home at 8 am with 20 or so drug-affected kids Mum would be worried. 'Luke, your father will be home at lunchtime. They can all stay here but please get rid of them by then.' Mum was always there for me: whenever I needed anything she'd drop what she was doing and help me out. We have the best relationship: she's always full of laughter and I absolutely adore her.

'Yeah, I promise, Mum. They'll be gone.' I'd have every intention of getting rid of the boys, but once the bottle shop opened at 10 o'clock and we started drinking I'd be less worried about Dad's reaction. Being drunk and off my head lessened all my worries for a time, although it compounded them for days after. We would get milk crates full of wine and sit in my granny flat or in the backyard drinking, and it wouldn't be an hour before arguments broke out or someone did something stupid.

Craig, a friend of ours who wrote, was new to the group but he fitted right in with his daring behaviour. The first time I met him we punched on with each other. I was travelling in a car when he walked past and shouted something at me. I jumped out of the car, then he turned around and it was on. There is nothing quite like traded blows to break the ice.

Craig was a loose cannon and we could encourage him to do anything. He was older than us and could also handle himself well. He was short but stocky, and his head was bald and round. His chest and arms were covered in tattoos and his appearance was menacing. When you're chatting one on one with guys who usually seem violent it's funny to see the real person come out and share their fears and weaknesses. When they are broken down everybody has a kindness, but in our group we considered kindnesses to be weaknesses. One morning as we sat in my granny flat after a big night out, Craig revealed that he wanted to get away from it all.

'Punchy, I get too excited. You boys gee me up and it's like I want to impress every time. I'm going to end up fucking killing myself.'

I listened and watched as his ego took a back seat. For the first time I saw the real person deep inside him. I agreed and told him to do what he felt was right. Much later, doing what he felt was right saw Craig commit an inexcusable act. The truth was we probably all wanted to get away from it; we just didn't know how.

CHAPTER 20

WHAT A JOKE

Taking drugs every week was an escape from my habitual, obsessive thoughts. When I was under the influence it was as though my mind and pure self called a truce, ceasing their arguing and letting me be for a while – until I came down from the high, that is.

I was a week away from turning 18 and we planned to celebrate at a rave, so we met up at Snap's house and popped two pills. When we arrived at the rave I had a third pill before going into the dark, hot, sweaty room. The air was choked with fog and coloured lights flickered on all the happy faces.

I had another five pills in my pocket. Being an extremist, I would often get caught up in the moment and take silly risks, hoping others would notice. This time I put three of the five green pills on my tongue and swallowed them, and an hour later I felt as though I was bathing in a flowing spring. I struggled to keep my eyes open and caught people pointing me out to their friends, laughing at how buckled I was.

I went to the toilet and tried to pee; I was busting to go but nothing would come out. I was disoriented and had forgotten where I was. *Ah, that's right, I'm at a rave,* I remembered as I walked out of the toilet. I started to dance and would have looked pretty fragile, but I felt untouchable.

The state I'd get into used to worry even my friends. I was always trying to better everyone by having more drugs, and when others stopped I would keep going as I didn't want to face reality. I was constantly pushing my body to the edge of life and my mind to the edge of sanity.

That night I ended up having even more pills and endless lines of speed. It was freezing cold and, as so often happened, I was still there when night turned to day. My legs ached from dancing as I looked around the room. The lights had been turned on and a few people remained on the floor as others danced around them to no music. I hugged myself to get some warmth, watching on as the spiritless spooks trudged towards the exit.

We headed for a planned morning at a friend's place. I didn't want this party to end, so while others smoked on bongs I lined up a row of drugs, chopping away like a chef preparing a meal. As the effects of the drugs and alcohol wore off reality began to close in. The pills I took that morning had very little effect as they'd already caused a huge release in my brain of serotonin, the neurotransmitter that plays an important role in the regulation of sleep, pain, emotion and appetite and other behaviours. That's what created the blissful experience, but after a night of heavy drug taking I was immune to the pills' effects because my brain was now drained of serotonin.

Alcohol, however, can wreck you at any time, and the bottle shop would be open soon. I headed out then returned with two bottles of rum I had pinched. Everyone cheered: the day was still young and we had plenty of party hours left in us. I poured shots, although many of the boys passed on them. I was happy to have theirs.

* * *

When I woke up I was confused and my mouth was sticky. I looked down: I was completely naked and was in my parents' bedroom. *What am I doing at home? What happened?*

I looked at my phone; it was 6 am. Mum and Dad were cleaners and got up extremely early, so they would have been at work. I needed some answers. *I hope I didn't muck up.* When I sat up the room began spinning. It felt like the bed was a roller coaster that was flipping me from side to side. I had a faint memory of a police officer and was sledgehammered in the face with a massive dose of depression.

'What did I do?' I screamed. The unknown was killing me, so I called my friend. 'Grant, it's Punchy. Man, please tell me I didn't play up.'

'Man, you fucked up!'

'Mate, I'm sorry. What happened?'

'I don't know what happened to you,' he continued. 'You were drinking then you just lost it. You just stood up and started pissing on the coffee table.'

'Bullshit!' I laughed, hoping to God he was teasing.

He didn't laugh. 'You did, mate. You hopped up and just went everywhere. You were blaming someone else for it while you were doing it!' He kept talking, and with each nasty description I sank further into a dark hole. 'We didn't know what to do with you so we called a taxi. Base jumped in with you but you pushed him out, so we told the taxi driver where you lived and gave him the money to take you home.'

'What about the police?' I asked.

'What police?'

'I don't know; I can picture police. So I didn't get into any trouble?'

'No, we put you in the taxi and the driver took you home.'

I hung up and stared at the ceiling. It felt as though my life was ending, and I still couldn't get the police out of my mind. Then my phone rang.

'Luke, are you okay?' It was Dad.

'Yeah, I'm fine, just tired,' I lied. My body was shaking and my head ached. I wasn't fine.

'What did you take, mate? You were off your head,' he said, in a slow, beaten voice.

'I was just drunk. I had two bottles of rum.'

'That wasn't alcohol, you were tripping out!' Dad's frustration was evident. He sounded as though he hadn't had any sleep, and now he wasn't being told the truth.

'I just didn't sleep. I was drinking for two days and it must have affected me badly.' I hated lying to Dad; we were close, but I didn't want to let him down.

'Even the police said you were off your head!'

Shit! 'What happened with the police?'

'I've got to get back to work. Your mum will be home soon.' He hung up.

My body continued to twitch and soon I was vomiting uncontrollably, crying and talking to myself at the same time. I promised myself I'd never feel like that again. Coming down after a two-day bender was always hard and I'd get severely depressed, but this was something else. This time I'd stuffed up big time and my parents had seen me all messed up.

I heard footsteps coming up the stairs and watched as the door opened to reveal a tired, sad lady. My bottom lip quivered; it upset me to see Mum like this, and it was all because of me. 'Mum, I'm sorry.'

'How are you feeling: are you okay? Dad wants me to take you to the hospital.'

'No, I'm okay, Mum, just hung-over.' I put the bullshit out there to see her response.

Mum broke her silence to reveal my credibility was in the toilet alongside the vomit. 'Luke, you were on drugs. The police said it.'

'What happened with the police?' I closed my eyes, not wanting to hear the answer.

'We got a call from Mascot Police Station asking if there was a history of mental illness in the family.' I had a little chuckle inside. Even in this situation I still thought it was pretty funny that the police thought I was insane. *Am I?* I couldn't imagine the feeling my parents had had after getting a phone call like that. 'They said, "We have your son here and he's completely out of his mind."'

It turned out Snap had given the cab driver $50 to take me home, but instead he took me straight to the police station. When Dad came to pick me up I was sitting in a corner talking to myself, and after a while I noticed him standing there. I stood up and shook his hand like he was an old friend, which was when he knew I was on drugs.

When I got home Ruben got his friend over to witness his brother totally messed up. Ruben thought it was funny, and if it had been him I would have done the same thing.

'How did I get naked?' I asked with no enthusiasm for the answer.

'You called Lucas to pick you up.'

Lucas was the friend I'd met through playing sports when I was 12 years old. He was different from my other mates in that graffiti was rubbish to him and he would rarely hang out with me when I was with the crew.

Even so I had an open, honest and understanding relationship with Lucas and we had a strong bond.

He was my escape from the crazy world I was in and the first person I'd ever heard talk about the powers of the universe. He'd say we were all an energy field and that the reason I kept getting into fights and why drama filled my life was because I was putting it out there. 'Your ego is massive; it's all made up in that big head of yours. You control everything that happens in your life and the universe provides.' I'd roll my eyes, having no idea what he was talking about.

Mum said that when Lucas arrived after I'd called him Dad told him to leave. I was in the shower, but when I heard Lucas's voice I ran out yelling. Not wanting any piece of this mayhem, Lucas drove off and I ran up the road with Dad behind me. By this time I'd dropped the towel and my big fat arse was bouncing from side to side for all to see.

Dad had to lie to settle me down. 'Luke, I'm dying. I've got to go to the hospital tomorrow, I'm sorry to tell you. I don't need this at the moment.'

It worked. I crumbled, crying and screaming, then hugged him. He led me inside the house, put me in his bed and laid next to me. I kicked and screamed for hours as Dad lay by my side. When you're on drugs it's near impossible to rest. Your eyes may be closed but you're never fully asleep, and it means a night of terrifying visions as your mind creeps from a bad dream to reality and then back again.

'You can't remember any of this, Luke?'

'I can't. Seriously, I don't know what happened. I was too drunk!'

'Well, one of your idiot mates must have put something in your drink,' Mum said. Never underestimate the power of denial.

'Yeah, you might be right!' I said, trying anything to get out of the shit I was in. My poor mum didn't want to believe her 17-year-old son had lost his mind on drugs. Our conversation was cut short when I jumped up to run to the toilet to violently throw up. Mum stood behind me the whole time, her hand on my back trying to comfort me.

The boys rang me all through the day, laughing about what they'd witnessed the night before, then Dad arrived home.

'Mate, don't bullshit me: you were on drugs,' he said, in a tone I hadn't heard before that was worried and disappointed all rolled into one.

'Mum reckons my drink was spiked.' I hoped Mum's circumstantial evidence would see me acquitted. Dad looked at Mum then walked out of the room: guilty as charged, your honour.

I spent the next week on the couch. My body was aching all over and there was cramping in every muscle, and my cold, sallow face was restless on the lumpy pillow. Once when I was half-asleep I overheard Sarah and Mum talking.

'Look at him, Mum,' Sarah said. 'He keeps shaking. Is he going to be okay?' A full week went by when I didn't see the light of day. I'd missed out on a whole week of painting and going out on stealing adventures, so I called Base.

'I'm back. Let's go out.'

CHAPTER 21

ANOTHER CLOSE CALL

'Wow, look at you: you look terrible!' Base said when we met up.

I still felt sluggish, debilitated and forceless but it was going to be my birthday the next day and I wanted to head out. I wouldn't be doing any celebrating, though, so instead we opted to go shoplifting. We'd been stealing expensive clothes for a while. We never had any money to live the lifestyle we wanted, so we thought stealing was our only option. Other boys were dealing drugs but that never interested Base or me; we preferred to go out on an adventure for the day.

We decided to go west to pinch some clothes from a new department store that we'd been getting clothes from for a few weeks. The shop was open but still under construction, so we thought the surveillance cameras weren't working. We walked casually through the store without being noticed. Tradesmen were still building storage for the clothes we were there to steal.

One man at a cash register noticed us and looked twice in our direction. They were always on to us, so we just had to be better. We separated: Base went around one way while I went the other. I grabbed a pair of dark blue designer shorts and quickly stuffed them down my pants, and I looked at other clothes as though I was contemplating buying them. I met up with Base and we headed towards the exit.

'How'd you go?' I asked.

'Nothing: too many people.' I laughed and told him what I'd got. 'Damn, I missed out,' he replied. We exited the store cheerfully.

'It was a pair of blue shorts,' I heard a baleful voice behind us say. I looked out of the corner of my eye and Base did the same: a man in plain clothes was talking into a walkie-talkie. He quickly turned it off in the hope it hadn't blown his cover.

I walked slowly for another few seconds to compose myself then boom! I took off at a sprint and scooted out into the street. My opposite number hesitated, shocked by my sudden bolt. I was running downhill, which was to my advantage. My 100 kilos gave me momentum and I gained pace, but I could feel the sweat dripping off my sick body.

'Just drop the shorts! Drop the shorts!' the man shouted. I reached down inside my pants and threw the shorts behind me, as I was happy to part with them if it meant he'd stop chasing me. I glanced back: my assailant had stopped and was bending down to pick up the shorts. I was breathless, but seeing he'd stopped chasing me gave me some life back.

I got to the bottom of the hill. I was still recovering from the week of near death and this was the last thing I needed. In vain I desperately tried to catch my breath and stupidly failed to look behind. A taxi drove by and I called out to get it to stop. A flash of red from the rear lights raised my hopes of an escape and I jumped into the back of my saviour mobile, although the driver smelled worse than me. I was about to direct him away from the crime scene when I heard: 'Get out of the car!'

The door was tugged open and I slid across the back seat to attempt a second evasion, but then the other door sprang open and another man stood waiting to grab me. Both men reached in and almost tore me in half as they pulled from both directions. I yelled loudly in a dismal attempt to intimidate the store security guards then, attack being the best form of defence, I forcefully jumped out of one door. I managed to break free but didn't make it a step before I was tackled to the ground. I still didn't give up and scuffled, grunting, trying to show force, but by then both men were on top of me.

'All right, all right, I'm done.'

'You're fucking done, all right.'

As the taxi driver sat watching the show they lifted me up off the road and led me back towards the store with my arms pinned behind my back.

I walked slowly, my head down, giving them a false sense of security so they would release their grip a little, then like a greyhound bounding out of the gate I exploded, breaking free of one guard and pushing the other. I ran a couple of metres. I felt free: there was nobody holding on to me and I was in the clear. It didn't last, though, and I was soon smashed to the ground.

'That's it, you scum, you piece of shit.' They ground my face into the footpath. I deserved it: I was scum.

'Okay, this time I'm definitely done,' I said with a little laugh.

They lifted me up again. 'If you try that shit again we're going to flog you.' They had me in a hold not even Houdini could have wriggled out of: one held my limp left arm behind my back while the other had my right arm twisted above my head. It felt as though my arm would break if I tried to run.

The guards radioed in on their walkie-talkies to boast of their capture. 'Yep, we've got him!'

I pictured Dad having to pick me up from the police station for the second time that week. I wouldn't turn 18 for about another 12 hours, so a parent would have to be called. *If only I was old enough to be charged without my parents being called,* I thought. Getting a criminal record didn't worry me, because as I was marched up the street all I could think about was Dad. One week off my head; the next charged for stealing? Dad would think I was a junkie, and that thought scared me. *My life's spiralling out of control,* I thought.

Base came zooming around the corner and headed straight for us. 'Let go of him!' It was like a superhero had come to save the day, and I swear I could see a cape blowing in the wind behind him.

'Back off, mate!' the two men yelled.

Base reached us and shaped up to fight. 'Let him go, you dogs!' One of them let go, and young Base was now toe to toe with him. I turned to the other.

'Don't even think about it, mate,' the guard said to me, but I heard doubt in his voice and it gave me a second wind. I smiled.

'You heard him: let me go!' I punched his arm, releasing his hold.

The guards were tired from the run and our wrestles. Base was fresh and I had a second wind, so we soon had them backing away. When there was a far enough distance between us Base and I turned and ran. Unable to believe it, the guards didn't budge. We hid in some bushland for a couple of hours. I was bleeding from my head, nose and mouth and was spewing up, but I didn't care.

'What took you so long?' I said, cheekily. Base always had my back but the truth was I was having way too many close calls, and it didn't look as though things were going to improve any time soon.

CHAPTER 22

WHO AM I?

Snap had taken steps towards a new life: he owned a car, a truck and his own catering company that delivered fine foods. He'd avoided the criminal life and rarely came out any more, and I admired his courage to break away from it all. When I first started painting I looked up to Snap, but when I'd gotten into the scene myself he'd turned into an equal. I now looked up to him again, this time as a role model for a positive life.

Sometimes Snap picked me up on the weekends and we'd go to a shopping centre for lunch, and I'd watch on as he purchased clothes. Whenever I entered a large store I'd be on edge, because it usually meant I was about to steal something.

'Punchy, don't go stealing anything. I'm buying stuff,' Snap would say.

After those words my body would relax – another example of the powerful effects our senses have over the body! It was a long time before I was able to enter a store without feeling anxious, as my subconscious mind remembered the surroundings and indicated to my body that I should be concerned.

Snap seemed happier, calmer, and even walked a little differently. His own business had given him a sense of self-worth but he was worried about me. One day he sat me down and gave me a talking to.

'Punchy, I know the painting is the best thing in your life. It was the same for me but, mate, you've got to start thinking about your future.' He spoke with a sense of urgency. 'You and Base are my boys and I care about you both. I've been hearing about what you've been up to. I know we taught you all this, but you boys are going crazy.' I just nodded my head.

'Please, Punchy, listen to me,' Snap said. 'You're fighting every couple of days. I know you like backing everyone up, but you can't fight all their battles. I can get you a part-time job with me.'

'Thanks, Snap, I'm just too busy studying at the moment.' Snap was right: we were getting carried away with everything. Even a few of the other older boys who I used to think were crazy had said the same thing, telling us to settle down. Coming from them meant we were getting out of hand. Billz had begun to see me as a liability rather than an asset to the crew: I'd fight for them all the time, which he loved, but I was causing more drama than he wanted. They had shown us the ropes and, as mentioned, anything I did I wanted to do well.

Still, seeing Snap with his chunky wallet and eagerness for a better life stuck in my head. Even though I was carrying on the way I was I knew that when I put my mind to it and wanted to change for the better I would, and I'd do it well. I just wasn't ready yet.

At least I was studying for my Year 10 certificate, but even then I only socialised with writers. I felt awkward when meeting new people and wasn't confident in fresh situations. When I met someone who wasn't a writer I automatically forgot their name, because instantly in my head I worried about what I looked like to them.

You didn't shake his hand properly. I hope I don't have something in my nose. Does my breath smell? I better stand back just in case. Oh, shit, what's their name? I hope I don't have to introduce them to anyone. Does it look like I know what they're talking about? Did I say that right?

Why? I'm not sure. I do know, though, that my friends all teased each other constantly, joking around any time anybody slipped up, so if we judged others I guessed others did that to me. When I did meet another writer I'd outwardly beam with confidence, knowing my reputation would back me up. I felt superior, and as I didn't care about them my head chilled.

My reputation was the only thing that attracted girls, so I'd only go to writers' parties. At regular parties I was just a fat kid with an attitude and didn't make for Casanova material, but at a writer's party I'd be sought after. The girls could see how my boys and I were treated differently to everyone else, so I played this card every time. We'd introduce ourselves by our tags, not our names, because our tags had merit.

'Oh, my god, they treat you like kings,' a girl said one night.

'They talk shit behind your back, though,' another said, trying to start trouble.

I knew we were talked about harshly behind our backs, but to be spoken about in any light boosted my ego. When you get a big reputation in anything you're always going to have your critics. Even when you're known for doing good and helping there'll always be jealous people who try to shoot you down.

When other people hear your name often they can see it as an attack on themselves. The mention of your name makes them feel that theirs is diminished and sets them off on a campaign to tarnish yours, hoping to bring you lower than their level. But only more anguish comes out of jealousy, especially because even more people will talk about the intended target. My attitude had grown to that of a complete arsehole: I thought I was better than everybody else.

Away from the writers' scene my life was peaceful. I'd hang out at Grandma's, sitting on her lounge and listening to her tell stories of her crazy neighbours. I'd watch as she burst into laughter and I'd feel sad for her, knowing she was lonely, then she'd stop laughing.

'You know me, darling. I love you so much,' she'd say, her look serious.

'I love you too, Grandma.' I'd stand up to give her a hug and a kiss.

I liked hanging out there because it was another escape from my crazy world and Grandma loved my company, but I'd leave her place feeling confused. I was her grandson who seemed like a nice young man. I even felt like a better person when I was there but as soon as I hooked up with one of the boys – bang! I was Punchy, a violent young man.

Who was the real me: the person who liked to chill out with my grandma or the person who inflicted pain on others and broke the law? Was I either of them? Was I living either of those lives or was I simply a witness to both, watching from another place? I didn't know.

CHAPTER 23

MY FIRST LOVE

We were at a writer's party when one of our boys walked over to introduce me to his girl.

'This is Anne. Anne, this is Punchy.'

I didn't look in the girl's direction: I was too arrogant. Anne was quiet as I shook her soft, tiny hand but I could feel an energy and finally looked in her direction. She was pretty and blonde.

'Nice to meet you.' I smiled, and Anne smiled back.

My mate noticed there was something more to it and was quick to get her away, but before I left I managed to get her phone number and I rang her the next day to invite her out to the city the next Friday night. She seemed to be impressed by the whole writer thing so showing her how I led a team of guys would surely dazzle her even more. Our first date would be the Town Hall steps and a huge bunch of other people. I was quite the romantic.

I'd need a new shirt and haircut. A piece of clothing or some new hairstyle can make you feel special and invincible to rejection. Of course nothing changes except your perception, but it can leave you feeling confident.

I stole a new shirt but I had no money for a haircut. I was desperate, so I decided to get a haircut anyway. I walked into a barber shop, one I'd never been to before and one to which I could never return. The barber, who looked Italian, was elderly. He wiped down the raised red barber's chair and asked me to sit down. I sat, looking at my reflection in the mirror while he put the gown over me and secured it with a tight knot at the back of my neck. If he'd known what I was about to do he might have strangled me with it.

The barber started trimming my hair with the clippers. A haircut for me was a number zero all over. 'Where you off to, mate?' he asked.

'Going out on a date.'

He smiled and looked up at the ceiling as though he was thinking about past dates. 'Enjoy your life, son. It wasn't long ago I was your age going out on dates. I'm now very old and I never changed anything,' he said in his broken English. 'I wish I enjoy life more. You good kid. Keep being one.'

'Mate, I'm not a good kid. To be honest, I've done some pretty bad stuff. It's hard to get away from.'

The barber stopped cutting my hair and looked into my eyes in the mirror. 'In Italy we have a saying: "*A goccia a goccia s'incava la pietra.*" This mean "Drop by drop the stone was hollowed out."' Noticing my blank face, he explained: 'Many small changes will make big difference soon.'

I'd been hoping for a barber who wasn't kind, but this man was a gentleman with an energy of gold. He finished my hair and sprayed me with scent, then he removed the gown and with a snap of his wrists shook off the loose hair.

I walked over to the counter to pay. He continued talking but I couldn't hear a word he was saying: my mind shrieked with regret. I stood at the counter, hoping somehow money would magically appear but it didn't, so I ran out the door. He didn't say a word. Years later I went back with a $100 note, thinking that would make everything better, but the shop was no longer there.

That Friday night went like every other – Town Hall steps, Hyde Park and back again. Anne was now with me, as the friend who'd introduced us hadn't protested.

I got along with Anne straight away: she made me laugh. A few weeks into our relationship she found out she was pregnant. We contemplated keeping the baby, but after a week we reasoned against it. I thought

I could get a job and be a good father; however, Anne was only 17 and didn't want her parents finding out.

Anne came from a good home, but once she was with me she soon became the black sheep of the family. When we first met she'd been a shy, innocent teenager, but now I was taking her out drinking and she'd go home swearing and carrying on.

She was acting and speaking like us.

CHAPTER 24

THE WORST DAY OF MY LIFE

'Grandma, I've got a girlfriend. I can't wait for you to meet her!' I knew Grandma would love Anne.

'Oh, me darling, bring her around any time, I'd love to meet her. Does she treat you good?' Grandma always looked out for us kids.

After living in Brighton-Le-Sands for a while Grandma had returned to her home suburb in western Sydney. She was happy there, but because she lived so far away I didn't get to see her as much.

One Thursday afternoon I was watching television when the phone rang. It was Uncle Phil, my dad's brother. I really liked Uncle Phil: he had a reputation as a fighter and us kids looked up to him. He made us laugh, too.

'Luke, have you talked to Grandma?' Uncle Phil knew we regularly spoke.

'No, not for a few days. Why?'

'Nothing, mate. Just haven't spoken to her. I tried calling her but there was no answer.' By the tone of his voice I knew what he was suggesting and I felt my body freeze. I could feel my pulse thumping and felt sick.

'She's probably up the shops,' I said, hoping and praying she was.

'Yeah, I'll go up and check.' Phil hung up the phone.

I kept watching television. Dad was asleep; he usually had an afternoon nap after work and I didn't want to wake him. My breathing was short and I could feel my face turning white. *She's fine,* I tried to convince myself.

Mum came in. 'Are you all right?' she asked.

'Yeah, I'm all good.'

Mum walked back out into the kitchen. I stared at the television but noticed her looking worriedly back at me, then the phone rang again. I stopped breathing, although my heart was hammering against my chest.

'Nooo!' I heard Mum in a crying scream.

I rolled off the couch onto the floor and begged. *It's not true; it can't be.* I had a vision of the last time I had hugged my grandma and my head shook as I wept. I couldn't imagine that I'd never see her laugh again. I just didn't understand. I heard Mum open the door to the room where Dad was sleeping.

'Huh, what are you saying?' Dad was half-asleep. I went into the room. Dad stood still, looked at me and then back at Mum. 'Wait, wait: so you're telling me my mum's dead? My mum's dead!'

I didn't know what to do; the house was full of tears. Sarah had overheard everything and came into the room. Dad's my best friend, and I'd never seen him so disoriented or sad. He'd lost his mum. He walked around the room grabbing things and banging against the walls, sobbing uncontrollably and whispering to himself.

'Tell them not to move her!' he snapped. 'I want to see her. Tell them not to move her. Luke, you're coming with me. Sarah, I can't drive. You drive!' Tears flooded his face.

Sarah, Dad and I jumped in the car for the half-hour drive to Grandma's. We'd taken this trip countless times before but this time it was the hardest 30 minutes of my life.

'I can't believe it,' Dad said, putting his head down on his knees and crying. I felt incredibly sorry for him. I rubbed him on the back just to let him know I was there for him.

When we pulled up at the block of units I felt even sadder thinking about Grandma, who lived all alone there, the poor soul. Two police officers were standing near Aunt Carmen and Uncle Phil on the front porch. Dad walked into the unit while Aunt Carmen grabbed us.

'No, they're coming in,' Dad said. My aunt let us go and I walked past another police officer who held Grandma's door open for us. Dad collapsed on the floor and hugged his mum, who'd suffered a massive heart attack. Her lifeless body was in complete contrast to her usual bubbly attitude.

An ironing board stood nearby with some clothes on it she had been preparing to iron.

Dad held her silently, kissing her on the forehead. 'Kids, kiss your grandma,' he said after a while. I bent down and leaned in to kiss Grandma's face. She was usually so loud and full of life and I'd always put my arm around her and give her a massive kiss. 'I love ya, me darlin',' she'd say, but now her face was still and cold.

Dad stroked her hair. 'Oh, my pretty mum, I'm sorry,' he cried. I went outside to comfort Sarah. We sat down and watched through the open door as Dad hugged Grandma.

'All right, I'll tell him we have to take her,' one of the police officers said after almost an hour. He walked towards Dad as my aunt ran over.

'I'll tell him.' She knew that if this stranger, police officer or not, told Dad to leave his mum – well, we didn't know how he'd react. Dad can be a very peaceful man but also a wrecking ball, so we just didn't know. Dad walked out into my open arms, but a huge part of him stayed on the floor with Grandma.

After Grandma died, a night spent at home watching TV would be interrupted by tears from Dad followed by tears from me. We all missed Grandma; even as I write this I cry. She was one of a kind and it burns me to know she's gone. When Dad cried, Mum's face would also crumble; she loved Grandma just as much but her tears were more about seeing her husband so distraught. Those were hard times, but we got through them by being there for each other like we always had.

Grandma's death increased my own worries about death. I just couldn't get my head around the thought that I'd never see her again and then I'd feel a shocking bolt of nerves as I realised I'd be gone too one day. Where to?

We still had Mum's parents. Although they lived a long way away I loved making the trip to visit them. Elderly people have less ego; they don't care about the thoughts of other people. With them I could relax, dropping my tense shoulders and sitting with a smile. Mum would watch on, happy to see us all together and enjoying each other's company.

CHAPTER 25

A ROMANTIC EVENING

Base had joined the army and all of the boys, especially Snap and I, were super proud of him. Ever since I'd known him he'd been saying he'd join up one day.

'I'm not smart with school but I know I'll go well in the army,' he'd say, and he was right: it suited him perfectly. Even though we'd all muck up and Base would even sometimes push it a little bit further, he'd always had a mature streak. 'Pull up, Punchy,' he'd say when he noticed I was getting reckless.

I liked to cut corners but Base did things with military precision. Painting trains brought that out in him and I watched him plan different scenarios such as how our armed forces would attack our enemy, the train.

Before he left we had a party to celebrate our boy making it. None of us apart from Snap had a job, so seeing Base take this massive step towards an honourable life was pleasing. He gave us all hope. However, with Base gone and Snap working all the time my behaviour worsened, because I didn't have anyone who cared enough for my welfare to pull back the reins.

One night I was going to dinner with Anne at her friend Sophie's place and stupidly I decided to take Vert and Crazy Craig with me, because Craig drove and I wanted a lift. Sophie lived in a beautiful house near the beach. My crew believed that those with money thought they were better than us. It was a defence mechanism: cutting down people who were well educated or financially secure was our way of coping with the jealousy and insecurity we felt.

By the time we arrived we were already drunk. Anne was surprised, not only by the state I was in but also by the crowd I had with me. I was up for a big one and decided to try to get Base over too.

'Brother, you've gotta come. We're drinking with the boys.'

'Nah, mate, I'm too busy. I can't get out of here.'

'That's no good. Sophie's here. She's keen on you and she's sexy.'

Base succumbed. 'I'll be there soon.' When he arrived we hugged each other.

'Love you, brother,' we both said at the same time.

I watched in awe as Base walked into the lounge room to greet everybody else. He stood taller now, with a strong, solid build. I'd felt his back muscles when I hugged him. The army had turned our pimply faced, trouble-making boy into a sexy, strong, respectable man. I admired him as he walked around the room and watched how the others treated him, especially Sophie.

'You guys are messed up,' he commented after seeing us carry on for a while. Craig and Vert were arguing – Vert was joking around and Craig had taken it the wrong way, and Anne and Sophie were concerned. Sophie wasn't used to this kind of swearing and tension.

'Stop it, boys, this isn't our place. Stop carrying on,' I said. They stopped for a little while but were soon arguing again.

'Well, let's go out the front and sort it out,' Vert suggested.

'Sweet,' was Craig's automatic response as he bounced off the couch.

A clash was always on the cards in our group because everyone had a massive ego. We competed constantly over who was better than whom and when there was no enemy around we'd hit each other. A little joke could turn into a deadly attack because everybody was jostling for a position higher on the ladder, but it was a ladder that only existed in our miserable minds. In a group such as ours egos would flourish as they fed, not only on our own thoughts but on other people's mental disease.

Defending ourselves by attacking others was the only way our minds knew how to cope. It wasn't because we had no control over our minds that we couldn't let things go or not argue or fight; it was because we didn't know how to release our minds. A fight is the crazy mind in its physical form, and what we didn't know was that you can't control your own insanity but you can be free of it. An argument would see nobody back down and the only conclusion would be to stop it with violence.

Anne and Sophie watched from the front door while Base and I stood outside. *This is going to be a good fight,* I thought.

Vert and Craig were seasoned fighters, so the fight would surely be action packed. They measured up pretty differently. Craig was heavier with a stocky build and he knew how to use his pit-bull physique, getting close to throw looping hooks. He was a tackler and, like a pit bull, he wouldn't let go until he was dragged off. He was also good for a headbutt. Vert had a more formal fighting ability and would throw straighter shots and opt for trading punches rather than tackling and wrestling. He had a long reach, which he'd need in this one.

Keeping Craig at a distance would be the difference between victory and lights out. Vert's big heart won him most fights but a big heart in our group didn't mean you were caring or sympathetic: a big heart meant you had some ticker and you'd take on anyone and wouldn't give up. Even in clashes in which I thought he'd be beaten, Vert would manage to pull himself together and win.

'Just wait, I've got to take my track pants off,' Vert said.

He bent down to push his pants to the ground, revealing a pair of shorts underneath. As he attempted to pull one leg out Craig saw an opportunity and ran over, threw a punch and spear-tackled Vert into the stump of a tree that had recently been cut down. Vert landed flush on his back and gasped a short breath before going silent.

I bent down to see if he was all right: he was going in and out of consciousness. Base had just completed his first aid in the army so he took over, and my attention turned to Craig.

'Are you serious? You don't do that to anyone, let alone one of the boys! He was taking his pants off, you dog!' I threw a couple of punches. Craig fell back like the tree that had just been cut down. I tried to catch him but his limp body thudded to the concrete, his head taking the full force as it slammed into the pavement. He was soon snoozing.

When people get knocked out, occasionally they let out a sickening snoring sound. Their face gets all tense and, as a result, their mouths close. Craig's face did exactly that, and I immediately became worried about a possible brain injury. In a split second my emotions veered from complete hatred for what Craig had just done to a saddened love, hoping he'd be okay. Anne was on the phone to Emergency and I could hear Sophie crying. Craig was flat on his back, a pool of blood slowly forming beside his head and his face smeared with blood from a busted lip. I took my jumper off to slow the bleeding and cradled Craig's thick, bald head in my arms. His eyes were closed and, apart from the pool of blood, he looked kind of peaceful, which was in complete contrast to his usual manic behaviour.

I looked over at Base, who was cradling Vert's sleeping head. Four close friends, two of them knocked out as a result of three of them fighting. This sort of wackiness had become a regular occurrence.

Craig woke up after a few minutes and tried to stand, but he stumbled. 'What happened?' he asked. 'Got claret all over me fucking head?' He was smiling. Blood dripped into his open mouth, and when he spoke it filled with air and bubbled off his lips as though he was blowing bubbles with chewing gum. He looked completely bonkers.

Two ambulances arrived. The paramedics saw Vert on his back and rushed over to him. After putting an oxygen mask over his face they put him on a stretcher, loaded him into the big white ambulance and departed. We managed to convince Craig to get in the other ambulance and go to hospital.

'I don't need to go, I'm sweet,' he responded. Blood covered not only his head but also his shirtless torso. The sight of blood all over colourful tattoos is the epitome of trouble, and the worried paramedics radioed the hospital. Judging by Craig's docile face he wasn't comprehending the severity of the situation, and I felt sorry for him.

When both ambulances had gone and everything was dead quiet once more Base and I looked at the two girls and, shrugging our shoulders, walked inside. An hour later we heard a knock at the door: it was Vert with a bandage around his head.

'You should have seen Craig at the hospital,' he said. 'He was using his blood to do tags on the wall and they ended up kicking him out!'

There was another knock at the door and this time it was Craig, wearing a hospital gown. 'Someone fucking hit me,' he mumbled to himself.

Round two, I thought.

'You deserved it, mate. You nearly killed Vert while he was taking his pants off.' Base's words sliced the air.

'I guess I did deserve it,' Craig said, with a lisp caused by his fat lip. He kicked his shoes off, put his feet on the couch and went to sleep.

I should have known after that night that something was wrong with Craig. Sure we'd fight each other, but to dog shot and spear one of our own was different. We later paid the price for keeping Craig around. The truth was that while I liked to see a fight I didn't like seeing someone hurt, and the events of the night had reminded me of something that had happened earlier in the year.

Stintz called to tell me he was going for a prearranged fight against a writer who'd been trying to put it over him. Stintz had been convinced by everybody to fight the guy, but he was a tiny boy with a thin frame and he was nervous.

'Come with me, Punchy,' he said.

'Of course, mate, I'll be there soon.'

Stintz was a massive underdog going into this one. The other writer, who wrote Links, was chubby, older and bigger than baby-faced Stintz. To Stintz's credit, though, he was willing to back himself. He asked me for advice and the only words I had for him were to throw straight shots.

'Most people start throwing around wild shots, mate. Stay with straight, clean punches: they'll land first.' Stintz looked up at me, nodding his head.

The fight was in a back alley. Links arrived with two other people and when he was 10 metres away and saw us he stopped. Stintz was so nervous his body was tweaking from side to side but, like all our boys, he threw the first shot to get it started. He got caught with one of his own after trying to throw a big overhand right and missing, but he regained his composure.

'Straight shots, brother, straight shots,' I begged.

Stintz walked forward and threw two straight punches that landed clean on Links's face. Links backed up as Stintz hit him with continuous blows.

'All right,' Links said. 'I'm done.'

Stintz turned and walked away, an angry look on him that didn't suit his soft face. I put my arm around him and congratulated him.

'Well done, mate. You could have done better, though,' I joked as we walked away.

'Yeah, you reckon!' Stintz turned and ran back after Links.

'Come back here, mate, he's done!' I shouted, not realising how stirred up Stintz was from my comment.

Links turned just in time to see Stintz flying through the air. With a thud, his knuckles met Links's jaw and Links's head was aimed for the gutter. Crack! It sounded as though his skull had shattered and instantly there was more blood than I'd ever seen.

Stintz stood over Links, shocked. I pushed him. 'Get out of here, mate!' Stintz ran off up the road. I took my jumper off to stop the bleeding but it was no use, as blood was pouring from Links's head like an overflowing river.

I rolled him onto his side into the recovery position and he soon regained consciousness. A bus driver who'd noticed the commotion jumped out of his bus with a first-aid kit and began to assist. I heard the sound of police sirens, which was my cue to leave. I ran off and looked down at my blood-soaked hands. That man whose blood I had dripping off me, who I had just saved by rolling him on his side, would later almost end my life.

CHAPTER 26

'HE'S NOT BREATHING'

We were all excited to be going to a big rave at one of the stadiums built for the 2000 Olympics. The rave was on a Saturday night but we wouldn't stop until at least Tuesday.

Anne wasn't going to go as she never went to raves. I'd convinced her I didn't want to go out with a girl who was known to go to such places, but in reality I didn't want her to go because a rave was an opportunity to get with other girls and I was never faithful to her.

At these parties our reputation would see us benefit in many ways, and female attention was one of them. On this particular night all of our main crew would be there – Mick, Rod, Vert and Fund, plus 30 or so others. Base was away for training, his mind firmly on fighting for our country.

Meanwhile, the rest of the crew were fighting for our status. The rave was filled with the usual suspects dressed in fluorescent clothes and dancing with glow sticks. The girls had candy bracelets up the length of their arms and leg warmers the length of their legs. The odd bystander sucking away on a dummy would be ridiculed until they went away. There were gangsters from every background – Asian, Middle Eastern and Islander – a few respectful business people, some older people (who would dance more than anybody else) and lads, which were us. Everyone merged in this dark place filled with loud music, smoke machines and laser lights to escape their everyday lives and get completely off their faces.

We lads met at the front left speaker, and the area was a no-go zone for outsiders. If an unsuspecting individual in ecstasy-induced bliss somehow lost their way into our area they'd either become instantly aware of our attitude towards them and scamper off, or they'd receive a little jab in the face for their troubles. Even the area around a speaker was worth fighting for.

Soon we all felt invincible. Smiles were everywhere as the ecstasy manoeuvred its way through our hardness, and it was time to plan scat day.

'Hey, isn't that Robert?' Lisa, a girl I was seeing at the time, said.

I looked over. Robert, a young guy we hung out with regularly, was lying on his back. You would often see people spread across the floor at raves. Sometimes people would drop from a bad reaction to the drugs, but after they'd been attended to by the medics everything was usually okay. We used to look on and laugh when we saw somebody so messed up they couldn't even hold their own weight up. This time, though, it was one of ours. I looked more closely: blood was coming out of Robert's nose.

Lisa was a registered nurse, and she ran over and bent down to help. 'Get the medics!' she yelled. A couple of Robert's close friends ran to get help while a small crowd formed to watch. Lisa looked up at me. 'He's not breathing.'

Her mouth moved slowly as she spoke and the words tunnelled into my ears. They were all I heard, but they were met with blank faces. We were so buckled our minds didn't have the capacity to register their meaning.

The medics rushed over and their worried looks smashed me into reality: our friend was dying. The crowd was larger now, and I noticed strangers whispering among themselves with worried expressions on their faces, but everyone was so severely affected by drugs the grim reality hadn't really hit them. Some were even still dancing as they looked at my friend lying lifeless on the dirty rave floor.

As the medics started performing CPR I tried to imagine my friend opening his eyes and smiling. *Come on, mate,* I thought desperately. This boy's world was possibly about to end in a dark hole, the same dark hole that others used for entertainment and to escape the life this boy was fighting desperately to retain.

'Move out of the way!' Another medic carrying a large box burst through the crowd. The lights came on and the room was soon filled with people complaining.

'Man, that's bullshit! We paid good money for this!' I heard from behind me. I just wanted our friend to open his eyes.

'If you don't know him clear out!' the medic shouted. Soon there were only 10 of us standing and watching and hoping for life. The medic pulled two cords out of the box he was carrying and attached them to Robert's now shirtless body.

'That's fucking Robert,' was all Vert could say after catching my eye.

'I know. He's going to be okay, though.'

The medics stopped performing CPR. 'Clear out!' one shouted. A stillness swept over the near-empty stadium. Nothing happened for a few seconds, then a sickening bolt of energy sent from the box lifted our friend's body off the floor a couple of centimetres.

'Come on, brother!' I cried.

'Breathe, mate, breathe!' Vert begged.

Robert didn't move. Another shock went through his body, but again there was no response. Up until that moment I had every expectation that he was going to wake up.

'Please, come back,' a girl whispered.

Robert didn't come back, and his closest friends began to comfort each other and sob. A police officer asked us to leave, and another escorted Robert's sobbing friends away for questioning. We walked away slowly without saying a word, our heads were down trying to get hold of what had just happened. We walked out of the stadium into a bright sunny morning.

As we headed to the train station one of the young boys broke the silence. 'What the hell just happened, man? Was that real?'

I looked up and nodded my head. We all stared at each other: everybody was waiting for me to speak, looking to me for advice, but there was little I could say in a situation like this. Not only had we lost somebody close to the crew, but it was also a scary reminder that the fire we were playing with on a weekly basis had the capacity to kill us.

So what did we do? We all drank ourselves stupid for a couple of days. The comedown and sickness from those few days of drugs, alcohol and losing a friend had me scared like a little boy. Anne comforted me as I vomited and cried for two days straight.

The funeral was the first time I'd seen close friends cry. Chad, another one of the boys from the south-west I'd become close to, sobbed uncontrollably. He was close to Robert and it had hit him hard. Chad was a good-looking kid who always had ladies after him. He and I got along in any situation: when we were drinking or on drugs we'd laugh our arses off together, and when we were straight we'd have conversations that seemed to last forever, chatting deeply about life or girls. Watching Chad cry at the funeral just scared me more. We were living in a disturbing world and some of us were still just kids.

CHAPTER 27

BACK ME UP

I took a break from drugs and concentrated again on my graffiti. We had a beef with a couple of other crews, and that got us off our arses as we couldn't afford to get complacent and live off our reputation. Once competition came into play it was game on.

We were pretty ruthless when it came to battling other crews. If you were known to even speak to or hang out with those we had beef with then you were also the enemy and it gave us permission to fight. I had only ever fought if there had been a legitimate reason to do so but now I started searching for reasons, so Billz knew what my answer would be when he called me one night and asked me to back him up.

Billz picked me up and filled me in as we drove: some guy owed him money and when they'd last spoken the guy had laughed at Billz and hung up on him. We were going to a pub where this guy hung out, but Billz didn't know who else would be there. I already had sickening butterflies in my stomach that multiplied when I heard we were going to the other guy's watering hole. Billz rarely put himself in a situation where he didn't have enough back-up, just in case he was outnumbered. It didn't lessen my worries, though – you never knew what you were in for. I hated planned fights.

When we arrived in Newtown we double-parked on the main road outside the pub. 'We won't be long,' Billz said, as he jumped out of the car. When we walked into the pub I didn't know who we were looking for, but I soon found out. A bunch of people were sitting in a dark corner, and as we entered one guy whispered to another. We headed over as all six got to their feet.

'You want to hang up on me? Where's my money?' Billz said to his target.

I was sizing up the others, trying to work out a plan of attack. I didn't believe in weapons, so this wasn't going to be fun. The guy's friends stared at me and I stared right back. A man leaning on a pool table nearby looked as though he was trying to stay out of my line of vision. I turned and eyed him out, stopping him in his tracks. He concealed his alliance to our target by feigning a shot.

What's Billz gotten me into? This pub is full of enemy.

Billz and the guy argued as I watched a staff member behind the bar get on the phone. She glanced outside at our car and appeared to be describing it. Billz came up with what seemed to be the best outcome. 'You pick your best fighter. I've got one of mine. The rest of you stay in here.'

Sounds fair, I thought. I started looking at each of them more closely, trying to guess which one was my opponent.

'Okay, let's go.' A tall, stocky man with an orange ponytail who looked as though he was ready for war broke free of the others. He looked like a strong candidate to beat me: he didn't hesitate, as if he knew he'd be chosen as his friend's best fighter. His confidence rocked me a little as he led the way out onto the street. It seemed he was looking forward to it, that he was even a little angry we'd arrived late.

'They stay here,' Billz said to his opponent, pointing at the other friends.

Billz held the door open like a gentleman to let me pass.

'Thanks, mate.' I nodded my head, forgetting for a moment what we were doing.

The four of us were now on the street. Families walked by arm in arm, licking ice creams. A homeless man leaned against the pub wall as his three-legged dog sipped water from its bowl. I loved Newtown. I'd grown up walking these streets with Mum and Dad and it hadn't been so long ago when I had been arm in arm with them eating ice cream. Now, though, it was my battlefield.

Before a word was spoken Billz threw three fast punches, dropping the man who'd antagonised him. My tall friend looked at me and, seeing his friend beaten so severely, for the first time there was doubt in his eyes. His face turned to show pain as I headbutted him, and I followed through with an uppercut but missed as his body was already heading to the ground.

Four punches thrown and one headbutt, two victories.

We jumped in the car and sped away, yelling with excitement. The tension before a fight would later be replaced by either complete elation if you won or absolute misery if you didn't.

'Punchy, we can be unstoppable if we back each other up!' Billz said. I stared out the window with a smile on my face, but inside I let out a massive sigh of relief.

A couple of days later I was at it again when I got into a fight for Kon. 'Fucking hell, lad, who was that prick?' I asked Kon, laughing.

'Just an old writer,' Kon said. 'You take on anyone, don't you, Punchy?'

Kon was right: I did, because I thought this was how it was meant to be. I'd been hearing stories for the last couple of years about how many fights these guys got in, so I thought it was normal. But it wasn't. Sure, they occasionally had a fight, but I was doing it every couple of days. I'd fight anywhere – trains, shopping centres, streets and parks. If I saw an enemy it didn't matter where we were: I'd attack.

When we saw Billz later Kon told him about the fight. Billz was already impressed that I'd backed him up a couple of days earlier. 'You'll be running the crew one day, Punchy,' he said, before putting on his motorbike helmet and speeding away. Kon chuckled, but I knew he'd have been a little disappointed to hear that. I guess he thought that as Billz's brother he'd be first in line for the throne.

I was excited at the idea, imagining how people would talk about it, which I liked. Deep down, though, I felt fear, because from the outside looking in I appeared to be a strong, confident, happy young man but that image couldn't have been further from the truth. I hated myself. I was severely depressed and scared, and even though I was one of the head guys in a crew of many I still felt lonely.

I'd pray to God every night to be a better person. It was more than praying – I was begging. I wanted to escape the world I was in and start doing good to help people.

The ego finds it hard to impress when nobody else is around, so when I was alone a voice in my head would pipe up questioning my ego and all that drove it. It was a different voice from what I usually heard; it was more of a feeling than a voice. It gave me a tiny glimpse into who I was when my ego wasn't in charge and an opportunity to face the truth. Sometimes the discussion in my head when I was alone was pleasurable, warm and uplifting, but at other times it was a nightmarishly evil, dark debate.

CHAPTER 28

SET UP?

I was back into painting trains. One night Snap and I headed south to see a writer we knew who was respected as someone who had hammered the whole area. He wrote Tarn, and he was a worthy accomplice.

Being in a smallish city, he was well known to the authorities and had been busted numerous times for writing graffiti. I'd witnessed police stop him and call him by his tag, and recently he'd been in front of a judge. 'Paint graffiti again and you'll be painting walls in a cell,' the judge told him. He was on his last chance.

Tarn got on the drug ice, something I never touched. Having seen the effects of ice addiction, Base and I had promised each other we'd never go anywhere near it.

Tarn had local knowledge of the train yard in his area. We rarely painted down there, so it was an advantage to have his insight. There was trackwork along the whole line, which meant trains would be stationary for the whole weekend, another increased chance of pulling off a full-colour panel.

We met Tarn at a service station. He sat in the back seat and told us about the train. The spot was risky and well lit and backed on to neighbouring houses, but we were out of Sydney – Sydney's train yards were the hardest to paint – so we were probably too confident when we hit spots away from home and took risks we wouldn't normally take.

We watched the train for just a few minutes then jumped straight over a back fence and onto the tracks. We gave the yard a quick once-over then we crept up to the train, confident it was good to go. By that time I had to paint with glasses on because my eyes had worsened and my vision was terrible. I hated wearing my glasses; I was a big tough guy and they didn't go with that image. The funny thing was that they were only a piece of glass in a frame that sat on the bridge of my nose to help me see better, but from a young age the label of 'nerd' was one I wanted to avoid.

If I'd worn my glasses from when I had first been told to my eyes would be near perfect. Instead, I have to wear lenses with a strong prescription because, yet again, my actions had been determined by other people's thoughts about me. I've lost many opportunities, risked my life and even been close to ending the lives of other people all because I cared what people thought.

In any case, I'd lost my glasses weeks before when I'd been chased from a panel and slid down a hill, as they'd fallen off. Without them my vision was blurry. Tarn was to my right, Snap to my left. Halfway through my panel I looked up: I was happy with how it was turning out. My style was getting better and my colour co-ordination was improving every time. After I'd finished the background colour I got a little smirk on my face, and I started my final touch-ups.

'Boys, boys, boys!' Snap looked past me. I turned and squinted and made out two figures running towards us. They were roughly 20 seconds away.

'I'm nearly done,' I said, frustrated. I turned to do my final lines. We'd come so far to get there and I only needed one more minute. We'd been chased so many times by security we knew they usually just wanted to scare us off and were rarely willing to rumble for it, so I kept painting. Snap looked on from the end of the train as I painted.

Specks of paint landed on my tongue, the ball bearing rattling frantically as I nervously shook the near-empty can. I could hear footsteps slamming on the pavement that ran alongside the train: they were one carriage away.

'Fuck, they're coppers!' Snap shouted.

I didn't look. I headed for the fence we'd jumped over to get in but the police were already there, scaling the same fence to get over to us. They were easy to see because they were wearing reflective vests, so I ran the opposite way. We were being raided.

Noises crowded my ears – dogs barking, people shouting, train horns blaring. We ran frantically side by side. It was complete chaos, and all other thoughts left my mind apart from running away from the police who were in pursuit. Avoiding capture was my only aim as I ran blindly across train tracks, awareness for my own safety non-existent.

I ran towards the only area not swarming with police and reached a 3-metre high fence topped with sharp razor wire. I didn't give it a second thought, and my fingers clawed the thin wires as my big feet struggled to find gaps large enough to fit in. My leg caught at the top but I ripped it free and leapt off, landing hard on the other side.

I was in an area full of construction equipment: tractors, skip bins and portable toilets lined the yard. The boys had run elsewhere so I stood alone. The fence crashed behind me. Ten men and a dog were yelling at the top of their lungs not a couple of centimetres away.

'Stay there, you fucking mutt! Get to the floor!' Well-wishers they were not: they craved my blood.

It was a massive shock to my system. I'd been chased by authority before, but these rivals were within striking distance and screaming utter hatred as they slammed their fists against the gate. They wanted to eat me alive.

I was frozen with shock for a few seconds, then I snapped out of it and ran. They made for a different direction after deciding not to jump the fence, but I was desperate to get away from the frenzied, merciless men and was more than willing to risk injury or my life by bounding over another fence to get out of the yard. I was completely empty of any energy, but with a will to get away I raced on, vomiting from adrenaline and exhaustion as I always did.

I ran across a road and heard cars screeching around a corner and heading my way. Stumbling through a nearby cemetery, I reached a factory wall and hid between some bushes. I tried to slow my breathing. I could hear men shouting and car engines revving nearby. I looked up into a cloudless sky and silently begged. 'Please let me get out of this. I will never paint again. I hate this graffiti shit.' I lied even in my prayers.

You can be the toughest of the tough, but being in such a situation can result in serious distress and child-like fear. I watched the sky as my breathing slowed and my hopes for possible escape grew. Time ticked away. I could hear noise in the distance, but it seemed as though no one was getting any closer.

My shirt was ripped from under my armpit to the bottom. As my eyes became used to the darkness I noticed there was also paint down the front of it. I pulled it off so I was bare-chested. I was still hot from the chase, and sweat was dripping down my body into my shoe. My left foot was soaking, and I felt my toes wrinkling up as though I'd been in the bath for too long. I wiped the sweat from my leg then looked at my sweaty hand, but it wasn't sweat – my hand was covered in blood. The razor wire had cut deep and my dark red blood was gushing out of a thick, meat-exposing wound. My shoe was filled with blood, but I didn't care. My only concern was to avoid the ferocious, vengeful demons. My hands also had paint on them, so I chewed the paint off in the hope of ridding myself of any evidence.

Forty-five minutes passed. Always impatient, I decided to make my exit. I didn't have a phone, ID or any money as I'd left them all in the car. After hearing stories of people being chased from train yards only to find they'd lost their wallets and had the police knocking on the door the next day, I didn't want to risk that. I hoped I could make it back to Snap's vehicle in time and he wouldn't be gone.

I took a gamble and slowly walked out of the driveway I had been standing in and squinted up and down the road. There were some cars in the distance, so I decided to stay off the main path. Instead, I crept through the cemetery while listening for any noises. It was quiet and I tripped and stumbled, not noticing the fresh grave sites. I fell on my knees, heard a tree branch break to my right and saw two figures. It was Snap and Tarn, hiding behind a huge tombstone. I slowly made my way over to them. When they saw me they came out of their hiding spot.

'Get down, get down!' they shouted. 'Get to the floor.' It wasn't the boys. The police would loudly swear their heads off in an attempt to shock their quarry but it didn't scare me – I just had nothing left in me to run with.

'Man, help me. I was just being chased by a car full of guys trying to bash me.'

'Oh, really: from where?' They grabbed me and threw me to the ground. I guess they didn't believe my lame story.

My first pinch, I thought as I tasted grass. Pebbles and dirt dug into my bare chest. One officer's knee was in the back of my head, while the other put cuffs on me. I was enormously embarrassed about being shirtless. My big gut and chest were out for all to see, and even in such a situation I was self-conscious. I'd been able to hide my stomach for most of my life; the thought of people seeing me without a shirt made me lose sleep. Even at the beach or a pool I'd wear a shirt. Now, with my hands cuffed behind me, there was no hiding it. *Why do I care so much what people think of me?*

The police radioed in and a muffled response came back.

'They've got another maggot up the road,' the officer told his mate.

'So, which one was your tag? You put on a pretty big chase.' I didn't say a word and continued to walk.

A police car pulled up and two officers jumped out. I could see Tarn in the back.

'Do you know this man?' A police officer pointed at Tarn.

'Nope.'

'Do you know him?' the same officer asked Tarn. Tarn looked at me as though he was staring death in the eye. He looked back at the officer.

'Nah, I don't know him. I told you, I was just with my girl and we had an argument.'

'And what's your bullshit story?' The officer turned and stared at me.

'I came down here to meet friends but they didn't show up. I walked back to the station and a bunch of guys stood over me for my wallet and phone. I took off after giving it to them and they chased me in their car.'

'We'll confirm your details back at the station,' the officer said, rolling his eyes.

'Back at the station? What for: I've done nothing wrong?'

'Well, what's that paint on your hands?' He pointed.

'It's blood', I snapped back.

'Black and green blood?'

I looked closely at my hands. Sure enough there was still some black and green paint on my hands. I sighed and shut my mouth. As the officer looked at Tarn's ID I felt sad for him: his name in this area meant vandalism and he'd just blown his last chance.

'He's good to go,' the officer said. 'He was just fighting with his girl.' They let Tarn out and he glided off light as a feather.

What the hell? I thought.

Back at the station, I thought about the night that had passed. *Had Tarn set us up?* He'd wanted us to paint that spot and had acted funny all night. He'd been busted recently, so perhaps to avoid severe punishment he'd organised a set-up. To this day I'm not 100 per cent sure, but I never saw Tarn again.

I was charged with trespassing and defacing property. I walked out of the police station with no shirt on and a bandage over my left calf. Scratches, bruises and paint covered my body: I was a big fat mess. The biting winter air stabbed at my bare and now purple body. I didn't know what to do. Snap had surely left so I made my way to the train station, but when I arrived at the station I was reminded there was trackwork. No trains, only buses.

I huddled on a seat feeling sorry for myself, my body frozen and my eyes watering. Strangers waiting for the bus looked at me, a shirtless crazy man talking to himself. After 45 bone-rattling minutes the bus pulled up.

'Where's your ticket?'

'I haven't got one, mate. I lost my wallet.'

Ninety-nine times out of a hundred night-ride and trackwork bus drivers wouldn't ask for a ticket because they didn't want to risk an altercation so late at night.

'Well, get the hell off,' the driver said, rudely. I stared at him, furious: I'd have to sit waiting at the station for another hour, and I felt my face colour as my temper flared. I was about to explode.

'I buy you a ticket,' I heard in broken English. An Asian man jumped off the bus and walked over to the ticket machine. Breathing out and now relaxing, I watched as the man stood patiently putting his coins into the machine for a complete stranger. I looked back at the bus driver – his face was also now calm.

We can be so caught up in our own situation and our own mind. I'd think and contemplate some terrible, scary stuff when I thought I was being attacked. If I believed someone was trying to get one over me physically or emotionally my mind would decide they should be flogged.

The bus driver was no doubt an honest family man who, sick of scum getting on his bus without paying, was just doing his job, but to me that bus driver was a man who didn't care about the ticket. All he wanted to do, I thought, was defeat me in front of a bunch of people and that hurt my ego, which meant I had to cause pain. The whole world could have been full of roses and smiles, but all I had in my sights was that driver who had rightfully refused me access.

When I got mad it was as though a tunnel came over me and my target: nothing else mattered. The driver picked up on that energy just as this shirtless, bleeding man stared right through his rude, tough-man front, but this time the tunnel was destroyed by a calm, quiet and patient man. His soft voice alone was enough to get me breathing again. He put some life into an inhumane situation.

I felt embarrassed as the man handed me the ticket with a small bow of his head and not a word said. I smiled and turned to the bus driver. He also had a little grin on his face as he pulled the button to close the doors so we could finally depart.

I was sentenced to a one-year Section 10 good-behaviour bond, which meant that if I didn't get in trouble with the law during those 12 months my conviction would be wiped. I told Mum about the charge and conviction but we kept the information from Dad. Dad thought graffiti was childish and stupid, especially if it was going to get you a criminal record. He didn't understand the subculture and he didn't understand the pride involved, the pressure we all felt to stay on top of the ladder.

CHAPTER 29

THE LAST FIVE SECONDS

Anne moved into my granny flat with me. I'd grown to love her and enjoyed having her as my girl; she made me laugh and I appreciated how much she fitted in with my family. That meant everything to me, because if you didn't get along with my family then you wouldn't be sticking around for too long.

I still wouldn't let Anne come out all the time with us, leaving her in the granny flat and heading out with the boys for a night filled with alcohol, drugs, fighting and girls, but she was always there for me. Even when I returned from a big night she'd comfort me and make me something to eat, and I could see us getting married and having children. I'd always wanted kids, maybe just to pull me into line and so there was a reason to not go out. I certainly wanted a more relaxed life but I was in too deep.

The fact was I couldn't handle alcohol, which sent me into a deep depression. Drugs and alcohol had me thinking the worst scenarios imaginable, and I'd get incredibly paranoid. I was fighting every week and I knew it was bound to catch up with me. So far I'd been lucky, but my luck could change at any time. I could trip on a gutter and end up with my opponent's shoe in my mouth, or a king hit might land. The use of a weapon could finish me for good. It was only a matter of time before I'd be the loser.

I'd been kicked in the face plenty of times in brawls but I'd managed to avoid kicking anyone in the head. The noise it made was foul, like a cupped clap, and it left an ill feeling in my stomach.

'Never kick a man when he's down; it's what a dog does!' Dad had always told me, and I'd stuck to that rule . . . until one night at Town Hall steps. Anne was with me on that occasion and we were having a drink.

'Hey, Punchy,' an older boy who wrote Lock said. I gave him the same two-fingered handshake Kon had given me a few years earlier. 'What's been happening, Punchy?' Lock asked.

'Nothing,' I replied arrogantly, hoping he'd go away.

'What, you think you can take me on?' Lock said jokingly, shaping up.

I laughed and stood off the sandstone railing. 'Come on, then,' I said. We laughed as we mucked around, sparring. Whack! Lock accidentally punched me straight in the face and I immediately tasted blood. The crowd of onlookers gasped, and Lock noticed the evil look in my eye.

'Punchy,' he said.

I dropped him, and my next act had me losing sleep for a long time. As if time had completely slowed down, I felt all of my senses become active at once. I could smell the fumes coming from the busy street and hear Lock plead for leniency from his position on the ground. The cool air on my bare legs wasn't enough to douse my fuming temper. The silence of those watching spoke a thousand words: *Stop, Punchy!* But it was too late.

I put all of my weight on my left leg as I raised my right and pulled it back as though I was loading a slingshot. I fired the kick, and even as my foot thrust through the air I felt regret. The kick landed straight on Lock's face and I watched as his eyes rolled to the back of his head. In spasms his hand locked up in front of him. When I heard that heartbreaking noise as air was released through his tightly closed jaw I silently begged to have the last five seconds back.

Everything went quiet; there was no more cheering. I stood looking at Lock as one of the girls bent down to help him.

Anne snapped me out of the daze I was in. 'Run, Luke!' she bellowed, pushing me forcefully. I looked to my right and saw a police officer on the back of a horse approaching fast. As I ran down George Street I could hear the horse behind me, its metal shoes clopping on the concrete footpath. I dashed across the road but the horse and its rider stayed on the other side as they didn't want to risk crossing through the traffic.

I ran and hid in Hyde Park. 'You dog! You fucking dog!' I said to myself. 'Why would you do that? I hope he's okay!' I was now a person my dad would see as a coward, a person who'd committed an act he would consider inexcusable.

I heard the others arriving: whenever we were kicked out of Town Hall steps we'd head straight to Hyde Park to regroup.

'Man, you dropped him big time,' Mick said.

I looked past him and saw Lock walking with a couple of girls while holding a tissue to his nose. I walked over to him. He froze when he noticed me heading in his direction.

'Man, I'm so sorry. Are you okay?'

He nodded his head and stared at the ground.

'I really am sorry. You didn't deserve that.'

'I'm okay, I'm just spewing I lost my hat,' he said, trying to lighten the situation.

'Here, take mine,' I said, as I passed my hat to him. I thought that act made everything square. Lock placed my hat on his head and smiled a fake smile.

Lucas, my friend who spoke of the power of the universe, was blunt with me one night: 'Bro, you should know that you've turned into one of them.'

'One of who?' I asked.

'Those people we grew up hating.'

CHAPTER 30

RIGHT-ARM WAVE TO GAOL

Stintz had been getting into trouble: he'd been questioned about a few robberies and was subject to police attention. I was trying to keep an eye on him, but I was hardly a great role model.

'Bro, you're a good kid,' I told him. 'Don't let this life take you over. Mate, sure we fight and paint and carry on, but stealing and robbing people only sees you in gaol.'

'Yeah, you're right, Punchy,' Stintz said. 'I couldn't handle sitting in a cell.'

I knew gaol would be mentally tough on him as Stintz was unable to sit still for a second, and if he was caged he'd lose his mind. He really was a good kid, but he was *still* a kid. Other people his age were being influenced by sports stars or celebrities, while his mentors were leading him to gaol. When I stole paint and clothes I stupidly justified it because I stole from big-name retailers and they could afford it; I didn't steal from individuals. Stintz, being led by older boys in the crew, didn't have any boundaries.

One night I was having a drink with Vert when Stintz cruised up in a car, the problem with that being Stintz didn't have a licence and he also didn't own a car.

'Like my ride, boys? Jump in!' He fixed the rear-view mirror like a seasoned driver and his cheeky, child-like giggle made us laugh.

'I'm not getting in unless he drives,' I said, pointing to Vert, who was the only one of us who had a driver's licence.

'Yeah, I'm not getting in with you driving,' Vert said. Stintz jumped out of the driver's seat and into the back while Vert and I sat up the front. Stintz had stolen the car the night before and it already had a dent in the side that hadn't been there when he got it.

'Sweet lad,' Stintz hollered. Getting into a stolen car is just dumb – sheer laziness, and losing this gamble meant gaol time. I was still on my good behaviour bond, but I felt invincible because I was with the boys.

We drove around the city for half an hour before getting into a brawl with a bunch of guys walking past us at the lights. I hurt my hand in the fight and told Vert to take me home. En route to my place we turned a bend to see a row of cars being pulled over by police. My heart flew out of my mouth and was now sitting on the dashboard.

'Oh, get fucked,' Stintz shouted from the back seat. 'Punch it past them!'

'They might not check us,' I said, hopefully.

The police were randomly pulling over some drivers for breath tests and letting others by, and a dented car with three young guys in it was unlikely to be waved through. An officer motioned with his left arm for the car in front of us to continue on home and we drove forwards to our fate. I felt like a gladiator in ancient Rome: on my back, my opponent's sword at my throat, I could hear the crowd of onlookers screaming for blood. 'Lugula! Kill him!'

I glanced into the stands of the colosseum, hoping for a reprieve from the emperor. A left-arm wave would mean we were home free, while a right-arm wave meant gaol. The judge who held our future in his hands stared us dead in the eyes, and we stared back. He waved his right arm to gaol. Now the car felt claustrophobic as we turned and slowly pulled to a halt. Vert wound down his window.

'Take off, take off,' Stintz urged from the back.

'Shut up,' Vert said, like a ventriloquist out of the side of his mouth. I kept my left arm close to the handle and was ready to run. There were flashing blue lights and police everywhere: this chase was going to be big.

'Licence, please,' the officer said when he reached Vert's window. Vert pulled his wallet from his pocket, his hands trembling slightly, and handed the officer his licence.

'Busy night, mate?' I asked, trying to sound relaxed.

'Blow in this until I say stop,' the officer said.

The breathalyser gave a beeping noise as Vert blew.

'Yep, that'll do.' The officer looked at the breathalyser, then bent down and looked in the back at Stintz. Stone-faced, Stintz looked right back. A few tense moments ticked by and my feet could already feel the pavement of the chase. 'All right, good to go, boys.'

'Thanks, mate.'

We made our way home to bed. That was our life, where the thinnest of lines separated safety in bed or dead or in gaol.

CHAPTER 31

CLIMBING OUR EVEREST

RM was at full force and known everywhere: we'd built its status not only as a fighter's crew but one that got loads of panels done. We'd been battling some other writers, which got us doing deeds we wouldn't have attempted otherwise. One such deed was the mythical whole car – except we decided to do two whole cars. A double whole car hadn't been achieved in Sydney since I'd started writing.

To pull off one whole car in Sydney was near impossible, so to get two done next to each other would cement our spot in history. It was time to get one up on our competition, and we'd found a spot that had gone untouched for a long time. We nicknamed it the 'Mish' train yard because it was a huge mission to get to. It was a long drive inland so to go all the way there and not paint would be the worst, but after sussing it out for a few weeks I was confident we could pull off a double whole car.

Security at Mish train yard was inconsistent: some nights the guards wouldn't leave the train while on others we wouldn't see them for hours, but because the place was privately owned they weren't your regular, useless security guards. These ones wore black overalls and were armed with guns. With that in mind, I decided not to attempt the spot until we knew its workings back to front. 'We'll wait for the Queen's Birthday public holiday,' I told the boys. My thinking was that given the place was privately owned, on a long weekend the security might not be there at all.

During the week leading up to the public holiday we were pumped. Baby-faced Stintz was anxious at the best of times, and this week he was jumping out of his skin.

'Punchy, this is going to be hectic! You really think we can pull it off?'

'Yeah, mate.' I smiled and put my arm around him to settle him down.

Doing a double whole car was going to be a big job and we'd need many hands painting, so I organised two carloads of boys. As we drove to the spot we were all quiet, contemplating the mission ahead. The armed security guards worried me. Usually we could intimidate security with numbers, but these guys were armed with guns. It was nearly pitch black outside the yard we were going to paint, and young men running in every direction might scare a guard into firing a shot.

Finally, we pulled up in a back street a good walk from the spot. 'You ready, boys?' I turned to Base, the pit-bull crazy Craig and Mick, who were all sitting in the back seat. The other car pulled up behind ours and we all got out and walked along a fence line in our dark clothes, hoods pulled up. We were ready.

I blew fog in the cold air, my heart racing. We opened a nearby fence with our master key and made our way along the dark tracks towards the yard. As we approached I spotted a speck of light in the intensely black night. My entire body tingled in anticipation. Fifty metres further on, we knelt down and looked around for any movement. The security team's car wasn't where it was normally parked, so I thought we were good to go.

'We're sweet, boys,' I said. I stood up and walked slowly towards our target. If we were sprung by security now we'd be in a difficult situation. I'd put in countless hours night after night, watching and waiting, planning and preparing. Sitting without painting was like putting a stray dog in front of food and asking it not to eat.

Normally never so patient, I'd stifled my impulses, knowing that if I didn't paint and just watched the yard's workings our crew could pull it off and have everybody talking, cementing our ego. Now we stood on the pathway to the closed train shed. Through a high open window we could see a Tangara train. I looked at the others, wide-eyed, and our buzz doubled. Not able to control his excitement, Base punched my shoulder to relieve some tension.

The shed was completely closed up. On other occasions a couple of entrances would be open, but due to the public holiday we couldn't find a way in. This was good and bad: good because it looked as though no one was around, but bad because not only would it be tough to get into the place, if police or armed security came it would be hard to get out of quickly.

'Stintz, come here,' I said. 'I'll boost you up through the window and see if you can open the door from the inside.' Stintz was the smallest and lightest of all of us, but he looked at me reluctantly. 'Mate, if anyone grabs you I'll boot this door in. Don't worry, you know I've always got your back.' Stintz was optimistic and allowed me to boost him up to the window ledge, where he got the first good look of the yard.

'Lad!' It was Stintz's only word.

'What?' we all shot back at once.

'It's fucking packed with trains.'

'Is security in there?' I whispered.

Stintz looked left, right, up at the ceiling then straight ahead to see if anyone was about. We all stood like baby birds waiting to be fed, our necks bent backwards to look up at him. We hoped for positive feedback.

'I can't see anyone, boys.'

Those words sent a bolt of energy through us all. We looked at each other, grinning from ear to ear.

'Jump in and open the door,' I demanded, frustrated he hadn't already done it. Every second counted. Stintz leapt off the window ledge and started pulling on door handles. He was tip-toeing around, still not sure the place was empty.

'Beep, beep, beep, beep!' A loud, echoing alarm went off, signalling our night's end. A couple of the boys were startled and ran off a few metres.

'Wait, boys!' I screamed out, no longer caring whether anyone could hear me. The boys stopped and turned. Stintz was scrambling through the window but couldn't reach up.

'Spewing, what a waste of a good spot,' Azza commented. He was disappointed we could no longer paint.

'Damn, Punchy, that's shit. Let's get out of here,' another boy commented.

'Bullshit,' I responded. I turned and, with two kicks, booted down the door. I entered the large warehouse. Stintz busted past me to head out of the exit. 'Mate, we're still painting,' I said, grabbing his shirt.

'Come on, Punchy, the alarm's going off. We have to go,' a couple of the boys said.

'I've been watching this spot for months. There's no way I'm leaving without attempting it.' I put a ladder next to the train. The others watched on, still not happy with my decision to paint. I climbed the ladder and took a look around the yard: I felt like I was a king. I was daring to do what others wouldn't, but it was all for the ego. Capture or even a possible bullet wasn't going to stop me. I reached the top to sketch up the first letter then took a second to look around. The crew began to fill in the train. A couple of the boys stood back hesitantly, still not sure about it, so I motioned with my head for them to snap out of it and they soon joined the others.

I shook my can and started on my first line. Lowering myself down the ladder, I kept my eyes straight ahead. Green paint spat out to give the upper half of the train some life. The alarm kept ringing and ringing and seemed to be getting louder, angry that nobody had turned it off.

Still standing on the ladder, I looked across to see eight of my close friends hectically covering two Tangara carriages with colours. Their expressions were that of desperation, as they frantically swapped empty cans for new ones to continue their monumental effort. I was now sweating and tired, but adrenaline and the hope of finishing pushed me on. The sound of the alarm was piercing my brain and starting to make me feel sick.

A bang startled us all: Craig was headbutting the train. 'Not only are we painting it, but I'll kill it too,' he said. Craig was insane. The wet paint was on his forehead and we all laughed, which was a welcome escape from the edginess. Not wanting to waste a second, I begged everybody to keep going.

Forty minutes in I heard a few upbeat, satisfied words from the boys. 'Looking good! We got this shit covered.'

'Boys, I think we're home!'

I started to get that little confident grin again, but pulled myself out of it. *It's not done yet,* I thought. I didn't want to drop my guard, like I had a few months earlier when I found myself on the end of a charge sheet. I'd learned my lesson then and stayed focused on completing and escaping before celebrating.

I looked across at my main man, Base. He stopped and looked back at me, then nodded. I flashed him a satisfied grin, accepting we were close to pulling off this huge night. Both carriages of this now fully coloured Tangara had come together nicely, and this married couple only needed to say 'I do' to complete the ceremony. With a few more strokes I did some final touch-ups on one carriage while Azza completed the other.

We'd finally climbed our Everest. In the graffiti world, the RM crew were now legends.

CHAPTER 32

FEELING RESPONSIBLE

Ruben had a boxing fight scheduled one Friday night that was a three-hour drive south of Sydney. I called the boys and organised a few of us to go support him. Chad, the blond-haired pretty boy, Craig, the crazy pit bull, baby-faced Stintz, my main man Base and I all met in the city and had a few drinks before jumping on a train for the long ride.

It was a Friday afternoon and the train was filled with school kids, workers and business people. The five of us managed to get seats, and we sat drinking our case of rum and coke. Cruising past the spot I got caught, I pointed out to the boys where I had been chased. They all had their eyes on the spot as I recalled the story. 'That's where we jumped in. That's where the coppers come from.'

By the time the train got in Ruben's fight time was very close, so we ran to the club so we wouldn't miss the fight.

'Where's your ID?' Somebody grabbed me by my shirt. I turned and saw a man standing taller than me with a solid build and wearing a black security uniform. His facial expression told me he was looking for trouble; he'd found the right crew for that.

'Mate, I don't have any. I'm not going into the club. I've just come to watch my brother fight.'

'Well, unlucky for you. You can fuck off now.'

I kept my cool. Although this guy was testing my temper I didn't want to miss the fight. 'Mate, please, I just travelled here from Sydney.

My brother's fighting in one minute.' I saw families inside with kids and knew this guy was just on a power trip. 'Mate, people without ID can watch the fights. There are families in there with kids.'

'I know they can, but you're not coming in.'

'Don't worry, Punchy. Let's go watch it at the pub,' Chad said. Given the size of the security guards, Chad thought it best to leave without an altercation.

'That's right, listen to your girlfriend and fuck off.'

I snapped. After landing a few punches, Base pulled me away. 'Let's go, Punchy,' he said.

We watched the fight on a TV in a pub round the corner. Ruben knocked his opponent out and we celebrated, drinking and enjoying ourselves. Afterwards we walked back to the train station and found a train sitting at the platform waiting to depart. Just as we arrived we heard the guard's whistle, signalling for it to leave.

'Wait, wait,' we yelled, running up the stairs, but by the time we reached the platform the train had already left. What seems a tiny thing in life such as missing a train by one second can have a flow-on effect, creating unfathomable differences to hundreds of people's lives.

Chad scrolled his fingers down the timetable on the wall. 'Man, that was the last train.' The next one didn't leave until 5 am so we decided to go back to the pub, but soon the bartender was calling last drinks.

'Boys, I'm going for a walk. I'll get us home,' Stintz said. We watched him leave. It sounded like a good idea: riding in a stolen car home was a lot more inviting to a bunch of drunk idiots than sitting on a freezing cold station for a couple of hours.

A faint alarm rang out in the distance then my phone rang. 'It's Stintz,' I said. 'Get ready. He must have a car.'

I pressed the answer button to hear Stintz whispering, 'Punchy, Punchy, can you hear me?'

'Speak up, man,' I said.

'I can't,' he whispered. 'I'm in the roof of some office. Follow the alarm.'

'What?' I motioned for the boys to leave with me. 'Tell me if it's okay to come out,' he begged.

As we approached the sound of the alarm I had some bad news for him. Police and security people were everywhere, their cars parked on the footpath near the entrance of what looked like a computer firm's office.

'Mate, coppers and security are everywhere. They're coming in.'

Stintz had left the pub feeling like he was an intrepid explorer searching for a means to get us home. Sidetracked, he'd made the obtuse decision to break into an office in search of money. He hung up the phone to stay quiet and ready himself for capture. We sat and watched as the police entered the building with torches and spent the next 10 minutes searching.

'I think he's going to get away with it,' Base said.

'Quick! He's out! He made a run for it!' I shouted.

We heard crashing noises as the police scrambled and tripped on each other to get outside as quickly as they could. 'Did you guys see anyone running? Was that you shouting?' one officer asked us.

'We didn't shout anything, but I saw a guy running towards the station.' I was hoping to throw them off the scent of our boy hidden in the roof. They began to run towards the station, but a loud crashing noise inside the building stopped them.

'I've got him!' an officer yelled. The officers all turned and ran back inside. We looked at each other and shook our heads: our boy wouldn't be coming home with us.

Stintz sported a fresh black eye as he made his way out first, two officers holding his cuffed hands behind his back. We laughed to throw their suspicion off us, but I caught Stintz's eye and felt complete sorrow. He gave me a little disappointed grin that looked more like a frown and put his head down.

It hit me again that this little baby-faced boy was still a kid. I'd met him a few years earlier as an innocent skater boy looking for an idol and over the past year I'd watched as he stole cars, robbed people and bashed Links to a bloody pulp. Now he was heading to gaol. He was an innocent boy who had got in with the wrong crowd.

I'd tried to pull him in line after hearing of the harder stuff he was getting in to. The crowd he was with, that we introduced him to, were not right for this frantic kid who suffered from mental-health issues.

It wasn't the lure of fast money that dragged him into stealing; it was the belief that the better thief you were the stronger would be your reputation. The money was nothing and would be frittered away on clothes, drugs and poker machines anyway.

I was reminded of a remark Kon had made after a brawl. When he realised he'd lost a diamond watch in a mêlée he searched for it only for a couple of seconds. 'Easy come, easy go,' he said, before walking away. I'd heard that saying before, but until that moment I didn't get the true meaning of it. Kon had got the watch from wrongdoings, so he wasn't too fussed about its loss. If you get things easily you'll lose them even more easily, and if you get things via doing wrong then eventually you will be crushed.

Chad saw the distraught look on my face as I watched Stintz being taken away. 'Don't sweat, Punchy. It's going to happen to all of us anyway.' A couple of years later Chad was sentenced to life in gaol for killing a man.

CHAPTER 33

DEATH SCARES ME

Stintz had been refused bail, and because he'd turned 18 a couple of weeks prior to getting caught in the roof he was incarcerated in Silverwater, the big boys' gaol. When I visited him there he walked out wearing white overalls a couple of sizes too big for him. They didn't have any to fit this small boy.

In the end, because of his mental-health issues and his age he was sentenced to six months' gaol. It was a light sentence for the charge of getting caught in the roof plus a couple of other minor charges he'd managed to clock up. I knew gaol would be hard, but I thought it could be the best thing to have happened to him. I hoped it would straighten him out and help him realise that he needed to improve his life.

I had to do something to improve my own life. Things were getting serious: a couple of the boys had been bashed badly when other crews had found them alone and a few were doing gaol time. Snap could see that the world I was in was crashing down around me, so he asked me again if I'd work with him.

'Come be my offsider on your days off studying,' he said. He was reaching for my fingertips, desperately trying to keep me alive as I fell. Snap's business had taken over his life, so I rarely got to see him. He was busy, which didn't allow much time for painting or taking drugs, and he was hoping it would have the same outcome for me.

I doubted he really needed the help; he just wanted to get me on the right path. 'Yeah, okay, let's do it,' I said with a smile.

Base was away in the army, and Snap and I chatted about how happy we were to see him doing so well. Two of my closest friends had taken steps towards better lives. They were both more relaxed and happier while I was a mess.

Dad and I visited Grandma's grave together, and I watched as he removed dirt and fallen twigs. He put one of the fallen twigs in his mouth and kept his head down for a little while, as if he was talking to her.

'You know, Luke.' His voice was croaky. 'I'm going to be dead too one day.'

'Don't say that, Dad.' I hated talking about the death of my parents; it left me breathless as they meant the world to me. Death scared me.

'It's true, mate, this life is short. That's why we have to do everything we can to help the family and love each other.' We both kissed the plate with Grandma's name on it then, after wiping the tears from our faces, Dad put his arm around me and we walked back to the car.

On the trip home I thought about what he had said. I did want to help my family; they had done everything for us kids. Looking at Dad with Grandma's twig still in his mouth, I felt incredibly ashamed of myself. If he knew what I was getting up to he'd be so disappointed, although I knew he'd find ways of defending or excusing my behaviour because he always backed his boys up. But the stuff I was getting up to now would be hard to excuse.

CHAPTER 34

DENY

When I finished Year 10 at TAFE I decided to stay on to complete my Higher School Certificate. I chose a college far from home so I wouldn't know anyone or get distracted and I sat by myself most of the time, but I soon hooked up with some writers and my grades began to fall again.

Shaun was a Fijian-Indian writer who'd just moved to Sydney from Brisbane. Deny, who was a couple of years younger than Shaun and me, was excited to know that Punch was in his class. 'Man, I had no idea that was you! I've heard hectic stories, but all I see is you sitting by yourself studying.'

'Just trying to get through this year best I can.'

'That's fair enough. Can I meet any of the other RM boys?'

'Yeah, I'll take you out at the end of the year after we finish.'

'What? Awesome, can't wait!'

The year was now up. 'Punchy, we're finishing soon. When are you introducing me to some of the RM boys?'

'I'll take you out tomorrow night,' I said.

Deny had become a good friend. He was another innocent kid who just wanted to hang out with some older boys he respected. When he and Shaun arrived at my place we quickly got into our first bottle of rum.

'Why do you keep those?' Deny asked, pointing at the empty spirit bottles on top of my wall unit.

'There's a story in every bottle,' I replied. I hopped off the couch, and as I picked up the different bottles I explained each story the now-empty container held. Deny sat quietly and listened.

'I wonder what story this one holds,' I said, grabbing the rum out of his hands and taking a sip.

'Tonight's going to be sick!' Deny said. By the time we reached the city he was already extremely drunk. He was a young kid and the rum had gone straight to his head, and he was tripping over everywhere.

'Better get him home,' Shaun said.

I agreed. 'Boys, let's get out of here.'

'Where we going?' Chad asked. Not wanting to miss out on a night full of girls, this ladies' man wasn't keen on leaving.

'Don't know. We have to take Deny home, and then we'll do whatever.'

Down at the station there were transit police everywhere. These new grey-suited transit officers, who had replaced the failed Chubb security and whom we nicknamed the 'grey dogs', had power. They knew it, too, and they could be savage towards writers. It made for some interesting times.

As we purchased tickets the transit police watched on, waiting for us to slip up. I noticed their suspicious eyes following our every move and grabbed Deny tightly so he wouldn't stagger around too much.

'Hey, mate, just chill out. The grey dogs are watching.' Deny was playing it cool, but when we reached the escalator he stepped down one step and tripped a little. 'Mate, just stay still.' I grabbed him and leant him against the handrail as we rode down to the train platform.

'I need to piss,' Deny said. He pulled his pants down and without a second's hesitation started to go. We all giggled. Deny was laughing more than anyone, looking back at us by leaning and turning his neck a little and almost falling over.

'Hey!' We heard hollering from behind. Two transit officers were running down the escalator towards us. Deny scrambled for his pants and pulled them up while he was still going, which made us laugh even harder. It was no big deal; he'd get a fine for urinating in a public place but the transit officers yelled out as though he'd just committed a murder.

When they were a couple of steps away from us I turned to see whether Deny had run away. He'd reached the bottom of the escalator. The transit officers pushed us to the side and we watched Deny's legs disappear out of sight.

We ran down to see what was happening. When we reached the bottom we saw a train sitting stationary at the platform. The train guard's whistle sounded and the car doors closed. Deny wasn't thinking straight, and with two transit officers close behind and a stomach full of alcohol he jumped down into the gap between the platform and the train to escape.

Our laughter turned to screams as we pleaded for him to stop, but it was too late: Deny's small body vanished as he crawled under the train. Like a man waking from a deep sleep, the train shook a little as it readied itself to depart. I watched as in slow motion the monster crept along the tracks devouring our friend, who lay underneath.

'No!' I screamed.

'Fuck, he's dead!' A crying Shaun grabbed me. 'Punchy, he's dead!'

My head was hot and my body shook. My mouth opened just wide enough to feel the train's wind on my tongue. The train took what felt like years to move off our friend. I envisaged him being crushed with each wheel as it passed over his bleeding body. Finally, the last carriage rolled on. Closing my mouth, I braced myself for what I was about to see.

The noise of the metal train's creaking and grinding was gone, replaced by the deepest, most agonising scream I'd ever heard. It was coming from a bystander who saw what had happened.

Men began pulling their partners away from the crowd of onlookers, not wanting them to see any more. I looked down onto the dark tracks. Deny lay on his back, staring at the roof of the tunnel. His eyes were open and his head rocked from side to side. His right arm had been completely sheared off a couple of inches above the elbow, and fragments of bone and veins were minced on the silver track near his head. His left hand had also been eaten up, diced into irreparable mulch.

He looked up at me with a ghastly face, his expression one of disbelief.

I jumped down onto the tracks, picked him up and pulled him to his feet. As I lifted him onto the platform he moaned and little murmurs of words came from his blood-filled mouth. The poor young soul was incredibly drunk and confused about what was happening.

Deny tried to lift himself off the ground with an arm that wasn't there. He was crushing the bone and veins onto the ground, so I pleaded with him to remain still. 'Just lie down, brother.' Someone took their jumper off and wrapped it around his remaining flesh.

'I'm dead, Punchy,' Deny's purple lips mumbled as I cradled his head in my arms. He closed his eyes slowly and took a step towards death. One more and he was gone.

'Deny! Deny!' I said, tapping his adolescent, freckled face. The lids to his eyes gave a little shake before slowly opening.

They flickered, and he took a step back towards life. He looked me straight in my eyes, his soul asking for help. 'I'm dead,' he repeated.

'Mate, if you live I'll put you in RM, I promise.' I knew he loved the crew and would have done anything to be in it, so I was hoping this desperate plea would work.

'You swear?' he replied, opening his eyes a little more.

'I promise, mate,' I said. He closed his eyes again. 'Deny!' I shouted as tears ran down my cheeks. I slapped him hard but he didn't open his eyes. 'Deny, open your eyes, brother!' I shouted more loudly.

He opened them. A rotten game of tug of war was being played out between his beating heart and mortality. 'Mate, if you close your eyes once more I won't put you in the crew.' What I was saying probably seemed stupid to the onlookers, but it was the only thing I knew he loved. It was barely working, though. *Where's the ambulance?* I thought.

For the first time I became aware of my surroundings. Deep pools of blood covered the grey-tiled platform, but I was in another world with Deny. One of my hands was cradling his head and the other was holding on to the tug of war rope, assisting his beating heart. I glanced over to see the transit officers who had chased him kneeling down.

'You mutts! You caused this over a piss on the stairs!' Chad roared.

The transit officers looked at me as though expecting me to shut him up, knowing I was the leader.

'Yeah, you fucking dogs, fuck off. You caused this.' I didn't really think it was their fault: it had been a drunken accident. I was drunk myself, and with my friend's veins and parts of his skin hanging off my arm and clothing I wasn't thinking straight. I lowered my face down to get closer to Deny. 'I love you, mate. Stay alive,' I whispered.

'Okay, step aside.' Two paramedics wheeled in a stretcher.

I kept holding Deny's face and whispering to him. His warm blood was smeared across my face. 'I know him,' I sobbed, hoping they wouldn't force me to move and knowing full well my words were keeping his eyes open.

Police arrived. I kept talking to Deny, who was now demanding I keep my promise and put him in the crew. This unfortunate child didn't know the full extent of his injuries, and he also didn't know that if he closed his eyes and went to sleep as he felt like doing he wouldn't wake up.

I felt an arm wrap around my shoulder. 'Move away!' a voice said. I shrugged the arm off so I could keep cradling Deny's face. 'I said, move away!'

Before I knew it I was being dragged away once again. After I made several attempts to get back to Deny's side one of the police officers sprayed something in my face. I dropped to the floor instantly, my face burning in agony. It was pepper spray.

My eyes were open when the spray hit and it was as though a blow torch had been applied to my eyeballs and entire face. I was thrown to the ground and had knees in the back of my head. I was dizzy from a lack of oxygen and it felt as though my lungs were filling with bubbling acid and my face had blisters popping all over it. I was handcuffed and pulled to my feet, then I was walked out of the train station and thrown into a paddy wagon.

I was charged with assaulting police and resisting arrest. Deny was put into an induced coma for a week. He fought like a true champion and survived.

CHAPTER 35

BEHIND THE LABELS

'Mate, that's the worst thing I've ever heard.' Base had called me from his training base in Brisbane. 'Punchy, I'm so sorry. Mate, how easy could it have been for that to happen to you, though? We tested the limits a lot, but now it's time to do something with your life. You're going too red hot.'

'Brother, it was just an accident, that wouldn't happen to me. You know I'm special. I'm alive for a reason.' I tried to lighten him up.

'Bro, that's bullshit! I've seen you drunk, you're a mess. You're just lucky nothing like this has happened to you. You're not drinking around me any more.'

Base's maturity had doubled since he had joined the army. He'd told me stories about having to iron his sheets and having an officer in his face screaming if he hadn't ironed them properly. I teased him about how bad he had it, but really I was just trying to take the attention away from my own miserable life.

'What do you mean, I'm not drinking? Who the fuck are you? What do you know, anyway? You've been away, you got no idea what my life is like now.'

'I'll speak to you soon,' he said, disappointed.

I lay on my bed for a while, condemning Base for attempting to control me, then I headed into the bathroom to have a heart to heart with myself in the mirror. I would do this regularly, especially after I'd done something I was ashamed of. If I hurt someone in a fight I would come home and look deep into the mirror and stare into my eyes.

This time my reflection shocked me: who was this person staring back? Luke Kennedy used to be a happy character who had been brought up to be a good person and help people, not hurt them, but now I was big, bad Punchy. 'What are you doing to yourself?' I asked. I didn't need any answer. Deep down I could feel my true self, which didn't harbour malice towards anyone, trying to get out. He'd been blocked by an ego that enjoyed being labelled a fighter, vandal, thief, alcoholic, drug abuser and leader. *These labels,* I thought, *are the only things I have. Without them who am I?*

I knew my life was meant for something else. I just had to keep believing that one day I would be free.

* * *

Dad was incredibly angry. We argued, and he begged me to stop drinking and carrying on. 'You've been charged by the fucking police!' he said. 'What if it was you under that train? You and your fuckwit mates think you're so smart!' Dad didn't know what to do. 'Luke, please, I've been through it myself. It's not worth it! Kennedys can't handle the drink. Please, learn from my mistakes! Get a job and start looking after yourself.'

I defended my actions, which started another argument. In the end I stormed out and moved in with Anne at her parent's house, but Anne was just as worried as Dad. 'Babe, your dad's right,' she said, gently, as we lay in her big, clean, comfortable bed. 'We don't want to see you killed. Things are out of control and it's getting worse. You're fighting all the time. It's only a matter of time before something bad happens to you.'

'I don't want to hear this shit from you too,' I said, angrily. Anne smiled and hugged me. She was my first love and I was hers. Although I was mean to her sometimes and we'd have some big fights, I did love her deeply and would do anything I could to make her happy. Like any young lovers' relationship, ours contained plenty of happiness but also plenty of fights. I'd go out all night and play around with other girls and she'd be at home, trying to call me or my friends and hoping I was okay. When I got home she'd be angry, but quickly just happy to see me.

Anne cried sometimes and it crushed me. I'd promise myself I wouldn't cause her any more heartache, but all it took was a few drinks and we'd be back to arguing. When we were both sober you couldn't find a more loving couple.

Mum and Dad hadn't given up on me; they missed me. 'Luke, please come home. I love you, mate,' Dad said in a soft tone over the phone one day. 'I just don't want to see you go down the same road I did.'

I was soon back at home.

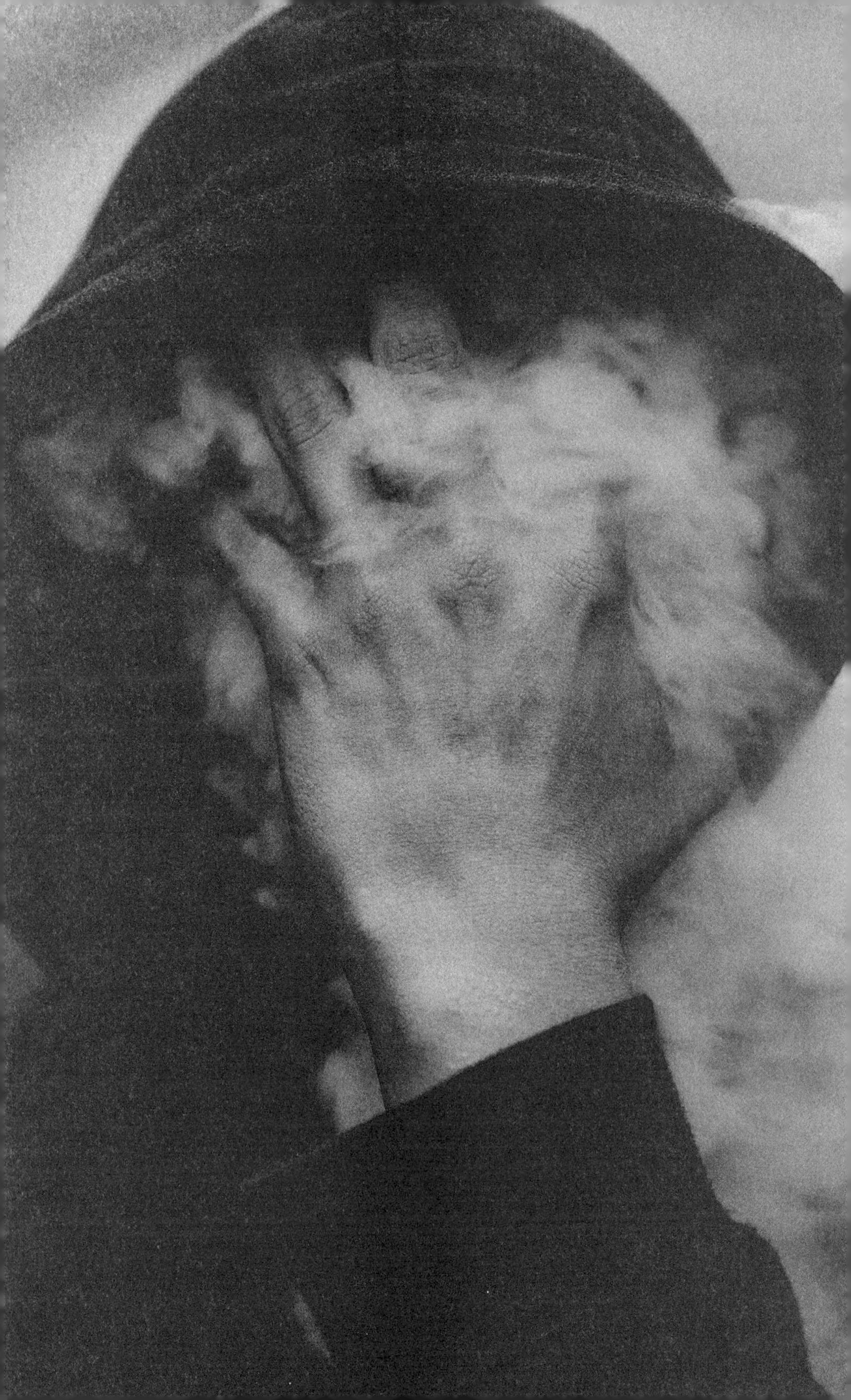

CHAPTER 36

INFIGHTING

Billz had been locked away in gaol for assault. He was a nice guy when I chatted to him man to man and we got along well. I spent endless days and nights at his place drinking and laughing the night away and our friendship had developed into a strong bond. Nevertheless, at least once a week we'd be close to coming to blows, though I'd sensed a new hesitation from him when we argued. He'd seen me win countless fights and, knowing what I was capable of, he avoided getting a piece of it.

It was hard to see him locked away. He'd backed me up a lot, as I had him. I once watched as he swung a machete at the head of a guy who was attempting to fight me. Luckily, the man ducked. Now Billz wanted me to take over leading RM while he was locked up. 'Kon's too busy with his music and, anyway, you're the man for the job,' he said.

I was happy to take on the label of leader and happy to look after the boys – I felt good after helping people. Besides, then they'd talk about me.

Our position as the top fighters in the graffiti world had gone unchallenged but now we were having running wars with other crews, some of whom had grown in number and muscle. A couple of crews that were sick of hearing about us and seeing their girls come over to our side had joined forces to take us on. The war between us and the other crews saw an increase in fights and painting, but we still had the upper hand. I hadn't yet been beaten.

'We have to step this shit up!' I told the boys. My confidence (and luck) was through the roof, but so was my anxiety. The next few weeks saw tit for tat fights that caused everything from broken bones to severe hospitalisation. When we were painting trains our nerves were already near crippled from looking out for security, but now with the war going on our anxiety was doubled as we also had to be aware that we could be ambushed by another crew.

Stintz was released from gaol. Crazy Craig picked me up and we went to meet him.

'*Stiinnttzz!*'

Stintz's child-like giggle was one that shouldn't have been heard inside a gaol. We hugged.

'Love you, my brother,' he said.

'My boy, I love you too.'

We took him home and the three of us sat around talking. 'Mate, it's time to pull up. You're upsetting your family and you don't belong in gaol,' I told him.

'You're just a fucking kid!' Craig chucked in.

'Punchy, you're right,' Stintz said. 'I'm going to stop all this. I know I'm better.' He was right: he was better than all this. His mental-health issues were no excuse for some of the things he was doing, but he needed some proper guidance. 'Punchy, you're worse than any of us,' he said. 'Why haven't you been to gaol?'

Stintz and Craig stared at me: I think it was a question they'd both been asking themselves for a while and I didn't know what to say. I finally broke the silence. 'Mate, to tell you the truth, I think it's because although I do muck up a lot I know my limits. You wouldn't have seen me up in that roof.'

Stintz smiled. 'What about all the fights?'

'Mate, they're something I do so I don't end up on my own back snoring. To me that's not a risk, it's a response.' I was trying to excuse my actions. I knew I was being a hypocrite but it was to protect Stintz, not me. I was trying to guide him away from the trouble we initially guided him towards. Easier said than done.

'Let's get out of here,' Craig barked. We decided to head out to the pub with Base and Kent to celebrate Stintz's release. All the crew from the south-west came too so it was the usual suspects – red-headed Mick, tall strong Vert, pretty boy Chad, Fund and Rod.

The night was set for entertainment. Craig and Mick argued over which horse to bet on while Base played the poker machines and Fund and Rod stood outside to have a cigarette with Kent. Chad was talking to two gorgeous ladies and had their full attention. We were all minding our own business having a good time, although the energy we gave off would have attracted drama from anywhere.

As Vert walked past a group of men one of them dropped a shoulder into him, said something and then pushed him. Vert didn't hesitate; he dropped the guy. Once more it was on. It was a major scrap – these guys could fight and Stintz was soon on his back getting kicked.

I pulled him up. 'Get out of here, brother.' I didn't want him getting into trouble again; the local police already knew him but Stintz didn't budge. Only the sound of police sirens in the distance saw us retreat and we went to the park to settle down. Chad had a bleeding nose, Stintz a black eye and Craig a broken hand.

'Stintz, what did I say, mate? You have to stay out of the shit. If they look at the cameras you're back inside.'

'You've told me I've always got to back the boys up,' he said.

'Yeah, you do. We were okay, but there are cameras everywhere. It's a massive risk.'

'It wasn't a risk, it was a response,' he cheekily replied, echoing my earlier words.

* * *

'Punchy, I got caught out. They got me in the city. Two of them had big pieces of wood,' Stintz moaned over the phone. He'd been caught out by some of the newly formed KS crew, which had merged with others to go up against us.

'The dogs! How bad are you, mate?' I hated people using weapons and encouraged our boys to fight with their fists, because when weapons were used it opened the gates to death.

'Yeah, it's pretty bad but I'll be fine. I'm gonna crush them, Punchy!'

I couldn't picture Stintz saying this: to me he was still a young boy with blond hair and a child-like face. As he talked I pictured him as a small child standing on top of a chair to reach the house phone. The fact was, though, he was now a strong, fully grown man with tattoos surrounding his thick neck and he was looking for retribution.

After he recovered we got all the boys together and went to Sydney's Royal Easter Show. It was something we did every year to get drunk and cause some ruckus.

'You think KS'll be there today?' Stintz asked on the way, rubbing his hands together as if he was warming them up for use. The sparkling new watch he wore halfway up his arm told me the person he'd stolen it from was a lot bigger than he.

'Maybe,' I replied. I hoped they weren't, because we were out for a laugh and a good time. There were kids and families at the show, and I hated mixing my crazy world with people's normal lives.

'I'm ready for them if they are,' Stintz said, giving me a cheeky smile. Judging from the way he had said it, I should have known he wasn't joking.

At the show Base wasted no time finding a bunch of girls. He was just back from training and was enjoying letting his hair down. My main man had grown in size and looked fit and healthy and was now extremely good-looking. The army had eaten up a trouble-making, pimply faced child and spat out a mature, proud man who walked with a confident strut.

'Watch this,' he whispered out of the corner of his mouth. He walked straight over and began chatting to the girls. I cruised over to back him up and tried in vain to get in on the conversation, but no flirty hair twirl was directed at me. I was big and fat and dressed with attitude, sporting a bum bag and a white baseball cap. These ladies had no idea who I was; they just saw a fat bastard.

A shout from behind us put a stop to the smiling and giggles: it was Stintz and the boys. Stintz had a hammer in his hand and had just missed another writer's head with a fast swing.

'You want to hit me with wood?' he screamed. I noticed a couple of KS faces, and one looked me in the eye before turning and running. They were outnumbered this time. Craig had one on the ground and was pounding his head even though the guy had already been knocked out. Families and carnival workers looked on in disgust, and parents pulled their children closer to block their vision of the insane violence.

'Get out of here!' I yelled at the boys, then I grabbed Stintz. 'What the hell are you doing?' We retreated.

From that day on Stintz carried a hammer down his pants. After getting jumped with planks of wood he didn't want to risk more pain, so he'd decided to hammer anyone who came near. The thing with weapons is that it just escalates. To avoid getting hammered the enemy progresses to a knife, and after that? A gun.

I didn't want the floodgates to open on weapons but I was losing control.

CHAPTER 37

NO STRINGS ATTACHED

After the Royal Easter Show Crazy Craig and I went back to my place to drink. 'This is the shit that's doing my head in,' Crazy Craig said to me in desperation. 'I don't want to do it any more.'

'Mate, you backed the boys up. It's what we do,' I said, trying to make him feel better.

'Yeah, but I take it too far. I'm over it.' Crazy Craig was still sporting a scar on his upper lip from where I'd whacked him after he dog shot Vert. 'When does it end?' He put his head in his hands. His right hand was forever in the flexed position because it had been broken so many times in fights. Craig had had enough; his non-stop fighting had left him full of regrets and I should have realised he was at breaking point. He was searching for an out with no return and he soon found it.

The very next night I got a call from him. 'Punchy, it fucking happened again. Stintz and I just demolished some KS boys and Stintz used the hammer.' The tone of Craig's voice made me worry. It was as though something really serious had just happened or was about to.

'Mate, chill,' I replied. 'I'll be there soon.' I didn't want Craig talking that crazy stuff over the phone; he knew better than that. A couple of friends had been phone tapped by police and had ended up locked away. I called Brad to pick me up and suggested we got Base on the way.

We cruised up to Craig's house but couldn't get close because it was surrounded by police cars and wagons full of police dogs. Speechless, we drove past. Detectives in their suits stood around chatting away and looking over clipboards. Clear plastic evidence bags leant against a fence and I saw a hammer in one of the bags. I felt sick to my stomach: what had happened? Then I saw poor Craig being brought out in cuffs. We'd only spoken the night before about him getting away, and now it was too late.

Base looked me. 'Brother, it's where you're heading. You've got to stop this. You're smarter than these guys.'

Stintz's house was also raided that night. He was still on parole for the roof incident and now he was back inside, this time for a lot longer. *At least he'd get to hang out with Craig,* I thought, ruefully.

I was eating breakfast the next morning when my phone rang. 'Punchy, it's Craig.' I recognised the voice on the phone, but thinking that Craig was locked away at first I didn't register it was him.

'Hey, what's doing, mate?' I asked. 'Have you spoken to Stintz?'

'No, mate, he's locked up. Where are you?' He sounded like a lost puppy.

'Just at a family friend's place. What's going on? No, don't answer. I'll come see you.'

'Nah, Punchy, the coppers are right on to me. I have to go away. Stintz bashed those guys pretty bad with the hammer. I didn't do anything wrong, I didn't do anything wrong!'

'Mate, I'll come see you. Where are you?'

'I have to go.' He hung up.

I stood tapping the wall, trying to get my head around what had happened. *Why is he free but Stintz is locked up? Maybe because Stintz is on parole,* I thought, hoping my suspicions weren't true. *Maybe because Stintz did all the bashing?* I was trying to come up with a reason but, judging by Craig's hesitance to meet me, I knew: he'd given Stintz up!

'Mate, you know I wouldn't say this lightly, but I think Craig snitched,' I told pretty boy Chad.

'Bullshit! No way, Craig is one of the staunch ones!' Chad called Craig but his phone was disconnected. 'Let's go around to his place and front him,' he said.

We marched over to Craig's house where, only the day before, I'd watched detectives itemise his possessions. We slammed our fists on his door. Eventually, his brother hesitantly opened it, half his body shielded behind it. 'Hey, boys, Craig's not here.'

'Where is he, is he okay?' I tried to sound as though I was concerned for his welfare. 'We're worried about him.'

'He's gone away for a while,' Craig's brother replied, looking scared.

'Where to?' I asked, my voice showing more aggressiveness.

'Not sure.'

I stood thinking about my next move, but I couldn't hold it in any longer. 'Tell him he's a fucking dog!' I screamed as Chad punched the closing door. It was final: Craig had given one of the boys up. 'I can't believe it!' I kept repeating as we stormed off.

'It can't be true!' Chad echoed. We were hoping it wasn't. We tried hopelessly to come up with a reason for Craig's suspicious disappearance. 'What if he's on the run from the coppers?' Chad suggested.

'Maybe, but his brother was dodgy just then,' I tried to reason. It was a massive call and we couldn't be sure until we had concrete proof.

'That fucking dog gave me up!' This time, sitting there in the visitors' room, Stintz looked older. He'd grown into the white overalls.

He had ended up using his hammer. 'It was Craig's idea to get them. I swung the hammer and it landed hard on this mutt's knee. The sound was like a tree branch snapping! He dropped like a ton of bricks. The others hesitated, then the bitches all ran. They left their mate. I chased them for a bit. When I came back Craig was on top of the guy who'd just been kneecapped. He bent down near the guy's face. I heard a scared scream from the guy. Craig looked up at me with something in his mouth.' Craig had bitten the sobbing rival's ear off.

They ran back to Craig's house, which was nearby. Stintz stashed the hammer in the kitchen and then jumped the back fence to get away. 'He started the brawl, and he bit the prick's ear off. Now I'm in here and he's gone away!' Stintz smashed his hands on the table, which caused the prison guard to look up.

The police had gone around to Craig's place to question him and he'd crumbled, showing them where the hammer was and telling them who'd used it. For months Craig had confided in me that he wanted an out, that he wanted to travel overseas or head to Western Australia to work in the mines. Now he had an escape with absolutely no strings attached. He couldn't return.

'You might be in here next week, Punchy,' Stintz said, in reference to my upcoming court appearance from the night Deny had had his accident. Stintz seemed excited about the possibility.

Stintz got 18 months' prison time. The evidence was in the brief in black and white: Craig had rolled over. It was a shock to us all, as we'd been close to him, but now it was as though he'd been our sworn enemy for years. We heard rumours Craig had moved interstate, and I pictured him making a new life working and keeping to himself. What he wanted.

I visited Stintz regularly to try to keep his spirits up but I noticed a change in him after a few months – his language and outlook on things had become grim. 'Mate, try to stay clear headed,' I said. 'You'll be out in no time.'

My own court case was coming up. The night Deny had almost been killed I'd been arrested for assaulting police and resisting arrest. 'Can you believe that bastard is trying to sue you for twenty-two dollars!' my legal-aid solicitor exclaimed.

'Who?' I asked, surprised.

'The arresting officer. He said that as you turned to go back to your friend a link in his necklace broke. He wants you to pay for it!'

I couldn't believe it. When I'd had a few run-ins with the police when I was a teen I felt a huge amount of hatred towards them, but after working with organisations to help youth I'd met a lot of cool coppers who had saved kids' lives. At the time the charge seemed ridiculous, but my lawyer recommended I plead guilty to all charges.

'You're on a good behaviour bond. If you're found guilty of assaulting police and you haven't pleaded guilty you may find yourself locked up.' I knew it would absolutely crush Mum and Dad if I was locked away, and I had a vision of Mum sitting in the visitors' room with a red face, crying, as Dad cradled her in his arms. I didn't want that. As it turned out the judge was surprised by my guilty plea.

'The circumstances of your friend gave just cause for frantic actions. However, seeing as you did struggle with police and your guilty plea, I have no option but to sentence you to another twelve-month good behaviour bond. This rubbish about a twenty-two dollar necklace link is not to be paid. I hope your friend has recovered from this life-changing experience. If you come before me for laying hands on any form of authority again you will go to gaol.'

CHAPTER 38

'HE GOT ME'

Some of the people we hung around with were level-headed and I enjoyed having conversations with them. One of them, Skye, was emotionally intelligent. She'd read my thoughts in situations and call and discuss them with me later, and I'd let my guard down.

One day she rang and was blunt. 'You're a smart man. Why are you doing this?' she said.

'Same reason you are,' I replied. 'It's about the excitement: I get off on the daring stuff. It makes me feel alive!'

'Don't give me that shit,' Skye said. 'You're a leader and this is the best way you think you can use your skills. You know better than all of them and yet you cause more violence than any of them.'

'Hey, I don't hurt anyone without a reason!'

'Keep telling yourself that, Luke,' Skye said. 'Reason or not you still cause violence. You're on this earth for a reason, so make sure you find the right one.'

Skye was right: I knew I could do right in this world and one day I would. The conversations I had with Skye made Anne jealous and think something was going on between us, but there wasn't. Anne thought there was something going on between me and a lot of girls, and in that she was right.

Another time Skye rang, still worried. 'Far out, mate, everything's going hectic,' she said. 'It's all falling apart. You guys are going to gaol, separating and fighting each other.'

'It looks worse than it is,' I said. 'All right, Stintz's locked up, but that's happened before. Craig's gone, but he's a dog anyway. Nothing's gonna make us fall apart,' I said, confidently.

'That Links guy bashed one of the younger guys,' Skye pointed out. 'None of you guys used to get bashed, but now it's becoming one for one.' Links was the writer Stintz had almost killed after dropping him into the gutter years earlier.

'Fuck Links!' I snapped. I was sick of hearing about people testing our stance. KS didn't go anywhere near the big boys, but because of the amount of bashings they were carrying out it seemed as though we were losing the battle.

Next Links tried to stab Mick. 'He rushed me first, the cheeky dog!' Mick said. 'He tried to stab me with something, then jumped off the train and ran.'

'Wait until I see him,' I said. I'd helped Links the day he'd almost drowned in his own blood, but this time I was going to finish him off.

'Come to the beach, Punchy,' Mick said. 'I finish at two. Come meet me.'

'Yeah, sweet.' I didn't like the beach but I did like Coogee – the ladies there were phenomenal – so I caught the bus out. Mick and I hung around soaking up the sunshine. I felt immense happiness, as the bright blue sky and beautiful ladies in their bikinis made me smile.

Eventually we got bored and decided to catch the bus home. As the bus pulled out I turned to talk to him and noticed a couple of striped shirts through the window. Striped shirts could mean other writers. Mick noticed me looking past him and turned to see four guys walking away from the beach.

'That's fucking Links!' Mick said.

I felt a little sick with excitement and anxiety. There were four of them and only two of us, but my hatred towards Links dismissed those odds. I pushed the red stop button and the bus pulled over, then we hopped off and watched as our prey turned casually into a back street.

'Let's run up this way and cut them off. Links is mine,' I said. We ran across the road and around a building, hoping to see them coming up the street. With a skip in my step, I turned a corner to find all four of them facing us. Their smiling, talking faces slowly turned to shock. One motioned to run away but then acted staunchly after seeing his friends stand strong.

I pumped myself up and stood tall, my jaw clenched in anger. I didn't take my eyes off Links. 'Let's do this, you fucking dog!' I growled.

As he looked me in the eye Links put his hands down his pants. I could see his face trembling a little. He pulled out and unfolded a knife, which gave him increased confidence, and he smirked at me. I'd known Links for years and didn't think he'd use it, so I ran towards him. I stopped a couple of metres short.

'You think you're going to stab me? Well, go on then, bitch!' I raised my arms, confident he wouldn't do it.

Links took a step forward and swung at me with the knife. I had to suck my stomach in and lean back a little so the blade caught my shirt but missed my flesh. I was shocked: I'd been so sure he wouldn't attack with the knife. Even though we were enemies I didn't think he had it in him.

'Put the knife down and fight like a man!' I said. I shaped up, and he did too. He still had the blade in his hand, but I leapt in and threw a left-right. I hit him with the left but skimmed him with the right as he moved to the side a little and threw his own punch. Suddenly he froze.

What's up? Why has he stopped fighting?

My back felt warm and I looked at him. Links held the knife in the air, his mouth open and his eyes wide, staring at me. I looked right into them. There was noise around us but all I heard was dead silence. I turned and looked over my left shoulder: blood was bubbling out of my back.

He'd stabbed me.

I put my right hand over the wound to try to stop the bleeding and glanced back at him. 'You're fucking dead now,' I gasped. Links's face was pale as he turned and darted off. The blood was pouring through the gaps of my fingers and I could see people running in every direction. Links's friends had taken off too.

'See that, Punchy? I crushed his mate!' Mick was nodding his head, proud of his efforts. 'What's wrong?' He noticed I was struggling.

'He got me.' My breaths were getting shorter.

'Oh, fuck, no, Punchy. No, Punchy! What do I do?'

'Put pressure on it. Try to stop the bleeding!' I pulled my phone out of my pocket and called for an ambulance. 'There . . . there's been a stabbing,' I said. I squinted to see the street sign, then told the lady where we were.

'Who's been stabbed, sir?' she asked. I heard her typing on a keyboard.

'Me.' Darkness began to descend on my vision. 'Brother, I think I'm gone.'

'Don't say that, Punchy, please,' Mick said.

'It's either your heart or your lung,' I heard behind me from a shop attendant who was standing there.

I was getting dizzy and needed to sit down. I couldn't breathe and was nearly blind. I looked in Mick's direction and gave a slight smile to make him feel better. 'I'm sweet, brother. The dog got me, though.' I shook my head. Death felt close.

What's about to happen? Being scared of death and always getting into altercations, I'd imagined this moment for years. Did I manifest it? I'd pictured myself knowing I was about to die and how I would react, but this wasn't how I thought I'd be. I just sat there, not talking, not asking for salvation; just coping with it. Death was knocking and it seemed I'd opened the door wide to let it walk in without even wiping its feet. *Where do we go when we die? Am I about to find out?* I wondered.

I looked down at my feet. I was wearing my $250 shoes. I held them so dear I'd even scrubbed them occasionally with a toothbrush. Nikes were what writers wore, and the newest shoes seemed important to have. If I didn't own the newest I would be seen as somebody who couldn't lead, but now as my dark blood dripped onto my shoes they seemed incredibly insignificant. Possessions.

Our self-worth is determined by different things that we own. Why? Our minds prefer the wanting of something than actually possessing it, as wanting something feels more alive. Once we've attained that thing our minds move on to the next. Contentment: is there such a thing?

Blurry, blue flashing lights approached. The loud sirens just a couple of metres away were a comforting distraction from my thoughts of dying. A police car was behind the ambulance.

'Don't tell them who did it. Say it was a robber,' I told Mick. Such was my hatred of snitches I didn't give anyone up, even a man who'd just stabbed me.

The police jumped out of the car with their guns drawn, yelling at us to get down. A blood-soaked Mick raised his hands in submission, then they raced over and tackled him to the ground.

'It's not him, he's my friend,' I gasped as the paramedics sliced my shirt in half with a pair of scissors and began working on saving my life. Mick lay flat on the cement with knees in his back, then he bent his neck up and looked at me. 'You'll be fine, my brother!' he shouted.

I was stretchered away. Inside the ambulance the brightness of the light stung my pupils. 'How am I looking?' I asked the paramedic.

How did I get to this point? How did I end up in the back of an ambulance struggling for breath? I'd been born pure, an innocent young child, but graffiti had opened doors to insane violence. Was it graffiti that got me to this point or was it my ego begging to be noticed? I didn't know any other way to gain respect than to fight for it. I enjoyed being talked about after my first fight and it just got out of hand from there. A couple of wrong decisions ended with a blade sliding straight into me. Some of those decisions had seemed minor, but a few wrong moves and here I was almost welcoming death.

'You'll be sweet, my brother,' I heard from the front seat. It was Base! *Was I tripping out? How did he get there?* Base was supposed to have met us at the beach but we hadn't been able to get in contact with him. 'Sorry I wasn't there, brother. My phone died and I couldn't find you. Fuck, man!' He'd arrived just in time to see his main man being stretchered into the back of an ambulance.

Base came to the hospital with us; I felt more secure with him there. In the hospital a nurse reported that it was, indeed, a punctured lung.

'Who was it?' Base asked, leaning in.

'Links.'

The muscles in his jaw flexed and his shoulders rose. 'Don't worry, we will get him.'

Which way?

'Mum, I'm going to be okay.' Mum was sitting next to Base, tears running down her beetroot-red face. Dad put his hand on my chest, but he didn't say anything either.

'We have to insert a drain under your arm. If there are no complications you should be okay,' the nurse said. 'You were very lucky: the blade missed your heart by a couple of centimetres.' Mum exploded into tears.

'Luke.' It was Sarah.

'Sister!' I jovially said, trying to cheer her up. She too had obviously been crying.

Mick walked into the room sheepishly and greeted Base and my family before hugging me. I flinched in pain.

'Fuck, sorry, mate,' he said. The police had taken Mick back to the station, thinking he was the one who'd stabbed me. 'I told them how the junkie tried to take your phone and how you wouldn't let him so he stabbed you and ran.' Mick sounded like he wasn't confident with the story. I looked at Dad, who glanced at me then stared at the floor. I wasn't looking forward to hearing what he had to say.

The police arrived, wanting to question me, and Mick stood back looking worried. Although I was the victim of a knifing we were still lying to the police to protect the identity of the man who'd stabbed me. This worried me more than the outcome of my injury. I gave the police the same bullshit excuse and waited for their response. They were asking leading questions that seemed designed to catch me out, but after they realised I wasn't interested in talking they left.

'When the fuck is all of this going to stop?' Dad snapped after they'd gone. Base and Mick saw that as their cue to leave.

Mum started crying more. 'Rube, please don't,' she asked.

'No, I'm sick of this. It has to be said. Every weekend you come home with your idiot mates with a ripped shirt, a busted hand or a black eye. Are you trying to kill yourself? It stops now!'

'Dad, it wasn't my fault. A junkie –' I didn't get a chance to finish the sentence.

'Don't give me that rubbish. I don't know who did it, but you're going to tell me.'

I looked over at Mum as Sarah hugged her. I felt terrible, as I'd created this heartache for my family. This near-death experience was a fork in the road: I could go one way towards a new life away from all the drama or I could go the other way and dig myself even further into the shit. Unfortunately, I chose to swim in the shit.

Was it one of the events, though, that led to awareness? Was observing my shoe and its insignificance in life a small opening into me, into presence? The seed had been planted but it would have to wait, because the shit I was digging into wasn't the kind to help this plant grow.

I was in hospital under observation for a few days as the blood was drained from my lung. As I lay there I planned my revenge. All boundaries had been crossed, which meant there were now no rules. Gaol would be the only outcome for what I was planning, but why was I planning this? To save my reputation, and to ensure others wouldn't doubt me. I was prepared to be locked away just so the voice in my head wouldn't nag me with doubts. I preferred my physical body to be locked away in a cage if it meant my mind would be free. *They'll think I have no heart.*

The word had already gotten around, and I knew I had to respond quickly. Once again I was the talk of the graffiti universe, but this time it was because I'd been dealt with. Links had been a no name before he drove that blade deep into my body, just missing my heart and piercing my lung like a pin popping a balloon. His fame had grown overnight because he'd stabbed Punchy out of fear. The graffiti scene was waiting for the next move – well, so I imagined.

'Give it a couple of weeks,' I told the boys. I didn't want an instant and unplanned attack as the police would charge me immediately, knowing it was my retribution. If I hit him straight away I may as well phone the media and inform them of the time and day. Even if I left it for a few weeks everyone would still know it was me, but that was a risk I was willing to take. I didn't know what I was going to do when I found Links. What I did know was that I'd have to have a weapon.

Dad was trying to get it out of me who did it but I wouldn't tell him. 'Mate, don't you go planning anything!' he said. I didn't respond. 'Are you listening to me? If you end up in gaol it will destroy this family. Let it go.'

I was extremely selfish. I knew my next move would determine the quality of the remainder of my life but my ego overrode everything, and

I knew my family would never be the same again if I did what I was planning but I wanted my revenge.

My mind convinced me that the burning sensation deep in my gut would disperse once payback was achieved. With the desire to rid myself of that feeling, no words from Dad were going to help. It was ludicrous. It wasn't because Links had stabbed me that I hated him so much, it was that he was a nobody who'd had the balls to shank me and make me look bad. I envisaged my enemy sitting around laughing at my misfortune. I knew everyone was talking about it, and I knew it made a large number of people happy to hear I'd finally got mine.

I was going to show them.

CHAPTER 39

REVENGE

I'd been home for a few weeks and fully recovered when Mick rang. 'Punchy, Links is at a rave on the North Shore.'

'Sweet, come and get me.' I pulled myself up and started to put on my shoes.

Anne was in the bed next to me. 'Where are you going, babe?' she asked in a tired, sweet voice.

'The boys are picking me up. We're going for a drive.'

'Everything okay?' She sensed there was something wrong.

Okay, I thought. *He's at a rave. There'll be security there. He no doubt has a knife. He'll be with a bunch of the KS boys and they'll have weapons too.* I went to the kitchen and pulled a carving knife out of the drawer. I rested it on the bench where Mum had prepared countless dinners with this exact blade; now I was going to use it as a possible murder weapon.

Is this what it's come to? I thought. *Are you going to do this?* I put the knife back in the drawer. *You're going to go to gaol if you do.* Was my pure self getting stronger? Maybe, but with all its experience my ego jumped in straight away. *What are you: a bitch? The boys are coming to get you. What are they going to think? Everyone's talking about you: are you going to step up?*

I took out the knife again and put it down the front of my pants. 'Fuck him!' Anne looked fearful, so I kissed her. 'I'll be back soon, babe.'

She didn't say a word, but I could see tears in her eyes and it made me sad. This could be the last time I'd ever see her. The night was going to end with either gaol or death. The truth was that I was risking my life just to ease my thoughts. My ego was my life: my mind had made up a world that was worth dying for and my real life didn't exist. It's scary to think of the power the mind can have over you and your environment. Realising this power is the first step towards being free of it or using it for your advantage.

A car pulled up out the front and I jumped in. Base, Mick, Chad and Vert shook my hand. 'Hey,' was all they could manage. They were doing their own contemplating.

'You know they're going to have weapons, boys.' They took turns to pull out what they were armed with. This was a new thing, a gateway, because each time a weapon is used it progresses to the next. There was no going past the weapons that were in the car that night.

We drove north and headed through the city. People on the street were smiling and having a good time. I was jealous – their lives looked so easy, and in contrast we were driving towards a nightmare. As we drove over the Sydney Harbour Bridge I looked back and caught Base's eye. No words were needed: we'd grown from young boys into violent men and were possibly facing a long term in prison together. Base had started a new life away from all this garbage, but there was no way he would let his main man go into battle without him. He looked at me, his face pale. He closed his mouth and sighed through his nose.

I had succumbed to the fact that we were indeed raiding this rave for blood. I sat nervously tapping my right foot on the stained carpet in the car. Rave music in the distance was getting closer, the blaring music indicating the whereabouts of our target. We pulled up in front of the warehouse. The thumping music and flashing lights immediately pumped me full of adrenaline as it always did, although it was for a different reason this time – not drugs, just death. My heart was racing.

At the door security guards were patting down a line of people. We were armed and I felt ruthless. I didn't care for the guards: they weren't going to stop us. 'Let's go.'

'Wait, brother.' Base grabbed my arm. 'There's a side entrance.'

A side door was a better option than the front door, where we'd have to fight with security to get in. We jumped out of the car and I ran ahead without a second's thought. My mind was purely on revenge, with no thought about the consequences. A single ego can be mean, and when you mix it with others on the same path the result can be pure evil. The thick, dirty, violent energy can kill any moral thinking and result in catastrophe.

The rave scene was full of regulars. Links never used to be one of them, but after he stabbed me he had newfound confidence and believed he was untouchable. He was about to find out he was wrong. I found the side door and kicked it with my fat foot. It crashed inwards, nearly hitting the DJ. I stormed through, armed with a knife and wearing a ski mask. The music stopped instantly.

'Get to the floor! Where is he?' I shrieked. My face was covered but people knew who hid behind the mask. Everyone dropped, their eyes staring at the floor. I stood with all my boys next to me, scanning the people lying face down. It was a small rave, roughly 100 people, and not one of them was moving. We searched the floor but couldn't find Links. I finally spotted him.

'You motherfucking dog!'

My boys stopped moving to watch. They knew how much hatred I had inside me and they knew this wasn't going to be tame. I grabbed a fistful of Links's hair and pulled his head up into an unnatural position. I wanted to see the dog's face before I finished him.

'Fuck!' It wasn't him. Staring up at me was a man with tears in his eyes.

I pushed the tearful face back into the ground. 'Where the fuck are you?' I screamed. Outwardly I acted as though I was disappointed that it wasn't Links, but inside I was relieved. Each time I pulled someone up only to find it wasn't Links I let out a delighted sigh, because the truth was I didn't want to find him. I didn't want to do what I had planned; I wanted to go home.

Some of the KS boys were there and Mick exploded, taking care of a couple of them with two big kicks. They played dead. He was fuming about the stabbing as well, and he wanted his own revenge. I'd met Mick with his orange hair a couple of years earlier at a rave when he'd backed me up in a simple brawl, and now he was backing me up to commit murder.

I will forever thank God that I didn't find Links that night. I quiver just thinking about what life would have held for me if I had spotted him. I later found out he was in the toilets, and when he heard the commotion he jumped out of a window and escaped with his life. If he hadn't gone to the toilet at that particular time I'd most likely be writing this story from prison.

I made it home and sat in my parents' lounge room, thankful for how the night had turned out. It had been the best possible outcome and people would still talk about it, saying how crazy we were for raiding the rave. They would talk about Links running for his life and I would get cheap credit without having done the deed. Links disappeared for a while after that, a decision I applauded as it felt good not to have to worry about him. Everyone knew he was away, so there was no pressure on me to get him.

Our crew was now flooded with weapons, which was something I'd wanted to avoid from the start but we couldn't stop. My recklessness increased: I was drinking and taking drugs more than I ever had before. Did I feel invincible after pushing death back out the door that had opened so wide? Maybe, but it would come knocking a lot harder next time.

CHAPTER 40

WHERE HAVE I BEEN?

I contemplated asking Anne to marry me as I thought our relationship was getting stronger. Even though I still cheated on her I justified it by saying I'd stop if we got married. I loved her with all my heart. We'd fight and hate each other when we hung out, but when we were apart it was like I loved her more. Once again my mind relished wanting more than having.

One night I was drinking in the city with Shorty, one of the younger boys. We were walking up a back street when a car narrowly missed hitting him, so he booted the side of the car as it went past.

'What are you doing, you dickhead?' I said to Shorty as the car stopped. The younger boys would cause drama then look at us to back them up. I knew I'd be the one doing the fighting and I hated fighting for no reason, so it pissed me off when someone started trouble for nothing.

The man in the car jumped out, looked at where his car had been booted and started yelling.

'Mate, we're sorry. You nearly hit him, though,' I said, defending Shorty's actions, which just made the man angrier. He interpreted my apology as weakness, and his confidence grew and he came closer so it was time to show some strength. 'Back the fuck off before I put you on your arse!' I yelled.

That shut him up. He turned and jumped in his car, sat for a while contemplating then drove off.

'See, you idiot? All that for nothing. You shit yourself when he jumped out!' I said to Shorty, pushing him a little. A few minutes later I heard a speeding car behind us. The relentless revving of the engine spelt an altercation and immediately all I could think about was attack. The energy triggered a tension in my body – it knew I was about to fight. I had no interest in self-security as I stood waiting. It was the same guy, who jumped out of his car wielding a metal bar.

Shorty retreated.

'What did I say? I told you to fuck off!' I yelled.

He sprinted towards me, holding the bar above his head. I was slow to react because his eagerness caught me off guard. He took a winding swing, and with an earth-shaking crash thudded the bar into my arm as I held it up to stop the blow. I heard a loud cracking noise, but adrenaline was pumping and I didn't feel a thing.

I forced him onto the bonnet of his car by holding the bar with my left hand and hitting him with my right. I stopped punching as my attention turned to the bar. With both hands I attempted to pry the pole out of his hand as he punched me with the other. He held on, his grip on the bar a matter of life and death. I was finally able to slide it out of his fist and leave him clutching at air. I felt a complete deflation in my opponent's soul. He gave in and went limp, his body, not his mouth, begging for mercy.

I hit him with his own bar and split his head open as he leant back on his car bonnet. He started to cry, strings of bloody saliva in his mouth as he sobbed.

'Sorry,' I mumbled. The energy from my single soft word stopped his crying, and his eyes said thank you.

'Let's take the germ's car!' Shorty said, jumping into the front seat.

'Bullshit, let's go!' I said as I ran. My arm was pulsating, throbbing with pain. The blow from the metal bar had completely snapped the bone, and now that the adrenaline was wearing off I began to shake. I felt cold. 'I have to go to the hospital.'

* * *

'We were playing hockey in the park and I got hit with a club,' I told the nurse. She'd noticed blood on my shirt and obviously didn't believe me. She turned in her chair and spoke to a bald man with glasses, who looked over at me. 'Let's get out of here,' I said to Shorty.

The next day I went to the local hospital. 'That's a baton wound,' the nurse said.

'No it's not, it's from playing hockey,' I said.

'Yes, I heard you, sir. These kinds of injuries are called baton wounds, like when a police officer uses a batons on someone and they put their arm up to defend themselves. It doesn't mean that happened to you, it just describes the injury.' Boy, did I have a guilty conscience.

When I got home Mum and Dad were in the lounge room watching television. Mum turned to look at me first and saw the bright blue cast on my arm straight away. She looked over at Dad, obviously wishing that somehow he wouldn't see it. Noticing Mum's expression, Dad turned and looked at me.

'Sit down, Luke.' Mum and Dad were really the only ones who were still calling me Luke, and when they said it I was forced back into reality a little. My world as Punchy had taken over; I'd left Luke behind long ago.

'I got hit playing hockey with the boys.'

'It doesn't matter what happened.' Dad had had enough of my lying. 'Let's go for a walk, Luke,' he said.

He opened the side gate and let out our dog Spotty, who was over 13 years old and an integral part of our family. I got her for my seventh birthday and we used to be inseparable. Every day as a youngster I sat in the backyard with her and chilled out, but I hadn't done that for a long time. Now I would shoo her away any time she came close, and she was so used to it she rarely came up to me to say hello.

'Do you miss Grandma, Luke?' Dad asked as we walked Spotty down our quiet street.

Just hearing those words brought tears to my eyes. Dad knew about the life I was living, and he often brought up Grandma in an attempt to remind me who I really was. I nodded my head. I didn't want to talk because I knew it would make me cry. I couldn't remember the last time I had cried, because my label as a tough guy wouldn't let me.

'I still can't believe she's gone,' Dad said, a little crack in his voice. 'Both my parents are gone. Can you imagine your mother and me gone?'

'Don't say that, Dad.'

'Mate, it's going to happen,' he replied, just happy to get a reaction out of me.

'I don't want to talk about it.' I hoped he would stop.

'We're going to be gone one day, Luke, you can't hide from that.'

As we walked I tried to imagine life without my parents, and a wave of fear came over me. I felt as though I was suffocating. I knew that one day they would die but I preferred to hide from that thought. When it popped up I'd shake my head and try to force it out of my mind.

'Why are saying this, Dad?' I lifted my tearful eyes to look at his.

He pointed. 'Look at Spotty.' She wasn't running ahead like she used to but was walking slowly by our side, enjoying our company. 'She loves you but you don't ever give her any time.'

I didn't understand.

'What I'm getting at is that you've turned into a person who doesn't give a shit,' Dad said. 'Spotty's at the end of her life. She's been loyal to you for most of your life and you haven't even noticed her deteriorating.'

I looked down at my dog. As if she understood what was being said, she turned and licked my shin. I bent down and gave her a pat on the head and she looked up at me, shocked that I'd touched her.

Dad watched on. 'Mate, she's going to be dead soon. Will you regret not spending time with her?'

'Yeah,' I said, nodding my head. I looked back down at Spotty with a feeling I hadn't had for a long time. I cared.

'You've been too stuck in your own world. How will you feel when your mum and I are gone? You haven't spent any time with us; all you do is make us worry. We lie in bed all night just waiting for you to come home.'

I could picture myself drinking with all the boys. *Is it more important to me than spending time with my parents? Is this whole talk just because he wants me to spend more time with him?* It was more than that. The world I'd created in my mind had eliminated what really mattered to me, and I'd made up a world that hid my fears. My fears were of death – my own and of those close to me. My new world was false.

Dad knew this and was trying to make me realise it. 'Well, what if we died: would you care then?'

'I love you, Dad. You're my best friend.'

'I don't want to lose you, Luke. Please start looking after yourself and getting your priorities right.' He kissed me on the forehead.

My priorities had always been about being there and helping my family. It's what Dad enforced, but now it seemed that drugs, alcohol, graffiti and fighting had taken over. As I walked slowly up that road with Dad by my side my mental chatter slowed down and my false world closed in on itself. I looked around and saw things as though for the first time. *Have I been walking around with my eyes closed?*

My dog had grey hairs and walked with a saddening limp. She'd aged considerably since the last time I had taken any notice of her. Dad had as well: he had wrinkles and his face showed his age. Even plants in the street had grown into big trees since the last time I had cared to notice them. *Where have I been?*

It felt as though the last few years had been made up, and they had. I'd been in my head escaping reality for so long, and now Dad was trying to drag me back.

That afternoon I got a taste of awareness for the present moment. I actually appreciated things, thinking only about what was in front of me. I felt happy.

CHAPTER 41

ANOTHER BRUSH WITH DEATH

Before heading out that night I had my regular one to one with the mirror. 'Okay, you're going out but I want you to have a grip on reality. Let's see if we can keep this feeling going.' However, by planning to be happy in the future by being present I was already defeating the purpose. I kissed Mum and Dad goodbye and ventured out with my freshly broken arm.

'Punchy!' Mick shouted when he saw me. He grabbed my cast. 'What the fuck happened to you?' He threw me two ecstasy tablets and my grip on reality was gone.

We headed to our friend Kane's house, where we'd go just to get messy. The table would be covered with drugs and alcohol and Mick and I would try to outdo each other, from how many drugs we could take at once to who could muck up the most.

'Please, boys, you can chill here but don't play up.' Kane's pleas fell on deaf ears.

'Mate, we won't do anything, we promise.' Mick stood behind him pulling faces, knowing full well we were in for a fun night. He and I challenged each other to scull a whole bottle of wine. Fund, Rod and Chad cheered us on while Kane watched, looking worried.

I was the winner, and I raised my hands in victory. The realness of the moment with Dad a few hours earlier had for now been spiked away. The boys clapped as I stumbled around. I was happy again but it was a counterfeit happiness, one that led to utter misery every time.

We started playing up pretty badly. I convinced Mick to break Kane's guitar over my head, and it was smashed into pieces. All the boys except Kane laughed their arses off.

'Come on, boys. Chill out on the balcony,' Kane begged, his patience now in pieces like the guitar at his feet.

Kane's house was double storeyed and stood on top of a big dirt slope, making it more like three storeys high. Even though his house was in the middle of bushland we could hear neighbours complaining. 'Keep it down over there! Your swearing's terrible.'

We laughed it off and kept partying. Kane came out to check on us then went back inside with an uneasy look on his chubby face.

'Brush him, he's carrying on like a sook,' Mick said as we both had another pill. The consequences of the first two and the sculled bottle of wine had taken full effect and my vision was now blurred.

Kane came out again. 'Boys, please keep it down a bit,' he said as another neighbour called for us to be quiet.

'Just go back inside,' Rod said. Kane was a prisoner in his own home.

'Why's he carrying on like that?' Mick asked, as if it was Kane who was doing something wrong. 'I'll give him something to complain about,' he said, going inside.

We watched through the glass door: our red-headed friend was utterly unpredictable. Mick disappeared into the kitchen and returned carrying a microwave, tripping on the cord on his way back outside. Kane sat on his couch and watched on; he knew a protest wouldn't go down well. We were messy and had no care for our safety or that of others. The poor guy just had to sit back and cop our shit in his own house. Mick came storming past us as we stood in the doorway and launched the microwave off the balcony.

'Watch this!' Wanting to outdo Mick, I grabbed a chair to throw off but it didn't get the same reaction. 'The barbecue!'

'Bullshit, I bet you don't,' Mick said.

Picking up a barbecue with a freshly broken arm would normally be nigh impossible, but I was high on drugs and alcohol so it was easy. I dragged it over to the railing, took a little run up and lifted it, but with the weight of the barbecue and my own momentum it was impossible to stop. I released the barbecue and turned, then felt the railing on my back and heard a cracking noise as it gave way.

'Oh no,' I said as I hung suspended in the air and facing the dark sky.

Mick recalled seeing me paused in the air like Wile E. Coyote chasing the roadrunner, running straight off the cliff and hanging there for a while before dropping. I was so intoxicated I thought I'd just tripped over and once I hit the ground I'd be okay, but the lights of the balcony were further in the distance and I realised I was in trouble. As I crashed to earth I felt I was being sucked into a black hole. I scraped branches of a tree on the way down. *Am I about to die?*

Bang! I landed flush on my back. It was pitch black.

'Punchy!' I heard numerous voices screaming. Mick's girlfriend was sobbing, thinking I'd been killed, and she got straight on the phone to call an ambulance.

I couldn't move, and I thought about a friend who would be in a wheelchair for life after taking a fall. I'd landed flat on my back on the soft dirt between the microwave and barbecue, which were under each of my spread-out arms. If I'd landed 15 centimetres either way I'd have destroyed my spine. I moaned and stood up.

The boys ran down and saw me standing. 'Are you kidding me: he's all right!' Rod grabbed me and noticed I wasn't talking. 'Are you okay?'

I smiled. 'Yeah, I'm just getting my breath back.'

'You've got nine lives, Punchy,' Mick's girl said through her tears.

For two weeks after the fall my entire torso was bruised and my movement limited. My purple body was begging me to stop attacking it. It hadn't been six hours since I'd had the serious chat to Dad, and I'd been so reckless and stupid I'd risked dying or never walking again. Why?

Even though I'd continued the craziness my conversation with Dad turned out to be a life changer, a stepping stone away from my ego and towards my true self. I didn't know it at the time, but I look back on that conversation as being a catalyst. It set me on a path of release and away from my false world.

That day with Dad I had no thought about the past or any anxiety about the future. I'd stopped to take note of things, which had brought me completely into the present moment for the first time. I still had plenty of releasing of my mind-made labels to do, but it was a start.

CHAPTER 42

LIFE DOESN'T HAVE TO BE LIKE THIS

Lucas asked me to go away with him to see his dad in Queensland and I jumped at the chance. We had a great time, fishing during the days and sitting around drinking, chatting and laughing at night.

One night we got talking about life. 'You control everything that happens,' Lucas said. 'The universe provides.' I rolled my eyes, having no idea what he was talking about. I was Catholic, and that was where my beliefs lay. 'You should read this,' Lucas said as he handed me a book.

It was *The Power of Now* by Eckhart Tolle. When I sat down to read the book Lucas had given me it just seemed like a bunch of words that didn't go together. I laughed out loud – it felt as though I was reading a dictionary back to front. The truth was that at the time I wasn't ready. Later I would be.

'Did you like the trip?' Lucas asked on the plane home.

'I did. It was good to kick back and chill. Should do it more often.'

'Yeah, for sure. Life doesn't have to be full of drama.' Lucas was trying to open the cracks in my ego even wider.

'I wish.' I looked out of the window at the clouds. 'Billz is picking us up from the airport.'

Billz had been released from gaol a few weeks earlier. I hadn't seen him since he had gotten out and was excited to have the chance to hang out with him again. He pulled up in a black Subaru WRX and Lucas and I got in the back seat. As we drove off Lucas sat silently, not saying a word. He was nervous around these boys.

As we waited to pull out onto the highway Billz asked me about the trip and was slow to take off. A black Holden behind us beeped its horn, so Billz fixed his rear-view mirror. The driver in the car behind us flashed his lights. We drove off, but the guy continued flashing his lights. Unfortunately, he'd picked the wrong car.

We screeched to a stop and Billz jumped out. Lucas shook his head. I followed Billz as he ran straight up to the car, managing to reach the driver's window as the driver was scrambling to close it. Billz threw two punches through the gap and landed them clean on the man's face. We jumped back in our car and made our escape. The other driver's head was on his dashboard.

I'd been away for a couple of days and hadn't seen a single argument. Now here I was back in Sydney for five minutes and only 20 metres up the road and someone had been punched in the face. A week later Billz was back inside for hitting the man who'd beeped at us. It was unlucky. I'd been in countless fights and gotten away with it, yet his last two had sent him to gaol.

The drama wasn't just around Billz. Kon and I had argued over a friend of his whom I'd knocked out, and we hadn't seen each other for a few months. During the weeks of tension between us he'd called me up and threatened to stab me.

I got a lift to his house to see if he'd be true to his words. 'Well, come on, then,' I hollered from outside his small brick home. I'd been stabbed before, so now I felt invincible.

'Go away, Punchy, go home.' Inside, a couple of Kon's mates were begging me to leave. Over crashing tables and shoving bodies I could hear Kon screaming at them to let him go. I'm glad they didn't. We finally met up in a pub and as soon as we saw each other a truce was called and we made up.

Kon grinned. 'Fuck you, Punchy, coming around to my house that night. You're off your head. You know I would have stabbed you.'

'I would have dropped you before you got the chance,' I said. We laughed and took a sip of our drinks. That's how relationships were in the crew: it was a thin line between joking around and literally killing each other.

* * *

Snap called. 'Punchy, come back to work with me.'

I'd stopped working with Snap because of my broken arm, but my arm had since healed. 'Thanks for the offer, brother, but I think I'm due to get a full-time job,' I told him. I'd been a bum for too long. I was drinking daily and taking drugs every few days and my weight was over 120 kilos. I was a fat mess. Mum and Dad had begged for me to get employed and it was time.

Billz was released on bail due to a lack of evidence and I didn't want a job to get in the way of partying with him, so I put the thought of working at the back of my mind once more. I was heading out for a drink with Billz when my phone rang.

'Punchy.'

'Who's this?'

'What, you've forgotten about me already?'

'Stintz!'

He had also just been released from gaol, and his first call had been to me. 'Mate, I'm going out with Billz. Come out.'

'I'm there!' I met up with Stintz and Kent. 'Stintz, my brother,' I said, putting my hand out to shake his. Stintz grabbed me and we hugged for a minute. I was excited to have my close friend out of gaol.

Billz arrived with a couple of other boys I'd met once before – Wayte and Natch. Wayte was a strongly built, olive-skinned man who walked with a slight limp after being shot in the leg. Natch was an overweight, angry-looking, dark-skinned guy with short black hair who'd been released from prison a couple of months earlier after serving two years for shooting someone. Both these guys had teamed up with Billz and were a force to be reckoned with. They showed little respect to any of the younger boys except me as they'd witnessed my fighting capabilities and knew I didn't take a step back.

'How you doing, boys?' I said, shaking their hands. 'Let's get a drink on.'

We walked to a nearby bottle shop and I came out with three stolen bottles of Hennessy. The shopkeeper had chased me until he saw the bunch of scary-looking men I was with. We sat in a nearby park, and in the company of two of my close friends fresh out of gaol and after a few drinks I was feeling jovial, which usually meant I'd drink too much and act crazy. I started sculling straight Hennessy.

'Slow down, Punchy,' Billz warned, knowing how unpredictable I was when drunk. I smiled and took another scull. I had a little argument with him but we hugged and sat back down, laughing it off.

Natch was a little quiet. He sat holding his foam cup in both hands as though he was keeping warm with a cup of tea and was deep in thought. Serving a couple of years in gaol made people a little anxious in group situations, especially when there was a 120-kilo drunk person who could fight hanging around.

I sculled another drink . . .

. . . then I was on my back screaming, flailing around in a well-lit room.

'Luke, Luke, settle down.' I heard a soft voice and felt a gentle touch on my right shoulder. I looked around and could see two security guards standing close by. Also in the room were a man in a dark-grey uniform and a lady in a white gown. I was in hospital. The alcohol was wearing off and I was able to get a grip on what I was doing. I stopped yelling.

'Luke, do you know where you are?' The pretty blonde lady with the lightly tanned skin and sparkling white teeth leant into my field of vision.

'I must be in heaven because I can see an angel,' I smiled, cheekily. She smiled back and both security guards laughed. I was still drunk but had settled down, and the security guards were hanging around until I stopped being violent.

'What happened?' I asked the gorgeous nurse.

The man in the dark-grey uniform stepped in. His face was covered in wrinkles and the bags under his eyes were more like suitcases. He looked as though he should have been the one in bed. 'You were attacked. You've been stabbed numerous times with a broken bottle.' My mind raced. 'Do you remember anything?' the man asked.

'Don't remember a thing, mate.' This was my automatic response, but this time I really didn't remember anything.

'Your injuries are very bad. The back of your head has large, deep gashes and is being held together by over one hundred staples. The top of your ear was put back on by the microsurgeon. We're hoping it was a success, but we won't be able to tell until it heals. You've got twenty stitches all up your arm. Whoever did this tried to kill you.'

My head and everything else was wrapped in bandages; I resembled a fat mummy. The doctor continued talking, but all I was trying to do was remember what had happened. I'd blacked out in a crowd of people you had to be on your game around. *Was it one of the boys? Did other crews we had beef with come down?* The unknown was killing me.

I heard a burst of crying before I saw her. It was Mum, again cradled in Dad's arms. 'Don't cry, Mum, I'm fine.' I was fine: I was sliced up everywhere but I wasn't in any pain. Luckily my injuries weren't on my face.

Dad had murder in his eyes. 'I spoke to Kent and he said it was one of your fucking mates.'

'Who, Dad?'

'Snatch or something.'

'Natch.' I sighed. It was indeed one of the boys who'd tried to kill me. It was a relief to find out who'd done it but gutting to know it was one of the boys.

'Yeah, that's it, Natch. We'll talk about it later.'

'Where's Stintz?' I asked.

He didn't get a chance to answer, as two men who were obviously detectives entered the room. I rolled my eyes and looked at Dad, who stopped the detectives before they could speak. 'Mate, he's only been in here a few hours. Leave him be.'

They looked at each other and one pulled out a card. 'Okay. We'll be back tonight. Here's my card if you want to speak sooner.'

My mental chatter was going wild. *What happened, why did he do this? I'm going to smash him. Where were the other boys? How did they let this happen?*

Billz and I were close, and I wondered whose side he took. He'd known Wayte and Natch for a lot longer than he'd known me, but I was always there as his right-hand man willing to spill blood on his behalf. He was the leader of the crew, although lately even he'd been calling for me to not take things too far. I hadn't cared: I'd set out to take the painting and fighting to new heights and I'd easily accomplished that. I'd changed the rules of the game and made it more thrilling.

Now a split in the crew might be imminent. *Don't get ahead of yourself,* I thought. I wasn't sure whose fault it was. *Did I deserve it?* A whole bunch of possibilities went through my frantic mind. I knew Natch was edgy when I was around, and although he showed me respect I always felt that he didn't like me. He didn't take shit, and I knew I could be a prick when I was drunk.

Did I start it? Was it retribution for all the violence I've caused? I was a violent drunk and my energy sucked drama towards me from every direction. Once again, though, I'd survived. *Why? Why was I always looked after, and by whom?*

Surgery and a blood transfusion had saved my life, but X-rays revealed glass fragments deep in my skull and they had to open up my head once again. 'The man who did this really wanted to kill you,' the surgeon said, holding up the X-rays.

CHAPTER 43

I STARTED IT

Stintz came in wringing his hands. 'Fuck, brother,' he whispered, not wanting other patients in the room to hear.

'What happened?' I asked.

'Man, that was the worst thing I've ever seen. There was so much blood.' He stared at the floor, visualising the night's events, then he told me the story.

After a few more drinks I had made a harsh comment about the suburb Natch was from. For those of us caught up in ego labels of any kind are worth fighting for, even the suburb we're from. Natch had broken his silence.

'What, you're talking shit about me too?' I had laughed and apologised and told him to settle down.

'Don't laugh at me,' he had said, his voice raised.

'Well, yeah, I am talking shit about you then.'

'Boys, boys, chill out. Punchy, sit down.' Billz knew what we were both capable of, so he had known that if this ego volcano erupted someone would be seriously hurt.

Being intoxicated, I had thought it a good idea to play on Natch's anger. 'Yeah, I was talking about you,' I had said. My conceited self-pride wouldn't let it go and I'd accidentally offended him, for which I was a little sorry, but I wouldn't take a step back after he challenged me. We'd never had a strong connection and now we would see what the other was really worth.

'I'm a bitch, am I? I'll show you a bitch.' He had started bouncing his knees up and down, psyching himself up.

'Stand up, then,' I had demanded, as the boys jumped in to stop us.

'What are you doing, Punchy?' Billz had held my face.

'Fuck him,' I had mumbled. Billz had held me back and I had tripped over. I was in disarray and unable to hold myself up.

A few metres away Wayte had stood by Natch, whispering. The sound of broken glass had cut through the swearing and Natch was gripping the necks of two broken bottles, holding the weapons out wide. 'Think you're a tough guy? Come at me now.'

Stintz paused in the story to say: 'You were blind, Punchy.'

'No way, I can't remember any of this.' Stintz went on.

'I'll take you and both those bottles on!' I had screamed aggressively, and I had run at him. Normal people would have headed in the other direction, but reality took a back seat to my maniacal ego. I saw myself as being the king of violence: I liked to be known as the one who wouldn't back down, especially with the crowd that was witnessing this mess. Death was a better option than to have a blemished image. I later wondered if I would have run at him if it had just been him and me in the park. Without an audience to show off to I don't even know if I would have stood up to him. My life was governed by other people's twisted opinions.

'You ran at him,' Stintz continued.

I had thrown a punch and Natch had taken his first swipe with a bottle at my face. Luckily, my extended arm had prevented the glass from coming into contact with my face but it had sliced through my arm like brand-new scissors through thin paper. We both had been instantly swimming in a lagoon of blood.

'I didn't know what to do, Punchy,' Stintz said. 'I ran over and Wayte forced me back with a big kick that dropped me.' Wayte was a former kickboxer. 'I got up and it was like we were watching a movie. I turned and told Billz to stop it. You boys were fighting and no one wanted to get involved. There was blood everywhere!'

A crazy-looking Natch had stood clutching two broken bottles and with my blood covering his face. He had spat some of the blood out of his mouth, so I had lunged at him again. I had stupidly jumped back in to throw more punches and had got caught with my head down. Natch had made four hard, skull-piercing stabs and the top of my right ear was lying on the grass. The carved incisions in the back of my head had opened wider, revealing my pearly white skull.

I had stood disoriented for a few seconds without saying anything. Blood had been streaming from the cavernous chasms in my head, the gaping wounds yawning like a tired mouth. Then I had fallen, the loss of blood collapsing my legs.

Stintz described it as being like something out of a horror movie. He had turned around to see Natch and Wayte attempting to push my limp body into the flowing stormwater drain that ran through the park.

'They were trying to get rid of your body!' he said. 'I ran over, lad. I ran over and pushed them away. Kent called the ambulance. Your head was in pieces around you. We all cried. You had your eyes closed. I thought you were dead, brother.' Stintz cried and stood up from his chair to give me a hug.

'What was Billz doing?' I asked, hoping he'd stayed true to me.

'He leant by your side and held your head.' That was comforting to hear.

'Fuck, Punchy, even the paramedics looked shocked. One of them pulled out a staple gun and began smashing it into your head. Blood was splattering all over them and the sound of the staples going in your head was crazy! The staples woke you up and you looked at the paramedic and said, "What the fuck are you doing that to me for?" They took you away and I heard one of them say they might lose you!'

Stintz stood up and gave me another hug. He looked up to me and I saw him as being one of my closest friends. Thinking I was going to die had really affected him.

'Have the coppers been here yet?' he asked.

'Yeah.'

'What'd you tell them? '

'What do you think I told them? Nothing. They're coming back, though. I'm going to tell them the truth.' I smiled.

Stintz leant back and pulled a funny face, not believing what I just said.

'I'm going to tell them I don't remember anything.' He relaxed and smiled too.

So I did start it. Once again, it had been my own fault.

Base and Snap were also at the hospital. Snap was wearing his bright orange work shirt and Base was in his camouflage army uniform. I hadn't seen either of them for a few weeks, but judging by their concerned faces I knew I was in for a strong talk. They both leant over and gave me a hug. 'My two main men.'

They still hadn't said anything: it was as though they'd been planning what to say but one was waiting for the other to speak first. I bashed the silence. 'What's wrong, boys?'

'Punchy,' they both said at once. Base nodded his head for Snap to keep talking. 'Punchy, we got a call from Stintz and he told us you were dead. You want to know what the bad thing about hearing that was?' I didn't say a word. 'The bad thing was,' Snap went on, 'it didn't shock me. It was something I knew was coming. I knew it was going to happen sooner or later.'

Snap sat down, as did Base. I told them the story, but all they did was shake their heads.

'Brush them, Punchy. You're going to die for these guys?'

'It's not for them, bro, it's for me. I've got to keep going. I'm running the show now,' I tried to impress on them.

'I've got your back forever,' Base said.

'Me too,' Snap jumped in. 'We'll both always be there for you, Punchy, but you've got to stop it all.'

They left, and once again I was alone with my thoughts.

I needed to go to the toilet from all the fluid that had been pumped into me. The nurse gave me a bed pan and told me to pee into the pan by leaning to the side. She left me and I tried to go, but I found it hard to do lying down so I decided to stand up. My urine immediately flowed out, as did the blood from my head. I blacked out and woke up on the floor, peeing all over myself. I'd fainted. Two nurses ran in and I spent the next 15 minutes being bathed by them. I was so embarrassed.

* * *

'Son.' An old woman was lying on the bed next to mine. She had a tube coming from her nose and her ash-grey hair was scattered on the white pillow. I stared. 'I've been listening in on what's been said. I'm not sorry for being nosey.'

She stopped talking so she could cough. A machine next to her beeped occasionally. 'I'm seventy-one and going to be dead shortly.' She looked a lot older than she was, and I don't know if she picked up that I was shocked to hear her age. 'The reason I'm dying and look so much older than I am is I've lived a life full of anger.'

The word 'anger' seemed foreign coming out of this sweet old lady's grey cracking lips. 'When I was as young as you my husband had an affair with my sister. I turned from being a relaxed, happy young girl into an angry old woman in a couple of weeks. I never spoke to my sister or most of my family again. I've struggled through life. I have been in hospitals so many times from ulcers in my stomach. I held all my anxiety and hatred in my stomach. You know being angry causes illness?'

I didn't say a word: her voice and what she was saying had me mesmerised. I didn't take my eyes off her, as I was totally in the moment and a rush of energy was going through my body as I literally felt what she meant.

'It does no good to anyone,' she went on, having noticed I was too withdrawn to answer any questions. Normally when someone else spoke I'd be in my head, thinking about what I was going to say. I'd always try and outdo their story, but this time I only wanted to listen.

'My whole life I've been mean to people, and look where I am: nobody has come to visit me and I'll soon be dead. My entire life is over. I may be seventy-one but I didn't live a day past twenty.'

I had tears in my eyes. My ego had disappeared for a few moments as she spoke, but as I wiped the tears away I was hoping none of my friends would walk through the door and see me crying. The woman noticed me wiping my eyes and checking to see if anyone was walking into the room.

'Who cares what other people think? Live your own life and be happy. Their minds are so caught up with themselves they don't care about you anyway. I didn't speak to my family because I cared about what they thought of me after I was cheated on.' Now she sounded a little angry, and she looked at the ceiling. 'I wish they were here now for me to hold.

Son, don't get to my age and have regrets. I have no family or friends. I thought I didn't care, but sitting in this bed has made me realise what a waste my life has been. Life is beautiful, if you let it be. I didn't.'

She started sobbing, and I did too. I couldn't get up to comfort her so I just stared at the ceiling as well. She sobbed for a few minutes before going quiet. I wished that one of her family might visit but they never did, and she died the next day.

* * *

The detectives were back. 'I can't remember a thing, mate.' One of the detectives was writing in his notepad, the muscles in his arms evident through his suit. The other detective, who was smaller and wore glasses, watched my face in an attempt to read my thoughts.

'I was blind drunk.'

'What about your friends: do they know who did it?'

'No, I spoke to one of them and they said it was a fight with some men who walked through the park.'

'Was it the guy who got you last time?' the detective wearing the glasses asked. I appreciated his upfront question as it gave me a glimpse into his thoughts. I looked at him. 'Cut the shit, Luke, You've been stabbed twice in a couple of months and also charged with a few assaults. We're watching you. We know what you've been getting up to.'

It was true. I'd been charged with assault after an altercation in the city and also for being drunk and disorderly after a run-in with the police.

'So who did it?' the muscly detective butted in.

'Mate, I don't know who did it.'

'I'm not your fucking mate,' he snapped at me, his frustration now evident.

'No comment,' I smiled.

'You're going to end up dead.'

'No comment,' I said again, this time without a smile.

'Good one, you idiot.'

They left. I may have thwarted them this time but their return was guaranteed.

CHAPTER 44

SCARRED FOR LIFE

I should have been dead. I'd come off second best in a battle with my ego and alcohol, but getting stabbed in the head was one more brick in a wall I was slowly building. Each time something like this happened another brick was added to that wall. The lessons I learned were the cement that held these bricks together to form the solid structure I now have, a structure that may sway from time to time but still sticks together. I've learned a lot: I know if these harsh bricks hadn't occurred I may never have looked for answers.

At the time these events elevated my ego. I had more people talking about me, and I wanted to hurt more people to make up for it. Later, though, living through this allowed me to let the tension go and forgive. I thought I was living my life, but the moment I let go of all the hatred was when my life really began.

So much chaos. My world was spinning.

What is everyone saying about it? Who's going to back me up? What are the police going to do? They've been watching me! My poor parents are crushed!

'This is him, this is him, cuz!' One of the security guards was pulling someone towards my bed. 'This is the one who was nearly dead and still tried to pick the nurse up. He called her an angel or some shit.' They were both laughing, and their jovial attitude cheered me up.

'Baby.' Anne stood in the hallway holding my favourite food at the time – pumpkin soup with sour cream. She shook her head, tears welling up in her eyes. Seeing her with her blonde hair and young face was comforting, and her tears made her look even more innocent. She sat down and put the soup in front of me.

'Baby, let's go away. Let's get away from all this stuff.' She'd obviously been thinking about our escape from it all.

'How can I? The boys need me.'

'The boys stabbed you!' Touché. 'You're too loyal to them and they don't return the favour.' She finished the sentence softly as though she regretted what she was saying; she knew I didn't like her doubting my crew.

'Shut up! My boys are loyal. He wasn't one of my boys!' Anne sat further back in the chair and kept her mouth closed. I took a spoonful of soup. 'Sorry, babe,' I said sweetly, trying to match the tone of her voice. She kept her head down. 'Please look at me.'

She raised her head and I could see her watery eyes sparkling in the bright hospital lights.

'Babe, I'm getting a job. I'm going to support us. I want you to have my baby.' She rolled her eyes: she'd heard it all before. 'I promise you this time. As soon as I'm better I'm looking for a job.' The poor girl held high hopes for us. She trusted me, or maybe she just didn't want to face the truth.

All the boys visited me in hospital and vouched to have my back, except Billz, so I called him.

'Hey, bro. I wanted to visit but I heard your dad was on the warpath. Listen, don't believe everything you hear. We were in a hard situation. You were blind drunk and we couldn't settle you down. When you started fighting he had a bottle. What were we supposed to do?'

'I heard you held Stintz back.'

'People were running everywhere and you two were fighting. You broke his nose. We stood back. I don't get involved in a one on one.'

'One on one where one has two bottles?' I asked.

'Listen, Punchy, I love you like family. I'll tell you how it is: you were in the wrong. Natch is sorry for what happened.'

'If you were in the wrong and you got stabbed I'd back you up,' I said. It was true.

'Punchy, it was a hard situation. No one was thinking straight. There was blood everywhere and it was over in a split second. I stayed with you until the ambulance came. We are a crew, Punchy. We stick together.' Billz could see the crew falling apart.

I wanted to sort it with another one on one fight, but they wouldn't have it.

'He stabs people or shoots them, Punchy. He doesn't fight.'

I hung up after telling Billz I was all okay with him. It was a tough position to be in as I had heard conflicting stories, but I took full responsibility for it being my fault. I still wanted to fight Natch, though, to sort it out. He'd shot someone and now he'd stabbed a man in the head, but that wasn't enough to stop my ego, which was thirsty for revenge.

Natch had attacked me because I had threatened his ego. With anything in life there are always going to be people who attempt to subordinate you, even those you think are close friends. It's not that they're bad people, but when you succeed at something their minds interpret that as you lessening them as people and their egos won't stand by and let such a thing happen. All pure, sensible thought processes about right and wrong go out the window. I was ready to do the same.

'Who cares about them, brother?' I said to Stintz. 'We're running this shit anyway. We used to look up to them, but we're the big boys now. Why do you think they're trying to bring us down?'

Anne was with me while the bandages around my head were removed. She had a scared look on her face.

'Your ear will get better as it heals,' the nurse said.

I grabbed Anne's tiny make-up mirror to see. The top of my injured ear was sticking out like a wing nut and I thought it was incredibly funny. 'Look at my ear!' I said, giggling crazily.

The nurse and Anne looked at each other, shocked by my uncontrollable laughter. The nurse held another mirror behind my head, and for the first time I saw the gashes. They were held together by metal staples: it looked like a network of train tracks, with the train departing from my ear to terminate down near my neck. It was gruesome and I stopped laughing. It was incredibly lucky that all these scars were not on my face.

'That's not so funny, is it?' Anne remarked.

When I got home from hospital Dad banned drinking in my granny flat. 'If any of you come over with alcohol I'll fucking flatten you!' he threatened the room full of boys who were there visiting me. It forced me to finally pull out my finger and get a job.

CHAPTER 45

MY FIRST LOSS

'I've got a job interview next week!' I announced to my thrilled parents. I could see how happy they were. Finally, I was making them smile. I'd put them through hell over the last few years and it was time to make amends.

'Boys, let's have a big one this weekend. I'm starting work next week so let's get on it.'

I organised a big session at Town Hall steps and once again we were a few pills into the night and carelessly roaming the streets. Another strong group of boys we knew through friends was with us and one of them, a large guy, looked as though he was itching for a fight. Some of his mates were cruising up and down the footpath on Razor scooters. He kept his hands in his hooded jumper and wasn't saying much then he started arguing with Kent, who, I knew, wouldn't be able to handle this hefty lad.

'Brother, pull up.' I separated them and spoke to the troublemaker.

'Fuck off or I'll stab you too!' he said.

Remember, Luke, always be first or you'll end up on your back before you know what's happened. Dad's advice rang in my mind. Whack! I hit him. The big guy pulled out a bottle, which made me hesitate. He launched at me with the bottle but I dodged it.

'Leave it one on one,' I heard Base scream as the guy's friends looked to jump in. The boys always called out to leave it one on one because they had full confidence I would come out the victor. Not this time: I threw a punch and the guy grabbed hold of my shirt by the collar.

'What happened, Mick?' We were stumbling across the street and I couldn't stand properly. I could taste my own blood. 'What happened?' I asked again.

'Ah, Punchy.' Mick looked at me, grimacing, not wanting to tell me. He stopped a taxi and pushed me in before jumping in the other side.

'What the fuck happened?' I demanded.

'Punchy, you got knocked out.'

I looked at him, my head swaying a little. 'Someone dog shot me?' I said hopefully.

He shook his head. 'Nah, brother, you just got hit by a big haymaker.'

I froze: I didn't know what to say. My boys looked up to me as the one who always won and I felt as though I'd let them down. It was my first defeat in a one on one and the only thing feeling pain was my image.

This time my other ear had a cut across it and there was another gash higher in my head. The big haymaker had put me out cold on the footpath, then one of my opponent's friends ran over and swung his Razor scooter into my defenceless skull. Mick had thrown his own haymaker, putting the scooter-carrying attacker on the ground next to me.

Mick had been so furious about the scooter attack he'd jumped on the guy's motionless head. We later heard that Mick's revenge jump resulted in a fractured eye socket and skull.

Base had run over and hit the guy who floored me then a massive brawl broke out. He'd looked over to see another person kicking into my lifeless body and was ready to kill the person, but after seeing murder in Base's eyes the guy had run off. Rod had managed to pry free one of the scooters and he began swinging it like a hammer thrower. At the end, all that remained were four victims of the battle lying dead still on the footpath. One was me.

'Man,' was all I could manage to say in the back of the taxi. Earlier in the night I'd been in a fight that had seen me king hit, giving me a black eye. Now my other eye was black and I had a couple of new injuries. When I entered Sydney's RPA Hospital, my second home, one of the nurses recognised me instantly and she shook her head.

I was back in a hospital bed but, apart from the obvious effects of being knocked out, I felt okay. However, the doctors were worried about possible scarring on the brain. A nurse came into the room to show me a whole bunch of pictures. The first was a flower, then a red car and an aeroplane. I had to remember them as a test to see if I'd suffered any memory loss due to a brain injury.

'Brother, you were just buckled from all the pills. You would have taken that guy any time.'

Mick was trying to come up with an excuse for me and I wanted to buy into it, but I hated it when people made bullshit excuses for getting beat so I took the rap.

'Lad, I just got caught. Everyone eventually gets caught with a shot.' The fact was, my luck had worn out. I'd been getting away with victories a couple of times a week, but this time I'd been beaten.

Base arrived an hour later with a huge cut in the back of his head. After he was stitched up he stood next to my bed just as he'd done a few weeks earlier.

'Punchy, my boy.'

'Mick already said: I got dropped.' I didn't want to hear it again.

The doctor came in with another man. 'This is the inhouse counsellor.'

'Mate, sorry, I don't want to hear it,' I said.

'Mister Kennedy, you have been in here a lot mostly due to alcohol and drugs. If you don't want to listen to me now take these and call me.' The counsellor handed me a couple of brochures on violence and alcoholism. I laughed and he walked out of the room.

The boys grabbed the brochures. 'Look, that's you, Punchy.' Mick pointed to a picture of a kid knocked out on the cover.

'You prick,' I said, smiling.

The nurse returned to ask me questions about the cards she'd shown me earlier.

'Do you remember the photos?'

'Yep, sure do.'

'Okay, great. Do you remember the order they were in?'

'Of course, easy done,' I smirked. The boys stood by.

'Can you tell me what they were, Mr Kennedy?'

'Yes. The first was a pencil, then a monkey. I think the last one was an aeroplane. No, wait, it was a bottle!' The nurse looked at me with the worst fake smile I had ever seen. She looked at the boys and they burst out laughing. 'A flower, a red car and an aeroplane,' I said, laughing. She wasn't impressed.

'Let's get out of here before those detectives come.'

I wanted to abscond with my brochures. I didn't want another clash with those abominable detectives from a few weeks earlier, who had said they were after me, but my first loss stayed with me. You're only as good as your last fight, and this was the first time my ability to fight had been called into question. Cracks were showing in the label I held most dear: the fighter label, the one I cared for immensely. It was the label that had seen me catapulted to fame and that had won me respect from those I'd grown up admiring.

I was now running the show, but getting knocked out in the street was the first dent in my mint-condition leadership. The man who had thrown that hard shot straight into my jaw, switching my lights off on impact, had relieved me of some of my superiority.

The good news was that like sun shining through a chink in a wall, the crack in my fighter label allowed a little light to shine on my true self. It put me on the way to releasing that and many other labels.

CHAPTER 46

WEARING MAKE-UP

Mum and Dad were devastated: once again their boy had been injured after a night out.

'You have a job interview this week,' Dad said. 'Piss off, I don't want to see you.' He was totally over it all.

I walked past them with my head down and headed to the granny flat, where I studied my reflection in the bathroom mirror. My face was all busted up – two black eyes from different fights, scratches and a fat nose. How was I going to get around this one?

I was anxious about the possibility of starting work, because I hated meeting new people. Job interviews were not part of my bailiwick as a street thug. What were they going to think of me?

Outside the lad and graffiti scene my social skills were minimal. I had good manners and appeared to be a nice person; however, I was too stuck in my head, worrying too much about what other people thought of me to allow my personality to reveal itself. I was also a terrible listener, as my mental chatter wouldn't allow me to take anything in. I was nervous meeting anyone, let alone someone who was an authority figure such as an employer. I could get along with anyone after knowing them for a while, but the first time I met somebody I'd be frozen with nerves. I was 21 and this would be my first-ever job interview.

The next morning my nerves had me close to pulling out. Mum helped me cover the black eyes and scratches with make-up.

'Looks good,' she said as I glanced in the mirror to have a look. It's funny – you see what you want to believe. I agreed it looked okay.

The job was for a picker-packer for a company selling women's clothing. During the entire trip I rehearsed my response to the different questions I might be asked. Each answer was more mechanical than the last, as I opted to attempt to sound intelligent rather than inspiring.

Once there and sitting in front of the young lady who was going to interview me I began to sweat. I noticed she kept glancing at my eyes with a funny look and I could feel the make-up running down my chunky face along with the sweat.

'I know you're looking at my make-up,' I blurted out. 'I played footy on the weekend and got hit with a high tackle and didn't want to come to an interview with two black eyes.'

She laughed. 'I didn't know what to say! I thought: is this guy really wearing make-up?' She giggled.

We both had a good laugh, which relaxed me. The make-up was there to disguise my black eyes, but it enabled me to reveal my personality. After having a laugh with her I began acting myself and answering the questions well without any nerves. The woman smiled and shook my hand and the next day I got a call: I had gotten my first full-time job.

CHAPTER 47

CANCER

After a weekend of fighting and drug taking I'd go to work and act the model citizen. One day I got a message on my phone from Skye: 'Call when you can. I need to talk to you.'

I knew instantly what it was about. A month earlier after a rave I had unprotected sex with her. We were off our heads and there was no thought of using protection.

'Luke.' The tone in her voice said it all.

'Hey, Skye, how you doing?' I tried to lighten the tension.

'I'm pregnant.'

I knew it! 'Really? Who do you think the father is?' It was a dumb reply. I was hoping she'd answer with someone else's name.

'Who do you think? It's you.'

'It can't be.'

'Look, I've been speaking to Mum: I'm keeping it. You don't have to do anything. I'll take care of my kid.'

'Bullshit!' I blew up. I'd been brought up to take care of my own, and I wasn't going to let my kid grow up without a dad. That's my blood. I didn't want it to get to that point, though. 'Skye, you can't keep the baby.'

'Luke, I want to keep it.'

'We were on drugs when we had sex. It might cause problems.'

'I'll deal with it.'

'Stop saying that shit!' I stopped short of saying 'It's my kid, too,' because I didn't want to cement that it was happening.

Skye hung up. I couldn't breathe. My legs felt shaky and I couldn't concentrate.

'Are you okay, Luke?' my boss asked. 'You look sick.'

What am I going to do? Anne's going to find out and I'm going to lose her and be left with a girl I've only seen as a friend and a kid to support on $550 a week.

Mum picked me up from the station as she did every afternoon – the 20-minute walk home was too hard for me. I sat in the car and didn't say a word. I hadn't noticed Mum's red cheeks and watery eyes.

Halfway home, she spoke. 'Luke, I was at the doctor's today.'

Those seven words dragged me from the world inside my head into the present, and suddenly I noticed every part of Mum's beautiful face. Her teary eyes looked beaten. 'They found a lump in my throat.'

There was a deafening silence. My own selfish thoughts were booted out of my mind.

'I have to have an operation. They think it might be cancer.'

'Mum, no way it's cancer. You'll be fine.' I was hoping my words would somehow magically make it all go away. I persisted with the positive attitude the whole way home.

After giving Mum a big kiss I walked into my granny flat, closed the door behind me and fell to the floor like a building imploding. I didn't cushion the fall – I wanted to be hurt, I wanted pain to dull my throbbing heart. I was crying on the floor. Eventually I got up and went to the bathroom to talk to the mirror, looking for answers. 'Why?' I begged my reflection, a face flooded with tears.

I called Skye, as it was one thing I needed help with before having to deal with Mum. 'Skye,' I sobbed. I told her about Mum and thankfully she agreed to have a termination.

Did I use Mum's condition as an out from a very sticky situation? It had to be done. Skye was in no way a bad person: she wanted to keep her baby not out of any malice towards me but because she wanted a child, and now I was able to give my full attention to Mum. I prayed numerous times a day that all would be okay.

On the day of the surgery nothing seemed real. After waiting for the bus to go to the hospital, I allowed people to push in front of me to get on.

A man seated a few rows down stared at me with an evil look. Normally I'd have stared back and said something, looking for a fight, but this time I smiled and put my head down. A lady sat on the seat next to me. Normally I'd get annoyed because, being so big, I'd want the seat to myself, but this time I just relaxed and we even leaned on each other a little. I didn't care. *What's the point of fighting? Mum's in hospital, nothing else matters.*

When you think your mum's going to die it puts everything into perspective. Other so-called worries don't even warrant a second thought, as it becomes clear how insignificant these worries are. How frantic we can be in life, getting pissed off at the stupidest things and letting other people control our emotions.

Was I going to be angry or worried for my entire life? Would it stay like this until I realised on my deathbed that I'd thought my entire life away? It would be too late then. Did I want to live and enjoy each moment, or was I going to continue to worry about tomorrow until there were no more tomorrows? Life is short. Did I want to spend this life worrying and fighting, in effect causing it to be even shorter, or did I want to be happy and make others happy?

'It all went okay. They got everything.' Mum struggled to speak as she lay flat on her back with a bandage around her throat. I smiled and sat down. I still wasn't convinced, as I knew Mum would tell me anything to make me relax.

The doctor came into the room and confirmed that they still needed to do some tests, but first impressions were that it was all okay. I stood up and hugged Mum. 'It's not good, is it?' she said.

'What, Mum?'

'Having to visit a family member in hospital.'

I knew what she was saying: I'd put her through hell during the last few years. Mum had had to visit me repeatedly in hospital after violence had caused my near death; I couldn't imagine what that must have been like. I wanted so desperately to make both my parents proud I was going to make it up to her.

'I love you, Mum.'

It was another lesson learned. Without this near-death experience for my mum I wouldn't have questioned the significance of what I'd thought were major things in my life, but after coming so close to losing Mum I realised so much.

CHAPTER 48

THE TASK FORCE COMES KNOCKING

'Luke, ring home.' It was a text message from Mum.

'What's up, Mum?' I asked when she picked up.

'The police and Task Force Graffiti were just here looking for you.'

'You serious? What did they want?'

'They left their number. They want you to call them.'

'Was Dad there?' I hoped he wasn't.

'No, you're lucky they left just before he came home.'

I called them straight away. I didn't want them going back to my house looking for me as Dad would have killed me. I hadn't been painting as much since I started my job, as partying and work had taken over.

'Hi, it's Luke Kennedy.'

'Are you at home, Mr Kennedy?'

'No. Don't go there, I'll meet you somewhere.'

'We're located in the city. Meet us at Hungry Jack's at Central Station.'

I hadn't been busted painting for three years. *What did they want now?*

As I walked through Central Station I worried that I'd be seen talking to authority. There were always people I knew in the city, and I didn't want to be seen talking to the law and have people think I was a snitch. I wanted to speak to the police, though, so they wouldn't come back to my house. I spotted them straight away: two detectives, a male and female, wearing plain clothes. Both had a bulge at the waist where a gun was stashed under their clothes. They shook my hand.

'I'm Detective Mills and this is Detective Baker.' Detective Baker was red hot, her sexiness doubled when she was standing in her smart suit.

'Sit down here, Punch,' Baker said.

A detective addressed me by my tag! I felt sick to the stomach.

'Huh?' was all I could blurt out.

'Look, we know who you are. Please sit down.' *Are they going to arrest me?* 'Mate,' Mills said, 'we know you're the leader of RM. We know you boys have been hurting a lot of people. We also know you're withholding information about who stabbed you.'

I laughed, trying to hide the seriousness of what had just been said. 'Who's RM?'

'We're here to speak to you as a human being. Don't treat us like anything less. We know you're not going to tell us anything, but just keep an open mind.'

I looked on, the fake smile wiped off my face.

'The guy who stabbed you, he's going to do it again. What if he kills someone? You could have prevented that.' I didn't know who they were talking about. I'd been stabbed twice: did they know that? 'You're leading RM. If someone gets killed by your crew you know you're in shit yourself.'

As we were seated in high chairs around a small table we were practically in each other's pockets. They were reasoning with me, and I was grateful for their honesty but I was on a constant lookout for anyone I knew walking past. The scene reminded me of a mafia movie I'd seen: a detective met an Italian man to warn him not to carry out what he was planning. It excited me.

'You seem like a decent bloke, but all this has to stop.'

I broke my silence. 'Look, I work now. I'm planning a family with my girl and this graffiti stuff is something I did when I was younger. I don't know who stabbed me. Honestly, I'm out of all the rubbish. A few things have happened lately to make me get away from that life.'

'I hope so. We're teamed with Task Force Graffiti and we're closing in on you all. You seem like you've got a head on your shoulders. I don't want to see you going down.'

These cops were like normal people! I shook their hands and said goodbye, as though I'd just met friends for lunch.

As I was growing up I'd viewed police as aliens from another planet, speaking a different language and trying to crush my lifestyle. After years of being chased, arrested, sworn at and pepper sprayed and seeing them take my friends' freedom, I'd come to believe they were a clique of ghastly demons that met in bat caves to decide how they were going to rip me apart. Of course, if I'd been an upstanding, law-abiding citizen I wouldn't have been in the situations that warranted their attention.

These two police officers weren't just trying to get close to find out information. I could sense they really were genuine people, people just trying to stop violence and help the community. I'd had a conversation with them just like I would have with any other people such as a mum or a dad who was working for their family and doing the right thing.

I hadn't been painting for a while, and the meeting with the detectives made me take another step back from it. I was going to let it settle down before attacking the trains again. Unfortunately, Links had been getting up to a lot on the train lines and it burned me deeply having to sit idle for a while.

'What are you going to do to him?' Chad once asked with a smile.

'Kill him,' I'd replied.

Chad had stopped smiling and nodded his head. 'Yeah, fuck him, lad,' he said.

I was now close with Chad, who had grown from a short, chubby, blond-haired pretty boy into a tall, chubby, blond-haired pretty boy. That night we met up with the main boys: I was looking to get totally loose to eliminate thoughts of the law closing in. We drank the night away and spent the next morning in Hyde Park, drinking even more. A guy arrived with a bag of ecstasy and I grabbed it off him.

'How many do you think I can do at once, boys?'

'Three! Bet you can't do three!' Rod said, knowing I'd take on any challenge.

'I've done three before, brother.'

'Do four, then!' Chad yelled.

'It'll kill him! Don't do that shit, Punchy!' Vert said.

'All right, I won't do four: I'll do five!' I threw five pills into my mouth and swallowed before anyone could stop me. Some of the crowd cheered while others were silent and had questioning looks on their doubtful faces, wondering whether I was going to be okay.

'If they're really good they should kill me,' I said, grinning.

I always wanted more and I strived to outdo everyone. My ego wanted the others to be worried about my safety. Their concerns reinforced my view of myself as someone who people cared for when, really, they just didn't want to be a part of death. I'd literally seen people die from having one pill and I'd just dumped five.

'Mate, have your phone ready to call the ambulance,' a worried Base said to Vert.

CHAPTER 49

NEW TERRITORY

A couple of mates from another crew were planning to head down south to Melbourne, a 10-hour drive from Sydney. Melbourne was renowned for its graffiti, which was more accepted there, and the city's back streets were covered in full-colour murals. It was also easier – or so we thought – to pull off big panels and whole cars, which was why we were heading down.

Throughout my graffiti career I'd had friends return with stories about hour-long panel spots and also tell us how easy it was to steal clothes and other big-ticket items. I was finally going to see what all the fuss was about.

I always said I'd tag for my whole life: 'Even when I'm a grandpa I'll still do the odd little tag,' I said. It was our life – what would we be without it? But I hadn't painted or stolen anything for months and the detectives' attention had left me worried, so I was nervous about the trip ahead.

I thought about the detectives. I'd told them I was out of it all, and I felt that if I got busted I was going to let them down. It was funny: after hating authority for so long I'd met a couple of good cops and didn't want to do wrong by them.

***

I always think back to that now when I'm working with kids in trouble. I try to break through their belief that all police are bad and can't be their friends. With this attitude it's no wonder these troubled kids continue to break the law. It's an 'us versus them' mentality, and it's so important for police to visit schools so kids can see them as human beings rather than aliens or the enemy.

If kids see police as being on their side they're more likely to want to do the right thing. I get it, though, as I've seen police do some heavy things and even seen them hurt members of my family. I've watched them lie in court and pick on kids, but there are dickheads in every area in life. I've never been stabbed by a police officer.

Through my work with youth I've met police officers who have saved hundreds of kids' lives and put their own lives and those of their family at risk by doing so. Like I said, there's good and bad in any group of people.

* * *

We all put in money and hired a brand new red Holden for the drive. Terz was the driver. A friend from western Sydney, Terz was a lot older than me and I enjoyed his company. Like the others who came on the trip he wasn't into the fighting – he just loved painting. I liked his maturity but also his funny outlook on things.

Another Westie who came on the trip was Ragz. Although he was also a lot older than me he didn't have an inch of maturity about him. I could sit for hours and listen to tall, skinny Ragz talk: he was incredibly funny. Deztiny, from Sydney's northern beaches, was another travel companion and then there was my mate Kent.

This trip was with guys I really liked. Sure, they had the typical graffiti ego; however, it was more to do with spreading their tags than being arseholes. I'd also taken the precaution of packing a bag of speed and 20 pills for the trip.

Base couldn't come because he was too busy with the army, so we decided to hang out the day before I left. We had hot chips and gravy just like we'd done a thousand times before, but I had a plan. 'Here, have one of these.' I threw Base a yellow ecstasy pill, and he laughed and swallowed it. It was only lunch time, but the time of day didn't matter to us.

'I've got an idea,' I said. 'Let's wait for these to kick in, then we will go get our eyebrows waxed and plucked. It'll feel amazing!'

Base laughed and agreed. The drugs themselves weren't enough of a high any more, so we'd try different things to enhance the experience.

It worked: as I lay flat on my back at the beautician's I was tingly all over. The contrast between the ecstasy's effects, which felt like waves of soft kisses over my body, and the slight pain of the cool metal tweezers pulling at my skin took me to a new level of high.

That night I barely slept. When I was on drugs I'd go from a scary dream to reality and get them mixed up, not knowing what was real. I'd yell out then realise what I was doing and stare at the ceiling. Drug sleeps are frightening – you don't know what to believe.

The boys were due to pick me up any second and I was feeling like trash, but it was nothing some speed wouldn't fix. I lined up the white substance and was soon feeling like I'd woken super fresh from a 10-hour sleep. I heard the car horn beep and a buzz of adrenaline hit me.

'Ay, Punchy!' Ragz shouted as he hung his head out of the passenger window.

'Oh, wait one second!' I said. I ran back inside and gave Mum a big hug and a kiss and told her I loved her, like I always did.

'Please, Luke. Your father and I are really worried about you going down there. Please be careful.'

I smiled. 'Mum, everything's going to be fine, I promise. Hey, hey, boys!' I threw my bag into the boot, jumped into the back seat with Kent and Deztiny and pulled out my plastic satchel filled with speed.

'Man, already?' Deztiny said. 'This trip is going to be the best.'

'Don't worry, I've got a bag too,' Kent said, laughing.

'We've got heaps for the trip!'

We were flying before we left the suburb. The windows were down and some Aussie hip-hop was playing over the stereo. I was overcome with happiness: the car was filled with boys I had no worries around who were just out for painting and having a good time. There weren't any thoughts about fighting.

'We have to get some paint, I know some spots on the way,' Deztiny announced. He'd been on this trip before, so he knew good hardware spots where we could score some quality paint.

At every store we stopped at we sat in the car park to have another line of drugs, then the five of us walked into the hardware store without an inch of worry. There was no time to make sure it was a good place to steal from and we didn't bother trying to distract the staff; we just walked in and stuffed cans down our pants. Soon the boot was full of the tools we needed to pull off our adventures, everything from spray paint to heavy-duty bolt cutters. We were armed for the cataclysmic onslaught we had planned for Melbourne.

We arrived in Melbourne just before midnight. I'd never been there before, and I was pumped up to visit a new city.

'Where are we going to stay?' I asked.

We hadn't got that far into the planning. The cold evening air and the speed intake had me quivering and we sat in the car feeling exhausted. We looked to Deztiny for answers.

'Let's chuck money in for a hotel tonight,' he said, 'then tomorrow we can look around for a hostel to stay in. They're heaps cheaper.'

We agreed and soon we were all tucked up in a two-bed hotel room, but it wouldn't have mattered if there were a hundred beds because none of us could sleep. Instead, the night was filled with cheeky laughter. I hadn't slept for more than an hour the night before, and this night I didn't sleep a minute.

The sun began peeking early through the blinds, which was devastating to anybody off their heads. The night somehow sheltered you from real life, when people frowned upon our dirty, chthonic existence.

'Let's go, boys. We can just chill today in a hostel and try to get some sleep so we're fresh for tomorrow,' level-headed Terz said.

'Screw it!' I yelled. 'Who cares how we feel! Let's run amok, boys. We're in Melbourne. Cheer up, you miserable bitches!' I was trying to trick myself into feeling less hung-over.

'Fuck, that one's full too,' Deztiny said. It was boiling hot and we were sitting in the gutter outside another hostel.

'Brush this; let's get drunk,' Ragz said. It seemed like a good solution so we made for the nearest pub, where Deztiny outlined the plan.

'We're going to chill out today, have some drinks then get some sleep tonight. Tomorrow I've got a daytime panel spot.'

Daytime trains were awfully risky, not only because it was easy to be seen but also because there were more trains running, which meant a higher risk of being hit.

'After the daytime spot we can have more drinks, then tomorrow night I've got a hectic spot where we can pull off a massive full-colour panel. Last time I was here we had over an hour there!'

'Hell, yeah!' we all responded, leaning in closer.

'The day after tomorrow is New Year's Eve. I've got another day spot then we can go out and party in the city.'

'Hey, look!' Kent pointed at a bunch of backpackers leaving a hostel across the road.

We had a room, but this was no five-star Hilton. The smell was horrendous, a mix of body odour, urine and alcohol. Determining the carpet's colour was a guessing game because there were more stains than carpet. All the occupants shared the same toilets and showers, which gave off an even worse smell.

As we walked down the corridor to our room it felt like a scene from a 1980s American college film. Open doors revealed drug taking and people kissing, and through one open door I saw a random guy meditating. It was the first time I'd ever seen someone meditate, and I had a brief look as I went past. It was as though his meditative state channelled into my mind: as I walked away I had a sudden yearning to see more.

I stopped and spun around without thinking, then calmly approached the open door to his room. It was like a magnetic force: I couldn't resist his ambience. The guy sat peacefully among the chaos that was going on around him, and his tranquil face was soothing to look at. I wanted that. Our room had no fridge, no air-con or fans and no TV; just stained carpet and six bunk beds.

'Perfect,' I said, as I threw my bag onto one of the bottom bunks. Again we stayed up all night chatting away.

'Far out, Punchy, it was too good, that speed. I just want to sleep,' Ragz said from the bed on top of mine.

'Me too, brother.'

It had gotten past enjoyment. I had only slept a couple of hours in three nights and I lay there quietly, angry at myself for getting the speed. *You've ruined the trip of a lifetime,* I thought to myself. *You wanted this trip to be the best, but you've ruined it. It's all your fault. Imagine how much better it would have been if you didn't get the drugs. They're all dirty on you because now they can't sleep.*

My mind was like that of a fat man at an all you can eat buffet – it had plenty of things to devour. I'd sit and think over every situation, suggesting reasons why it was my fault that things weren't better. I searched for perfection but never found it, because my mind would always find something to worry about. The mental disease was getting worse: with each passing day I was getting further away from the real moment and I was starting to feel depressed. My mind had won again.

'Boys, after today's panel let's get blind drunk and pass out. We need some sleep.' Ghastly pale faces stared back at me.

We started plotting our attack on the daytime train. Melbourne was going through a heatwave that summer and our room was sweltering. Our energy and enthusiasm were low due to the drug-fuelled sleepless nights so we were in no condition for the big adventure, but it was why we were there.

Imagine if we only pulled off a couple of panels: what would everyone think?

The plan was to bomb a terminator. This particular terminated train sat idle for 15 minutes on the middle of a train line behind an abandoned house. The driver sat inside waiting for the tracks to change and the red light to turn green to indicate it was time for him to continue the journey.

'The abandoned house is perfect, we can sit in the backyard and wait for it to come. There's one train that goes past twelve minutes in. I'll let you know when it's coming but let's try to finish by then.'

That meant we had about 10 minutes to paint, just enough time to pull off a one-colour, filled-in panel. We parked a couple of streets away.

'Oh, no,' Deztiny said as we walked across a road. 'The bloody house isn't abandoned any more!' He pointed to a brand-new house with a 'Sold' sign in the front yard.

'Let's do it anyway,' Ragz said.

We opened the side gate slowly, as we didn't want it to bang. The backyard was filled with kids' toys. I looked through the back door to see a lady with her back to us preparing food at the kitchen bench. We squeezed between a shed and the fence and sat huddled in a tight circle waiting for the train.

We could hear a slow metal clunking coming from the opposite side of the fence.

I pictured myself as a soldier going into war, readying my arms by testing my paint on the back fence. Then it was time to leap from the bunker into no-man's land, a land foreign to foot traffic but a land we were there to conquer.

Once over the fence we tried to get a better view, scanning for close foot soldiers or snipers in the distance but it seemed the coast was clear. Like pawns grasping an opportunity to defeat an unprotected king we proceeded for the slaughter and began our takeover. As I tossed my weapon, now empty of ammo, to the side it became clear this new land was ours. We'd defeated the king and it was time to retreat, but then a noise in the distance snapped me out of my stupid fantasy.

'Coppers, boys!' I spotted three men in orange vests running our way. I couldn't tell if they were police officers but I didn't want to find out. I looked over at who I'd imagined as my fellow soldiers. Their body armour was actually stained and ripped clothes, their weapons dented spray cans. My strong soldiers were just skinny white boys recovering from a night on drugs.

'Hey!' I heard screaming from behind and saw police officers coming from another direction who were very close. We jumped the fence into the lady's backyard, where she was hanging out clothes on a line.

'Sorry, we're just using a short cut,' I said, hoping to lessen her worries.

Out in the street we jumped into the car and successfully escaped the scene. Humble warriors we were not, each of us boasting about how impressed he was regarding his own weapons use. We celebrated my first interstate panel the only way I knew how: we got hammered.

Alcohol was our go-to for any situation. When we wanted to celebrate, we'd drink. When we wanted to sleep, we'd drink. When we were going out, we'd drink. When we were staying in, we'd drink. When we were happy we'd drink. When a friend died we'd drink.

Besides painting, alcohol and drugs were the only things that made us feel good. Nothing else gave us any sense of achievement, so we were always searching for other ways to feel good.

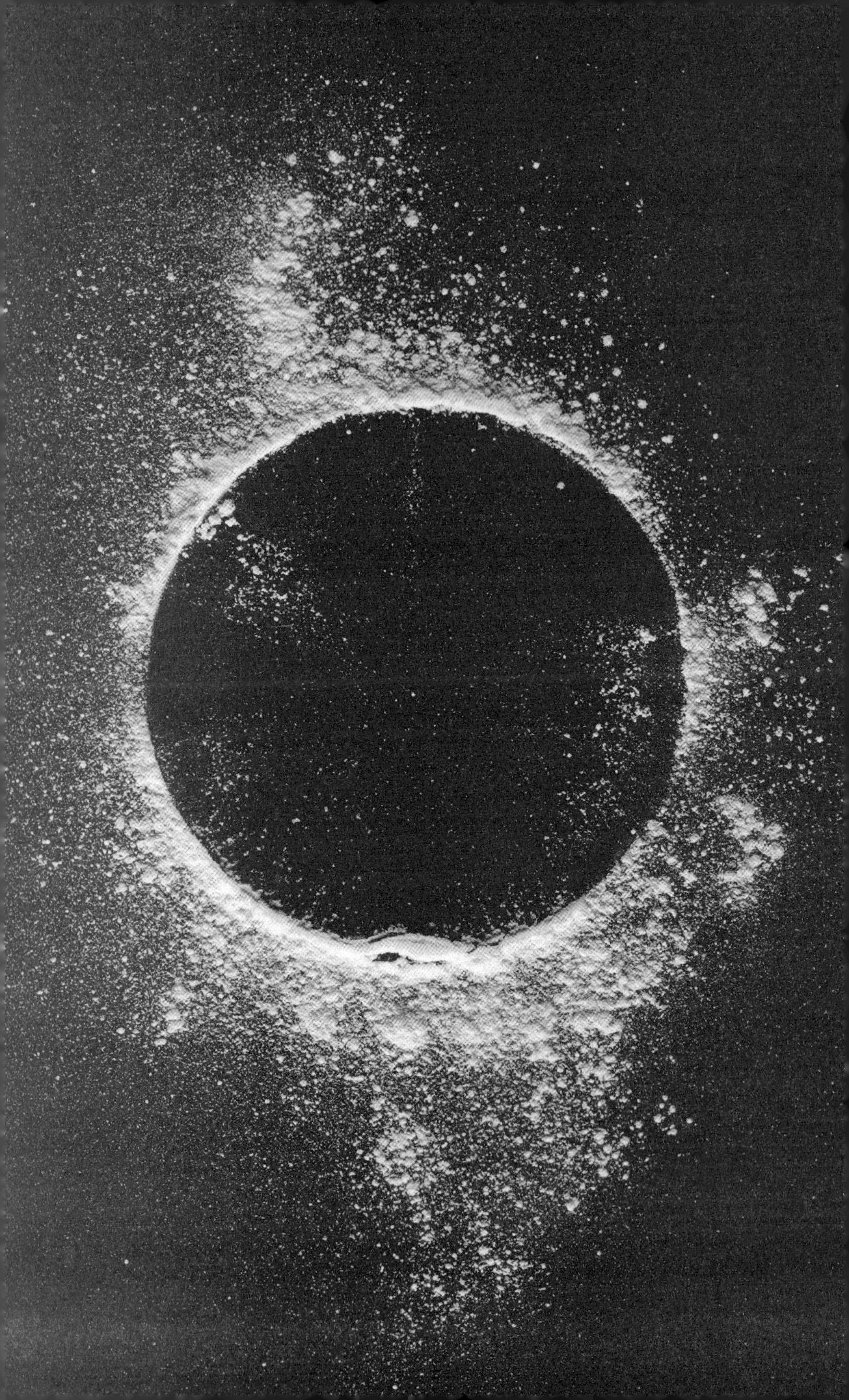

CHAPTER 50

ONE LAST PANEL

It was New Year's Eve 2006 and we had a huge night ahead of us. I'd planned to not have any more speed, but after seeing it lined up on a notepad I soon joined the boys and snorted the white misery up my nose. Next I pulled out a bunch of pills and shared them around. I was in a foreign city and completely off my head and I was happy. The drugs hid any depression and I was optimistic – until it wore off.

The day turned to night as we had another pill and more speed. The crowds were building by the tens of thousands every hour and we ran into several local writers in a park. They were excited to meet some well-known Sydney boys and fed us with free drugs.

'Lad, let's get to the main part to see the fireworks,' I said to Deztiny.

'You boys won't make it,' one of the local writers said. 'The crowd's massive. You won't get there in time.'

'Watch me,' I replied. I rallied the troops and we embarked on the impossible task of making it to the centre of the city in time for the fireworks. I didn't care for fireworks; I just loved a challenge. The street was split into three lanes by large concrete barriers, and the two outside lanes were filled with masses of partygoers making their way to or from the city. The middle lane was for the law – the police had an advantage in terms of movement and view.

The slow galloping of a horse as an officer rode from his raised position almost hypnotised me. The noise was beautiful as I stared, watching the horse's metal shoes hitting the white concrete.

'Forget this, Punchy, we're never going to make it in time.' Terz brought me back from my trance. He was right: the crowd wasn't moving. Everybody had left their run too late to get to the popular party spot, but in the centre lane officers on horses, security guards and other police strolled past.

'Let's run the gauntlet,' I said.

Terz's eyes popped out of his head. 'You serious, Punchy?'

'Yeah, fuck it. There's no way we're going to make it through this crowd. We can jump in, run around those pricks and jump back out further up the road,' I said.

'Really?' Terz responded doubtfully.

'Yeah, should be fine.' The drugs had made me delusional.

'Sweet, brother, I'll give it a crack with you.'

Terz and I made our way to the concrete barriers but a security guard already had his eyes on us.

'Hi, mate,' I said as we jumped the barrier right next to him.

'Hey!' he shouted, not at us but to get the attention of the police officers. I'd gotten away from an officer on a horse before, but that was through traffic and there weren't any cars here. We heard cheers from the crowd, which was just the encouragement we needed.

I dodged a short, chubby guard and raced up the path past another guard, whose hand slapped my passing neck as he attempted a grab. We sprinted with all our might and were soon in the clear. Guards were chasing us, flailing their arms, and three police officers were also closing in from behind as our sprint became a jog. The crowd roared as we progressed a couple of hundred metres, but men and horses were closing in from every angle and I knew we'd soon be crushed.

I looked at Terz, and it was as though our minds merged. We both headed for the safety barrier and jumped into the crowd, then we bent down and kept running. The crowd was still cheering and was happy to hide us. We'd done it! We'd made it to the city centre with 10 minutes to spare. We sat on a bench and watched different groups hug and kiss each other to celebrate the arrival of 2007. It marked my seventh year in the graffiti game.

Terz looked up at the fireworks. 'Can't beat this, brother!'

The other boys finally found us. 'I can't believe that: you boys are bonkers! Let's go to the pub,' Ragz said.

'No, let's do some panels,' Deztiny suggested. Our eyeballs were in the backs of our heads, but we still thought it would be a good idea to paint a train. We were in no condition to walk, let alone pull off a panel. This trip had been full of great ideas.

Nevertheless, after driving around for some hours we found a train yard where a train was sitting 20 metres from the fence. Once the painting started nothing else mattered; even drugs were no match for the in-the-zone moment of painting. The world could be ending or your brain could be frying, and the only thing you could think about was the panel. However, the moment I finished the last spray of paint to complete my panel the effects of the drugs took over again.

I sat and watched as the other characters stumbled and swore until they finally finished. After two days of painting, it was time to head home to Sydney.

'I think we do one more panel,' Deztiny said.

I was happy with our efforts on the trip. After a few close calls and being completely spent from almost zero sleep I wasn't interested in another panel mission, but the boys went for the idea.

It's the last one. You're in Melbourne; just do it.

'Yeah, last one. Let's go out with a bang.' I gave in.

As we drove to the spot it was as though life was suddenly different but meant to be. In fact, I was driving towards an outcome that was the beginning of the saving of my life. The sun was shining and its warmth hugged me. I was happy. I felt as though this had already been planned for me and I was just along for the ride.

We pulled up in a back street filled with industrial buildings. It was the weekend, and we were the only people on the deserted road. We made a dumb call: parking the only car in an industrial setting a paint spray away from the train wasn't something we would have done in Sydney. Yards were regularly patrolled by police or Task Force Graffiti, and a car nearby would be watched to see if its owners returned, especially a single car with interstate number plates in an industrial area in which no factories were open.

Deztiny led the way. There was not a cloud in the sky as we prepared for yet another attack. The train sat outside a train yard on top of a slight hill.

As we cut a hole in the fence the long shiny train sat still, looking nervous as it watched us prepare to kill it. I couldn't wait to get this done. We just had to pull off this last panel and we'd be home free. We crawled through a gap in the fence then crouched down to map out our plan.

'You two hit that carriage. I'm there. You boys have the next carriage.' I pointed to each man's preferred spot.

The train was out in the open for anyone to see including anyone in the yard, who would be able to spot our feet from the other side. A couple of bushes barely hid us from view from a nearby residential street. Nevertheless, we put all this to the backs of our minds and this group of optimistic criminals swallowed their suspicion. We started spraying with nothing other than hope.

As I applied my fresh colours to the train Deztiny stood by my side. He'd painted this spot before and looked confident. I had my piece filled in with three colours and began the outline. We were all taking our time, convinced we were one step away from home and it was as good as done.

'Yeah, boys!' Ragz's voice cut through the sound of hissing cans. We'd finished – mission accomplished! As I took a step back to view the work I felt light. The whole trip had been filled with close calls and now a weight was off my shoulders.

Those few days in Melbourne had been filled with drugs, anxiety, excitement, fatigue and an energy that seemed to guide my decisions like a plane on autopilot. I was in the cockpit, but my destination and my destiny had already been determined. This was all meant to be.

We'd be leaving for home in a few hours. We put our arms around each other and congratulated ourselves, then we headed for the fence and crept through it to freedom. I led the way back to the car as though I wanted to be first to reach the vehicle and be safe from capture, but as we entered the deserted street we saw two men fiddling with a lock on a factory gate. They were about 10 metres away and, like novice actors in a play, they looked out of place. Clearly they both had an eye on us.

The factories were closed. As I watched the two men pretend to open a gate my world completely slowed down. I glanced over at Terz as the realisation brushed over his body. I could feel what he was thinking: both our energies merged and words weren't needed to express what we both knew. Time stood still, and for a split second it was calming. The beauty of the moment was about to convulse into explosive violence.

'Don't you fucking move!' I heard someone roar from behind. The moment of grace became frantic movements of people yelling and running in every direction.

'Get down, get down!' Men in dark clothing jumped out and the actors who had been fiddling with the gate held up badges, as though that was going to make us stop. I ran for 10 metres but tripped on the gutter. I raised myself up to make another dash but was met by a boot to the face that smashed my glasses. I had two men on my back and my face was in an intimate meeting with the pavement. I looked up and saw Kent being chased through a park by two men.

One of the officers got off me and walked over to pick up a bag that had been left behind by Ragz. I took the opportunity to force the other officer away. He shouted for help and three different fists hit my head as I was tackled to the ground. I remember thinking how unfair it was: police aren't meant to hit you and I felt like a victim. Melbourne police didn't take any shit.

I sat in the gutter with my hands cuffed behind my back. I could taste my own blood.

'Don't report us for hitting you and we won't report you for pushing the officer, which would be another charge,' one of the men said to me.

'I'm not going to give you up. I'm not a fucking dog like you mutts,' I teased.

Whack! Another kick to my face broke my nose. I kept my mouth shut after that.

'There's one close by. I think he ran into the backyard,' one of the officers said over his radio.

Ten minutes earlier the street had been dead silent with not a soul in sight; now it was filled with flashing sirens and men hunting other men.

'We're sick of you Sydney people coming down here thinking you can get away with it. Whose car is that?' The officer pointed at our lonesome vehicle but I didn't say a word. He picked me up and threw me into the back of a paddy wagon. I thought of my parents but also of the two detectives I'd met at Central Station, who now believed I was away from all this trouble. They'd no doubt be told and have another reason to pay me a visit.

At the police station I was put in a room with bright lights. I sat there for hours without being attended to. It was spinning me out and I felt disoriented. The days filled with drugs had caught up with me and my brain felt as though it was going to explode. I stood up and walked around a little to try to settle down. I felt like screaming at the top of my lungs, but then I remembered the man who had been meditating with his door open when we'd first arrived at the hostel. He'd looked relaxed in frantic surroundings.

As I'd grown up I'd viewed meditation as being taboo, like witchcraft or something only spaced-out hippies did. I was Catholic and we prayed, but I thought: *meditation is for other religions*. I really didn't have a clue what my own religion was about let alone any other spiritual practices, but that man had looked so relaxed I gave it a shot.

I closed my eyes, which in itself was welcoming as the bright lights faded and my headache disappeared. My brain was still running faster than Kent as he tried to evade capture in the park. My mind wasn't stopping for anything, but it did slow down. I soon noticed the sound of a ticking clock, something I hadn't heard over the drumming thoughts of my mind. The ticking was relaxing and my brain slowed even further. Finally, I caught my breath and my anxiety lessened.

What if they raid my house? My parents will be crushed!

I meditated to find bliss, but I soon found dystopia and worried thoughts clawed their way into my mind. The anxiety was back and the ticking of the clock was gone as my thoughts echoed throughout my mind. *Does meditation work? I'm still frantic. I don't think it worked. Meditation is a joke,* I concluded.

However, my first instance of meditating had given me an opening to life. It was only for a few seconds, but it kept me sane at the time. I didn't meditate for a long time after that night, but the energy produced by that short stint of awareness began to build and gave me subsequent flashes of presence.

With a turn of a lock two detectives stood before me, one male and one female. They sat across the table from me and the woman put a bunch of photos on the table. There was one of the panel I'd just done and also of the one we had done after jumping the lady's back fence a few days earlier. They had us.

'So, Punch, will you agree you were arrested in Fits Road at 14.40 on 2 January 2007?'

'No comment.' They knew I was Punch, but I wasn't giving anything away.

They continued to ask questions but were soon sick of hearing my repeated 'No comment.' They'd been taking note of the panels we had done and were hoping we'd slip up, and we did. I was released after receiving numerous charges, plus a warning that more were coming.

It was 4 am and I had no idea where I was. I caught a taxi back to our hostel, but I couldn't see our car anywhere. I didn't have a key to get in so I shouted up at the window. *Have they left without me?* I wondered. I sat huddled in the gutter to think about my next move.

A backpacker stumbled past me and unlocked the door to the hostel. I ran up the stairs and banged on the door. Ragz opened it slowly with his eyes closed. Kent and Deztiny, who had both been asleep as well, were with him. I hated them for it. I'd just been locked up and interrogated and these guys were snoozing. *The lucky bastards,* I thought. *I wish I'd got away.*

'Where's Terz?' I asked.

'He wasn't with you?' Ragz asked.

'I saw him run into a backyard,' Kent said.

'I heard one of them over a radio say they had someone surrounded. It must have been him.' I filled the boys in. 'Get your shit ready, boys. They had photos of my other panels, so they're on to us.'

We heard a forceful knock at the door and, like ice sculptures, we all froze.

'Boys!' It was Terz. 'Fuck, lad, this is bullshit,' he said as he entered the room.

Terz had stayed hidden in a backyard for a couple of hours then, thinking it was all clear, he made his way back to the car. Just as he opened the boot he heard: 'Kyle, don't move.' They knew his name, so he thought it was no use trying to escape. They'd contacted the hire car company back in Sydney and managed to get Terz's name.

'They've impounded the car,' he said.

'What are we going to do?' Kent asked.

'We can't stay here. They probably know where we're staying by now,' I said as I packed the rest of my stuff into my bag. 'They'll want to get you boys too, so let's get out of here.'

We stood outside in the street with our bags packed and not a hope of knowing what to do.

'They said they'll call me when I can pick up the car,' Terz said. 'It might take a couple of days.' His phone rang, and he said a few words before hanging up. 'It's ready now. How come it's ready so soon?' he said suspiciously while staring at the sky.

I often stared at the sky myself. The stars in the universe mesmerised me and, while staring, my mind rested. It felt as though I was looking at my parents, the beings who had created me, and I felt as though I was part of the sky.

'Might be a set-up to get the other boys,' I replied.

'Yeah, for sure. You three stay here and me and Punchy'll get the car,' Terz said.

After an anxious visit to the impound yard we returned with a car that was completely covered by fingerprint dust. It looked as though a baker had been rolling dough over every inch of it. We hopped in and drove straight home to Sydney.

CHAPTER 51

FINDING LUKE

I moped around for a week after arriving back in Sydney, not knowing what to do. Court was a few months away, but I wasn't sure what would happen in between. As I was worried my home might be raided I decided to clear my bedroom of any evidence of my painting, the most damning of which was my photos.

A writer's collection of photos is his prize possession, dearer to him than any other thing on earth. Writing is about fame, and my box of photos was evidence of my fame. I'd spent countless nights showing these photos to anyone who ventured into my room because I loved watching as other writers, wide-eyed, flicked through the photos like young kids flicking through football cards.

'Punchy, please, man, get me a copy of this.'

'Man, look at this one! How long did that take?'

I'd proudly answer their questions, always exaggerating the story: 'Not that long. I did two other panels that night too.'

'Really? Far out!' It felt good.

Unfortunately, now I was certain the law would be paying me a visit so the photos had to go. I picked up the box and headed out into the backyard. Even though it was raining I stood in the rain and looked through my photos for the last time. Usually I'd never let them get damaged, but now they were getting soaked.

As I flicked through the photos I had flashbacks of my first panel with Snap and Base. We were just young kids back then. The night had started out with a brawl and ended with almost a whole train being painted.

I remembered scoping out yards, Base using a mirror on the end of a pole to see if anyone was coming.

The photo of the whole car on the country train fell onto the ground, so I picked it up and put it back in the box. I opened the lid of our bin, stared at the leftovers from last night's dinner then dropped in the box. It fell slowly before hitting the bottom, and photos spilled out onto the rubbish. They looked out of place, like gold bars mixed in with trash.

Not long afterwards I was at work dwelling on things when I received a message on my phone from Ruben. 'Man, you're in big shit. Call my phone. Don't ring the house.' I knew straight away it was about Melbourne. I hadn't told any of the family what had happened down there, but they'd sensed something was up. I rang Ruben.

'Hey,' he whispered into his phone. 'There's police here from Melbourne and the city. They're raiding the house.' His words echoed through my body like a sonic wave and my head felt hot. 'They're asking where your work is. Mum isn't telling them.'

The police had wanted to come to get me at work, which would have meant losing my job, so Mum had stood staunchly and wouldn't say a word. After hanging up I felt surprisingly good. *This is my out,* I thought. This could be a good reason to avoid the pressures of painting trains and fighting for higher graffiti status. I could use this as my reason to stop.

I expected to get a bombardment from Dad, and when I got home he was sitting in the lounge room. He stared at me as I walked in. 'Sit down,' he said.

As I lowered myself onto the couch I could hear someone in my parents' bedroom closing drawers. I glanced over to see who it was.

'That's your mother: she's fixing up our room. She just had strangers going through all her fucking stuff.'

'Dad.'

'Shut up and you listen to me,' Dad snapped back.

'No, please, Dad. I need to say this.' As he heard the calmness in my voice Dad's look softened a little and looked him in the eye. 'It's all over, I promise.'

'Diane, come here,' Dad hollered over his shoulder to Mum. 'You apologise to your mother,' he said, as he turned back to look at me. Mum came in and sat down next to Dad.

'Mum, you and Dad mean the world to me,' I said. 'I love you so much. I'm sorry. I mean it this time. This stuff will never happen again.' I normally would have bent forward and put my head into my hands, knowing I was lying, but this time I maintained eye contact.

Mum and Dad looked at each other then back at me. 'We love you too, Luke,' Mum said.

I looked over at Dad, who had a little smirk on his face. They'd picked up on my energy and they believed me. More than that, though, I believed myself.

Our house had been raided by Melbourne police officers, a Melbourne task force, New South Wales police officers and Sydney's Task Force Graffiti, who were all looking for more evidence in the hope of putting me away.

Some of the police who'd raided the house had left their details and asked for me to call them. One was Detective Mills, who I'd met with a couple months earlier at Hungry Jacks with his sexy partner Detective Baker. I knew they were good people, so I decided to meet with them. I hoped they'd give me information about what was likely to happen in court, but I also wanted them to notice the change in me. I wanted them to believe, like my parents believed.

I called the detective and organised a meeting at the same spot. He and Baker arrived at their makeshift office with another man I hadn't met before.

'This is Detective Slater from Victoria Police,' Mills said.

'Hi, mate,' I said as I put my hand out to shake his.

'I don't shake criminals' hands,' Slater said, with no emotion.

'Okay.' I turned back to Baker and Mills.

'You told us you were out of it all, Luke,' Detective Baker said in a soft, disappointed tone.

'Yeah, I seriously thought I was, but sometimes things just happen,' I said, shaking my scarred head. I felt I'd let her down. Detective Baker looked sympathetic, which I appreciated.

'Tell us who your damn friends were,' Slater butted in.

'Look, I stuffed up,' I said to Baker. 'You know what, though? I feel good about it. This is the last time I'll ever have to deal with you guys.

Things are changing.' Sick of all the drama and after the conversation with Mum and Dad, I knew I meant what I was saying.

* * *

'I can't come, I've got court coming up.' It was my response at least five times a week. The boys missed having me by their side, not only for painting but in case some drama broke out. They felt safe having me there. I was still taking drugs and partying, but I was free of an immense amount of expectation.

'Hey, Punchy, we need you.' I heard these words many, many times when I answered my phone. If the boys needed Punchy for a fight he'd be there in a second to throw punches. If they needed Punchy to help steal something he'd be there, planning the escape route. If they needed Punchy to paint a train he'd be there with a bag full of paint. Punchy was always the daring one who pushed things even further by adding some humour. Punchy didn't like to let anybody down. However, if I was going to start living my real life I had to start being Luke again.

One night when I was in bed watching movies with Anne my thoughts started to race about the upcoming court date. Anne was soon fast asleep, and I was left with the TV and my thoughts when the Adam Sandler movie *Click* came on.

Often seeds can be planted by other people to help turn things around, but it takes a deep self-reflection and realisation for lasting change to happen. Anne lay asleep next to me, and it was raining outside with occasional thunder. This type of weather and the darkness usually meant my thoughts would come in and suffocate me with a dark depression. It just made me feel lost, down, incredibly sad, but this night was no different.

You're a bum. Look at your beautiful girl: why do you keep doing the wrong thing to her? I'm going to die. What happens when we die: is that it? Fuck, my parents are going to die one day. We all are.

The main character in the movie was using a magic remote to skip through life. He skipped through the shitty parts – boring events, family dinners – and eventually skipped through his whole life without even living. He was constantly fast forwarding minor events to get to the next one. At the end of the movie he got really fat and died, leaving a life full of regrets. He didn't like life and life didn't like him, and he died without living.

Fuck, that's exactly where I'm heading. I'm going to die. I'm seriously going to fucking die. That's it; it's going to all be over.

My breath shortened and I had to sit up.

Fuck, what am I doing? I'm going to get to the end of my life and just die without doing anything in this life. That's it. What am I doing?

I looked around the bare room and felt ultimate regret. I had nothing; I was twenty-two years old and I had nothing: no accomplishments, never travelled, didn't own a car or even have a driver's licence. What I did have was a heap of regrets. Not only was I lacking in travel destinations and material things, but there was nothing I was proud of. The only thing I had accomplished in my life was becoming a notorious street fighter who hurt countless people. My life was a sham.

What am I doing?

In the movie the main character woke up and realised it had all been a dream. He went home, hugged his wife and kids and was finally appreciative of the little things. He realised how beautiful his life was and that every moment should be cherished.

What am I doing? We don't wake back up. This life is it: right now is it!

The deep awareness that this life was it, that I was wasting my life away, was the breathtaking moment I needed. It created lasting change.

'Love you, babe,' I whispered to Anne before falling into a deep sleep.

That night I made my mind up to make some changes. I wanted to start helping people instead of hurting them. I didn't want to die with the whole world hating me. I thought about how people might react if I died and imagined people saying, 'It was only a matter of time' or 'He deserved it.' I didn't want to leave the world like that: I wanted to be remembered for greatness!

I could picture myself being fit. I had always wanted to have a go at boxing, and as I peacefully closed my eyes and went to sleep I thought: *one day*. I had no idea about diet or exercise. When I was in my early teens I'd gone with Ruben and Dad to a boxing gym. We went for a run to warm up, but I didn't make it more than 200 metres down the road before I was almost sick.

I'd hated exercise from that day on and I was embarrassed about my weight, so I wouldn't go to a gym to lift weights. I'd imagine a gym full of big muscleheads laughing at me, so I kept away. The next day I decided to pack my own lunch for work: weighing in at more than 120 kilos meant I wanted to lose the weight.

'What are you up to, Luke?' Mum asked as she saw me making a sandwich.

'Just going to try and save some money by taking my own food to work. It's getting too expensive eating at the café at lunch,' I lied to Mum. I didn't want to tell Mum that I was doing it to try to lose weight. I don't know what it was, but I was embarrassed whenever I told someone about a goal I had so I always kept it to myself.

One Sunday I waited until everyone went out then I ventured into our garage, where Dad had some training equipment. I walked in and looked around for a few minutes: I had no idea what to do. I lifted the dumbbells and started pressing them above my head like I had seen Dad do. My breath almost instantly got shorter and I wanted to finish up and go back inside before anyone came home.

You're going to die one day. Do you want to actually fucking live or just be weak forever? Work!

With those thoughts I started going harder. Sweat was dripping off my face as I looked over at the boxing gloves lying underneath a boxing bag that swung from the ceiling.

Imagine being a boxer: what will people think? They'll look up to me. I can be a fighter. I'm going to be a fighter.

A month went by during which I trained regularly, and because of that and packing my own lunch I lost a bit of weight. I reached the 10-kilo loss mark and was proud of myself, and no longer cared about anyone knowing I was training in the garage. At the start I hadn't wanted them to know in case I failed but I wasn't failing now: I was focused.

'Luke, you've impressed me, mate. I've noticed a change in you,' Dad said to me when I walked inside after a training session.

'Dad, I want to be a fighter like you.'

I saw a little smile on his face as we walked over and hugged me. 'Luke, you put in effort and you can do whatever you want. I'll back you up in anything. If you –' He stopped as he had a thought. '– when you get back from Melbourne after court let's get into it.'

I hugged him and felt completely protected. 'Mate.' He separated from our hug. 'Whatever happens down there we will get through it. We're Kennedys, we get through anything.'

I was on the path of releasing bad Punchy in the hope of finding Luke. I saw my large figure as the Punchy everyone knew, and hoped that getting rid of him would allow me to release more labels.

CHAPTER 52

GAOL THREATENS

I trained hard for two months and lost more than 20 kilos. I'd never felt better, and it kept my mind off my court date. I'd occasionally go out for a drink but would then get right back on track with my healthy eating and training. After getting advice from different people, eating right for me was oats for breakfast and tuna, brown rice and carrots for lunch. After work I'd go home and have noodles with pumpkin. It was nowhere near the perfect diet, but it was a lot better than my daily intake of hot chips and gravy and a chicken burger with no lettuce but extra mayonnaise.

I was feeling healthy, positive and optimistic about my life but the fact was I was probably facing gaol time. I would be locked away in a different state separated from my family. I didn't care if I was locked away, but I did care desperately about Mum's emotions. In his way of trying to keep us out of trouble Dad had always told us: 'If you kids ever went to gaol it would kill us.' Thinking they'd have to travel interstate to visit me in gaol made my regret even more penetrating to my soul.

On the day I left for Melbourne I kissed my worried mum goodbye and told her everything was going to be okay. 'My solicitor said I'll have to pay a fine and that's it,' I lied. Out in the street Snap was waiting in his car to drive me to the airport.

'Hey, Punchy,' he said with a bright smile as I approached. I hadn't seen Snap for a few months; he'd been incredibly busy with his food delivery business and I wasn't venturing out much, preferring work and exercise. He did a double take. 'Fuck, look at you, brother! You look good, man.'

'Thanks, brother, I've been –'

'Luke!' Dad called from the house. I turned around and saw him standing on the tiny front porch of our green fibro home. He was asleep when I left and I hadn't wanted to wake him. 'Come here, mate,' Dad called, beckoning me in before walking back inside.

'Give me five, mate,' I said to Snap.

'Take your time,' Snap responded as I ran back towards the house.

Dad had retreated to the lounge room, and when I walked in he hugged me with his warm, secure arms. 'I love you, mate,' he said, before releasing his grip to look me in my eyes. 'You know, mate, you're my best friend. These last few months I've been watching you: you've turned into a man.'

I stared at him, feeling his love. 'You're my best friend too, Dad.' I hugged him again.

'Whatever happens down there we'll get through this. Like I said, we're Kennedys: we get through anything,' Dad said, sternly.

Hearing him say that made me feel indestructible. I stood taller and nodded my head. 'Love you, Dad.' I kissed his forehead and ran back out to Snap.

'Everything okay?' Snap asked as I jumped into the car.

'Never been better, bro.'

* * *

I arrived in Melbourne alone. Terz was coming down with his girlfriend and I wouldn't see him until court the next day. Instead, I met up with a Sydney writer who'd recently relocated and dealt with my emotions the best way I could at the time: I got drunk.

Rips was a fun accomplice in getting messy, and we roamed the city streets while drinking. Rips had grown up in a tough part of Sydney and had been constantly in and out of gaol. He'd had a child with his partner so he'd moved down to Melbourne to get away, but he soon came under police attention there as well.

'I want to get out of Australia, Punchy. I'm going to travel the world by myself. I've got to get out: there's too much temptation and I keep getting into trouble. I want to be a good role model for my kid. I'm going to find myself on this trip,' he assured me. 'I'll come back a new man.'

'Man, go for it! I'd love to do it myself, just get away from everything,' I said.

'Yeah, I'm going to do it.' Rips sat on a bench and stared at the ground. 'Hey,' he said, raising his head. 'You worried about tomorrow?'

'Yeah, kind of, but I think it will all be okay. You know what, though: whatever happens I know there's no way I'm messing up again. Life is going to be good.'

I sat and thought about court. Although I felt that everything would be okay, I imagined myself sitting in a cell reading letters from Mum and that worried me. However, like a flash flood the alcohol temporarily washed everything away. Worries about court: gone. Concerns for safety: gone. Money: gone. And Rips? I later found out he did get away, but his quest to save his life actually ended it and he died in a foreign country. Another one lost. I hope he was at peace.

The next morning when I arrived at court Terz and I shook hands. 'I haven't slept. I feel like rubbish,' I said.

Before Terz could respond we were interrupted by two men who I recognised from somewhere. One of them was the officer who'd kicked me in the face and broken my nose.

'We've got a couple more charges for you boys,' they said, handing over a large yellow envelope.

I smiled. 'Thanks for that.' Inside the envelope were photos of all the panels we'd done in Melbourne and a charge sheet. I glanced around the waiting room: the usual suspects stood around chatting, with hard-faced criminals looking out of place in smart business shirts, their collars not long enough to hide their neck tattoos. Suited-up solicitors joked with other suited-up solicitors with not a worry in sight.

'What you boys here for?' a skinny junkie asked. I looked at him but didn't respond, and he scratched at his scabby arm. 'I'm getting locked for sure,' he said, sounding like he was boasting. I looked away from him, not wanting hear it. 'Yeah, this bitch reckons I punched her and stole her car. I did steal her car but I hardly touched her.'

'Will you get away from me, you piece of shit!' I whispered, not wanting to attract attention. He was startled by my comment and was about to say something. 'Get out of here,' I said, nodding towards the direction I wanted him to head in. He wandered away.

What am I doing here? I thought. In the past I had viewed appearing in court as being something that was cool, and like the junkie I had just buzzed away I used to boast about my crimes. Not any more.

I don't belong here.

* * *

Courtroom number three was already filled with people. 'Sit here and wait until I call you over,' our solicitor instructed us.

An attendant asked us to all stand as the judge entered through a door behind the bench. He looked younger than I thought he'd be, with slick black hair and a confident walk. Everyone in the crowded courtroom sat down in unison as the judge sifted through his papers. I sat nervously, expecting a long wait, but my name was called first. I looked over at our solicitor, who waved me towards a seat at the front of the room that faced the judge.

I sat down as the prosecutor started with her evidence. I stared at the judge, hoping to gain some insight from his young face. Besides a couple of nods of his head and the occasional sneer, I didn't get much. After the judge had heard all the evidence he looked up and glanced around the courtroom while he straightened his papers. Finally his gaze rested on me, and he stared into my eyes. My mind was foggy: I hadn't slept the night before and the seriousness of the situation had me in a panic.

'I'll be delivering your sentence after a short break,' the judge said to me. 'Just to warn you, I'm considering a custodial sentence.'

I heard whispers and looked over at Terz, whose girlfriend was hugging him. Whatever sentence I received he'd probably get too. We headed outside to get some fresh air, because I thought that if I didn't I'd suffocate from the anxiety. My head was spinning, and I could picture Mum crying, and Dad kissing her forehead to make her feel better. It burned me deeply.

During these times in our lives when we live a fake existence in our heads we try to impress people, and we worry about what people think so we do certain negative things in case we miss out on positive opportunities. We do all this stuff because we're living a fake life that is stuck in ego but what suffers is our true self, our soul, and we're left to face the consequences, which is where regret comes in. I was living a false existence in my head, even telling people and myself that I didn't care if I went to gaol.

'Nothing can stop me.'

Upon being hit with the very real possibility of going to gaol the false self fell away and the big tough guy crumbled. What was left was me: I was left with my demons, I was left to pay the price and I was left to sit in a cell with my thoughts.

Our solicitor wobbled over, his head shaking slightly and a stupid look on his face.

'What the fuck happened?' I said to him.

'Boys, we knew there was a slight chance but I genuinely thought we'd be okay.'

'I've got return flights home,' I stupidly replied, as though that would help my cause.

When I walked back into the courtroom I looked over and saw the junkie staring at me with a huge grin on his face. I found my seat and sat down to rest my weak, shaky legs. As the judge entered I watched him closely, hoping he'd have pity on me. *I'm a good person,* I thought. *I've changed.* He lowered himself into his large, comfortable-looking chair.

'Please stand, Mr Kennedy,' he said in an educated voice.

I stood up. My feet were unsteady and my world was rocking from side to side; the night of partying with Rips had been a terrible idea. The judge began talking but I wasn't able to pay attention. Just as I'd done all those years earlier in front of the school principal, I ran through my acting straight affirmations.

Act straight.

Stand tall.

Keep your eyes open.

Nod your head . . .

'Snap out of it!' I said angrily under my breath. The judge was still talking.

'You and your co-accused organised a carload of men to come to our state to wreak havoc on our train system. You are a criminal gang who are a burden to this society. You should be locked away.'

I tried to look remorseful, nodding my head in the hope that by agreeing with the judge it would help my cause. I wanted to sit down, as I thought I was going to faint. *I should have slept last night.* The judge licked his finger, picked up some papers and looked at the photos of the panels.

'This "Punch" that you wrote on the train,' he said, 'I don't understand it all. Grown men painting on a train? It doesn't even look good.'

Why don't you lay the boot in while I'm down? I thought. I wanted to interrupt him to explain the culture of painting and that there was a lot more to it than just vandalism. I imagined people behind me rolling their eyes and thinking we were just immature men painting on a train who would be locked up for it. Then, with seven words, the judge saved my life.

'I will give you your last chance.'

The judge could have sent me to gaol, but instead he gave me an 18-month good behaviour bond and fined me $5,000. That decision shaped my whole life from that point onwards. It still amazes me that when he had a break to think his decision over this one man's train of thought determined the person I am today.

Before I broke the law the direction of my life was in my hands, but after I crossed that line I put my life into somebody else's hands. A gaol sentence would have taken me down a completely different path, effectively destroying a potentially useful citizen. It would have also destroyed my family. Instead, the judge allowed me to go free.

What he did lock away was my graffiti career.

I wonder how many lives have changed due to a judge's decision? Judges are like anybody else: their brains are full of mental chatter. 'Should I or shouldn't I?' is a common question we ask ourselves every day, but the way a judge's mind leans can make the difference between a quality life or one filled with drama.

Some of my friends have found themselves in a cell even though what they did was nowhere near as bad as the malice-filled activities I had undertaken. If they'd been given a chance could it have led to greatness?

Could it have led to a life in which contributing to the community was an everyday occurrence?

I walked out of courtroom without saying a word to anyone, and as I strolled down the footpath with the cool Melbourne air blowing on my face I felt ultimate relief. 'Eighteen-month good behaviour bond,' I chuckled to myself. He could have given me 18 lifetimes' worth. I knew I wouldn't break it.

When I pulled my phone out of my pocket I saw there'd been 16 missed calls from home, which made me smile. My family cared so much for me. *Why have I put them through this?* I wondered as I looked up at the sky. *Doesn't matter; we're making up for it now.*

'Hello!' Mum said loudly over the phone when I called her. 'Rube, it's Luke!' she yelled. 'Aw, we have been so worried. What –'

'Luke.' It was Dad, who'd grabbed the phone from Mum.

'All's good, my man. I got a fine and a good behaviour bond,' I said, calmly.

'I love you, Luke.'

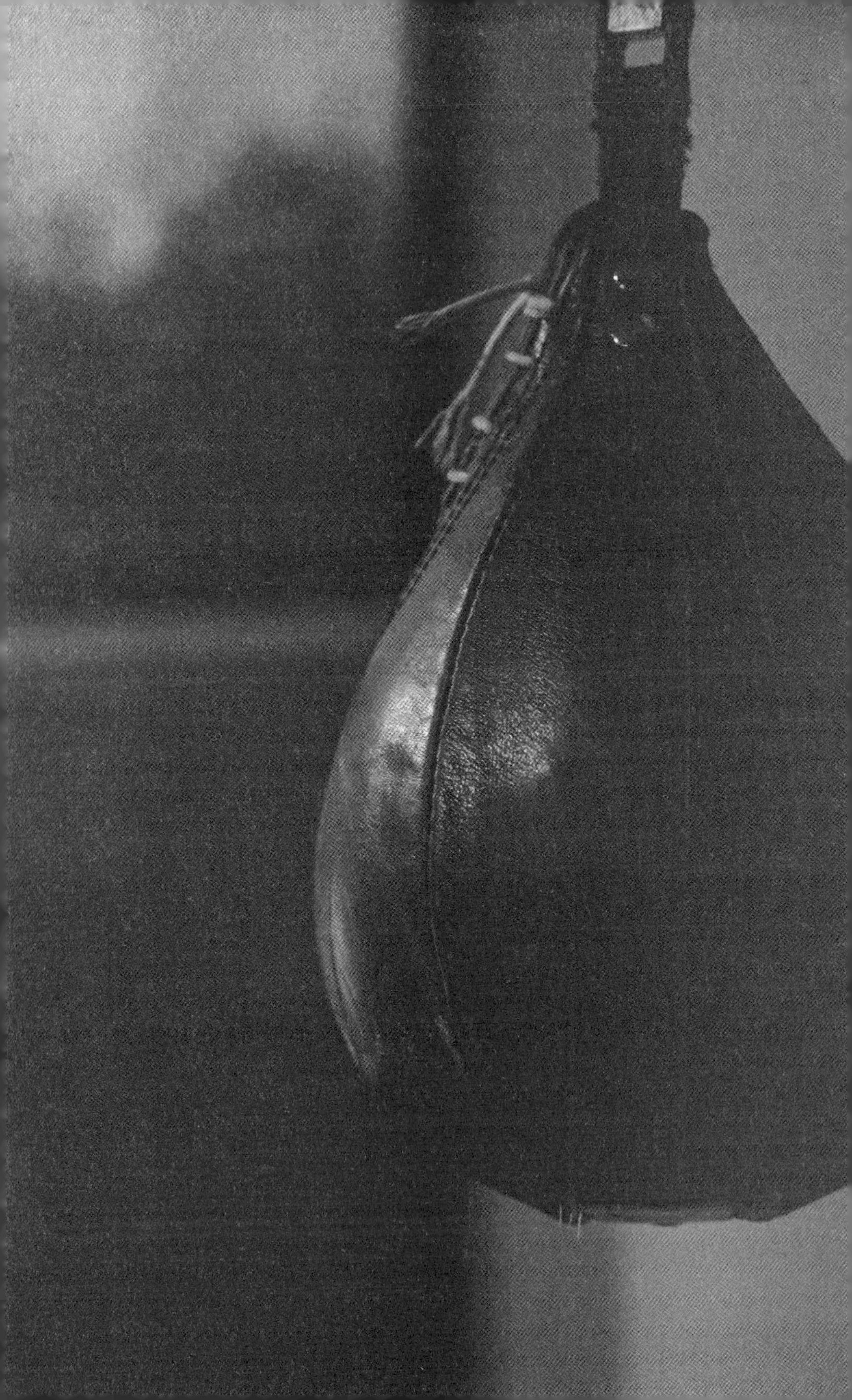

CHAPTER 53

THE FIGHTING DISCIPLINE

I trained even harder and could manage to run the whole way home from work. I begged Dad to hold the pads for me as I punched with gusto, and I was getting better. I'd lost 30 kilos, and my punches were getting faster.

'You think I could fight?' I asked Dad as he was taking the pads off after a hard session one day. He stopped in his tracks, and Spotty wandered up to sniff our feet.

'Luke, having a fight in the ring is something all men should do at least once,' he said. 'It teaches discipline. You have to give up certain foods, train hard and even stop hanging around people who might bring you down.

'You learn a lot about life when you train for a fight. A fighter has to set a date for a fight and train hard to get it right. It's the same as any goal you want to achieve. Mate, once you're in that ring –' He suddenly looked serious, as though he was remembering past fights he'd had. '– there's no one to help you. You're on your own.'

Dad had always believed in boxing as a way to improve self-esteem. As well as discipline he reckoned it taught you how to set goals and how to stand on your own two feet. In the ring you realised just how strong you were and that anything was possible.

'I'm going to do it, Dad,' I said, nodding.

A couple of weeks later we were again doing the pads in the backyard.

'Luke, if you want to fight you have to get into a boxing gym,' Dad said between rounds, a slight smirk on his face: he knew I wanted to avoid it.

'Can't you train me?' I asked. I didn't want to go to a real boxing gym to train for a fight because the thought of it scared me. What if they laughed at me?

'Luke, I'm not a trainer and besides, you have to get among other fighters.' I knew Dad was right: eventually I'd have to do some sparring in the ring. 'Go train with your brother,' he said.

Ruben was a professional boxer and had been fighting for almost 10 years. I loved watching him fight as he was short and thin and really quick in the ring, and he could avoid punches easily and counter with his own. He had a fight coming up and was training for it. When I put it to Ruben he was keen.

'Sweet, come tomorrow,' he said.

The next day Ruben drove me to the gym. I was incredibly anxious as we pulled up out the front. As I grabbed my bag from the boot I heard someone call out.

'Hey, Ruben! How you doing, champ?' A short, chubby man approached us.

'Stan, this is my brother Luke,' Ruben said.

Stan shook my hand. 'So you want to fight?' he asked, still holding on to my hand.

'Sure do.' I smiled.

As we walked up the stairs to the gym all I could smell was sweat. Inside, the walls were lined with full-length mirrors and posters of old fighters, and boxing bags hung from the ceiling. At the back of the room was a small boxing ring that I was itching to jump into. I copied Ruben's every move. He walked over to the skipping ropes so I did the same. He started skipping so I started bouncing right there next to him. He stopped so I stopped. Then he tossed me a new set of hand wraps.

'You can have these.' I watched him as he wrapped his hands, and when he'd finished he started shadow-sparring in the mirror. So what did I do? I shadow-sparred in the mirror. After shadow-sparring Ruben grabbed his boxing gloves from his bag, so I did the same. He put his gloves on and jumped into the ring, and I followed.

'Mate, I can't do the pads with both of you at the same time,' Stan said, laughing, as he climbed through the ropes.

Ruben also laughed. 'Bro, go warm up a little and hit the bag, and he'll do the pads with you when I'm done.'

I felt like an idiot as I climbed out of the ring, but after 20 minutes it was my turn. I jumped back into the ring enthusiastically.

'I've heard you punch pretty hard,' Stan said. I loved that comment because it increased my confidence, and I started punching as hard as I could. 'Settle, mate. Let's just take our time,' Stan suggested.

After the session Stan shook my hand. 'Good work today, mate. See you tomorrow,' he said.

I didn't know it at the time, but my quest for letting go had begun. I was feeling less anxious and I knew why: I wasn't partying as much. There was no more painting or street fights and I was feeling fresh. I had fewer worries and I didn't want any, but I felt slightly guilty about not going out as much with the boys from the south-west. I wasn't there to back them up as much, so my image as a fighter was beginning to disintegrate.

It was the label I held most dear, one I'd literally spilt blood for like nothing else. I felt I'd deserved the label, and I didn't want to let it go so easily. I'd seen how fighters were respected when I was growing up, and with this belief I'd been fighting in the street every week for years so others would think highly of me. Even though the truth was that I'd been risking my real life to enhance my fake one I still held on tight to the fighter's label. I could picture people talking about me, saying I'd lost my heart when I knew I was actually opening it.

Did I see boxing as a way to hold on to my fighter's label? I sure did. Through boxing I could rid myself of the worry that came with street battles but still maintain the strong-man image. Being a boxer was a positive label, one that would allow me to maintain respect without the drama. Replacing an image with another is not releasing the ego, but it was a better outcome – for the time being at least.

Every time I wiped a drop of sweat from my eyelids I knew I was doing the right thing, and for the first time in my life I felt proud of myself. I was getting rid of my fat but, even better, I was getting rid of the weight of worry I'd placed on Mum and Dad. And I was getting rid of bad Punchy. I smiled more as my solid brick structure became stronger. I was still in no way an angel, but I was less of a devil.

* * *

Chad called one night. 'Come on, Luke, come out. I'm not even calling you Punchy any more. You're "Luke",' he teased, hoping it would entice me to come out.

'I'll show you "Luke"!' I said. I hadn't gone out for a couple of months, opting instead to hang out with Dad and watch the football. It was the longest I' gone without having a drink since I could remember.

That night I got into a fight.

'Now, that's what we want see!' Chad said, as he put his arm around me. I flexed my hand, trying to rid it of the pain. I didn't feel good. Unlike previously, when I'd regret what I'd done only later when I was alone, this time I felt ashamed straight away.

'Fuck this, I'm going home.' I pushed Chad's arm off me and walked away. I'd had enough.

CHAPTER 54

BROTHERLY LOVE

One night during a training session in the garage at home I skipped in front of the mirror non-stop for an hour. I loved skipping – it was my alone time, a time when I could stare at my reflection as my frantic mind slowed down. When I'd finished I pulled up my shirt to wipe my drenched face and was shocked by what I saw in the mirror: stomach muscles. I quickly took my shirt off and stood there with tears in my eyes. I had abs! Having been obese for most of my life, I never thought I'd see my own ripped stomach.

'Dad!' I yelled, running inside. I stopped and showed him my stomach. Dad didn't say anything; all he did was smile. He hadn't seen me with my shirt off since he'd chased my naked body up our street the night I lost the plot. I'd been too embarrassed to expose my stomach to anybody and I never took my shirt off, but now I didn't want to put it on.

I'd lost close to 40 kilos. Apparently the rumour going around the graffiti scene was that I'd lost all the weight because I was a drug addict, but that couldn't have been further from the truth. There was a time when I'd have lost sleep at the thought of such rumours going around about me but now it didn't bother me at all.

When I was at the gym training with Ruben one afternoon Stan approached me. 'You're having your first spar today,' he said, with a serious look on his face. You can punch the pads as much as you want, but jumping in the ring with someone who's trying to hit you is a whole new ball game.

'Who am I sparring?' I asked confidently, knowing I'd won countless fights in the street.

'Me,' Ruben said.

I had more fights in the street than most people there had had in the ring, so I knew I could hold my own. Well, I thought I could. What I didn't know as I stepped into the ring was that street fighting and boxing are totally different. I've seen some great street fighters not last a second in the ring and vice versa.

Ruben was 15 kilos lighter than me and 30 centimetres shorter. *This'll be easy,* I thought.

'Hey, do I hit you hard?' I asked Ruben as he bent down to get his mouthguard from his bag.

Ruben burst out laughing and pushed me. 'Yeah, if you can.'

We got into the ring and Stan gave us instructions. 'All right, boys, nice and light. Take your time, and wait for the bell.'

I paced the ring, planning what punch I'd throw first. Ruben was in the other corner bent over to stretch. The bell rang, and it was as though a hypnotist had clicked his fingers. Both Ruben and I stopped what we were doing and headed towards each other. It was game on and the 'ding' called for complete presence. No other thought entered my mind, and for a split second I was at peace.

Whack! Ruben threw a punch. It felt to me as though an earthquake's epicentre was in my head. It didn't hurt but it was a complete shock, and the feeling was foreign to anything I'd felt before. Sure, I'd received plenty of punches in the street, but the thud of a boxing glove flush on your face interferes with all of your senses. I looked at Ruben and he smiled, revealing his green mouthguard. He knew exactly what I'd felt and now he was waiting for my reaction.

Like a street fighter I attacked, throwing punch after punch as he ducked and swerved. My thoughts were on the minds of those watching and I could hear them doubting me, judging me. *He's got no idea. He's hopeless.*

After a minute in I was completely exhausted, but I managed to last the round and walked back to the corner. The headgear felt suffocating. 'Get it off, get it off!' I gasped through my mouthguard.

Ruben and Stan were both laughing. I was bent over forwards and resting my arms on the ropes. Ruben walked over and tapped me on the shoulder. 'Man, this isn't a street fight. Take your time and relax. Work on your jab and I'll work on my defence this round.'

For the first time in our lives Ruben had given me some advice to help me. It felt as though he was concerned and wanted me to do better when previously our relationship hadn't been one of brotherly love. We preferred to tease each other rather than help. I'd have loved to have been closer to him but our attitudes wouldn't allow it, but now boxing was bringing us closer together. He helped me and I respected him for it.

'Hey, you're getting heaps better,' he said a couple of weeks later after a sparring session. He said it quietly, as though he didn't want others to hear. We'd be on a high after training and would chat about the session during the drive home together. Cruising with my brother was something I was thankful for.

One afternoon I invited Base to the gym to train and also to introduce him to Stan. 'Luke, why do some of the boys call you Punchy?' Stan asked later.

'It's just a nickname,' I said. Stan just saw me being as a skinny, innocent young man. He didn't know about my past, and I was happy with that.

My new life was taking shape. I'd met a whole bunch of people who also had no idea about my past, and it allowed me to give off an innocent and friendly appearance. I liked it. Sometimes I'd meet people who gave off the same energy I used to give, who seemed to be searching for an argument or fight. I'd extinguish the tension with some humour or a smile when a few months earlier I would have ignited it with a punch or headbutt. Maybe I was being tested by situations that I would normally respond to by fighting. After passing these tests with a smile they became less common as my new energy stopped attracting conflict.

While I was still deep in my partying days my sister Sarah had met a man she loved. She was the youngest child in our family but the most mature, and she had moved out of home with her husband and was now pregnant. It would be the first baby in our family, and Dad and Mum had a new skip in their step. We were all enormously excited.

I was asked to be a godparent to my beautiful niece, Allana. If she'd been born a year earlier I believe I wouldn't have been asked, considering the life I was living. It was the proudest moment of my life. I was on a roll; everything was working out. After endless nights of tearful prayers, it seemed as though they were now being answered.

I suppose my prayers had always been answered, even during the heavy and harsh events that had occurred. All of those moments in my life, although extremely hard at the time, were seemingly planned for me so I could become the man I am today, a man who is able to use his experiences to help others.

CHAPTER 55

MY FIRST BOXING MATCH

'I've got you a fight in seven weeks,' were Stan's first words when I arrived at the gym one day. He shook my hand. 'Congratulations, mate. You've worked hard to get to this point.'

It was true: I was now obsessed with training. I'd train with Stan five days a week and on the weekends I did my own stuff. Three times a week I'd get up at 4 am and head to a local park to do sprints. Most mornings it was freezing, and when the alarm went off I'd lie there and contemplate going back to sleep. 'Do you want to be a fighter or a pillow biter?' I'd say to pump myself up. 'I want to be a fighter!' I'd state enthusiastically before bounding out of bed.

It was now time to put all the training together and jump in the ring. I was still a beginner for whom sparring sessions could go either way and on occasion I'd go really well, but at other times I looked hopeless. However, I did want to fight.

That night I lay in bed thinking about how much harder I was going to train in the lead-up to the fight. *What if I'm beaten?* I thought. *What if I get knocked out and everybody laughs? You can take a punch. There's no way you're getting knocked out*, I convinced myself.

The next morning I leapt out of my warm bed into the frigid air and jogged through the dark streets. The only sound I heard on this fresh morning was the thud of my feet hitting the pavement. As I ran, I shadow-punched like I'd seen real fighters do on TV. I felt alive. I'd lost 43 kilos to get myself down to 79 kilos. I would be fighting at 75, but losing the last 4 kilos was tough. I was already overly gaunt and lacked any form of muscle tone, which didn't help my case for not being a drug addict.

I hadn't had a sip of alcohol for 10 weeks, and it was the best I'd felt in my whole life. The weeks until my first fight were ticking away and soon I was counting the days, but I was still worried about what everyone would think of my fighting ability. All the boys were coming to watch me slaughter an opponent, and I hoped I wouldn't disappoint.

'Luke, me and your mum are so proud of you,' Dad said a couple of nights before my first fight. 'You've shown discipline I didn't know you had.' I liked the idea of discipline: it was something a warrior would have. I wanted to increase my discipline and promised myself I would never again throw another punch outside the ring.

As I sat in the dressing room on the night of the fight a constant stream of people came in to wish me luck. Dad was shepherding his friends in to meet me.

'This is my boy. He's having his first fight tonight.' I could tell how happy he was to introduce me as his son. 'Mate, just work off your jab,' Dad advised. 'You've got a good jab – keep using it.'

The stage was set for the beginning of a new life, and the ring of the bell for the first round would signal my complete turnaround. As I walked out to the ring I heard cheers from voices I recognised as my boys, and I could smell the beer on the breath of those cheering.

'Here we go, Punchy!' someone hollered, slapping me on my back. They were all there to support me as always.

My body shook a little with anticipation, but a huge smile spread the width of my face. I jumped through the ropes into the ring and looked down at my feet as they bounced a little on the soft white canvas, which was stained with spots of blood. Outside the ring the crowd sat in darkness; I was lit up like Yankee Stadium.

I looked across at my opponent, who was dressed in blue. 'Fuck him up, Punchy!' Voices from the darkness cheered for blood.

The bell rang for the first round and I came out the only way I knew how: throwing a heap of punches. My opponent was doing the same, and I got caught with a massive shot. I heard the crowd moan as the thud of his landed punch echoed off the walls in the small arena. That made me mad, because it meant people thought I was being defeated. My head wasn't in the fight and instead I was watching it through the eyes of the crowd. I went on to get it over him. The ref stopped my onslaught in the first round after some scrappy punching resulted in my opponent being cradled in a corner.

I'd won!

I shouted and high fived Stan, who looked just as happy as I was. I wasn't yelling in delight about the win so much as my triumph over eight years of fighting, crime, drugs, drama, alcohol, stabbings and a relentless mind that wouldn't let me be. When the referee stood between my opponent and me waving his arms for the fight to stop, he was also waving away the old Punchy. My past was gone; my new life was about to begin.

I walked over to Dad, who congratulated me. 'Mate, you went well, but you've got to work on throwing that jab properly.' As soon as he said it I knew I hadn't looked good during the fight. 'I'm proud of you for getting in there, but we need to work on a few things.' He was right: I was a complete novice.

'Punchy! Man, we're so proud of you!' Snap and Base ran over to give me a hug. My two main boys had watched me crawl my way out of the dirt and I could see the joy on their faces, knowing I was setting a new standard for my life. Lucas walked over and stood nodding his head but not saying anything. He hugged me and I held on to him tightly, thankful for our relationship.

Mick and Chad came up, laughing, to congratulate me. 'See who it was you fought?'

'Who?' When my opponent took off his headgear after the fight I thought I recognised him, but I couldn't remember where from.

'You had a fight with him six months ago when he was picking on one of the younger boys.' How was that for irony? He'd only taken up boxing after I defeated him in a street fight six months earlier, then he'd come up against me in his first fight and the outcome had been the same.

I went looking for him, hoping to speak with him and apologise, but I couldn't find him.

* * *

'Hey, what about you yelling after the fight!' one of the boxing trainers said on my first day back at training. 'It was like you'd won a world title or something.' Embarrassed, I kept my eyes on the mirror.

'Hey,' Ruben said. 'If only you knew how far he's come. You've got no idea where he's been.'

'I was only joking, mate,' the trainer responded.

I shrugged my shoulders: Ruben's words were better than any victory in the ring. He'd revealed his true feelings about what I'd done and shown that he, too, was proud of me. Boxing had brought us closer together, and as our respect for each other grew our bond grew stronger.

CHAPTER 56

TAKING SHAPE

I won my next fight, also by knockout, and looked a lot better. I didn't care that much about winning; I just didn't want to look like a loser. Every decision I made began with worrying about what other people might think. It was a disease that had its ghastly green hands wrapped firmly around my throat, but I was loosening its grip one finger at a time. Hopefully one day I'd be totally free of it.

My new life was taking shape and my positive attitude building pace. After shedding all my unwanted fat, this previously weighed-down traveller was sprinting on a journey towards happiness. My head was clearer and my spirits high. I'd always questioned my existence and had been lost for a long time, but I knew I was now on the right road.

While I was trying to pull myself out of a deep, dirty hole, with my fingertips clutching the edges and my feet kicking to get a grip, Anne stood with a shovel to dig her own fresh hole to jump in. I'd turned Anne into a female version of my old self. She was drinking all the time and I had suspicions she was cheating on me, just as I'd cheated on her. She was hanging around the crew of people I'd formed even though I wasn't there any more and we were constantly breaking up and getting back together.

Even though the relationship was going nowhere, we had been in it for so long we found it hard to completely break up. I thought Anne was doing the wrong thing but I still loved her. In the end we did finally break up, because my fresh attitude, dedication to boxing and new outlook meant we had less in common and had outgrown each other. Anne would call me, crying, and it made me feel sad. I'd hang up the phone and try to think of how I could bring her on the path with me, but I couldn't think of anything that would work.

* * *

'I'm joining the navy.'

Mum stopped folding the clothes on the couch. 'Are you serious?'

'Sure am. I called them yesterday and I've got a meeting next week.'

Mum didn't need to say a word: her face expressed myriad emotions. 'Grandad's going to be so proud,' she finally said. She gave me a kiss and headed into the kitchen to call her dad, who had been in the army.

This was exactly what I wanted. I'd seen for years how my best friend, Base, was treated by his family and people in the community for being in the armed forces. Through holding a position of honour and respect he'd turned into a confident man, and that was what I wanted. For too long those close to me had been concerned about me for all the wrong reasons, and by joining the navy I believed I would be talked about for doing the right thing.

I wanted to replace the old negative labels with new hope-filled ones. At the time I didn't think I could release the negative labels without replacing them, because my mind was too hungry for more. What I needed to do was simply surrender the labels. Replacing the labels wasn't the answer or the final destination, but it was still big progress. All I knew was that I wanted happiness for myself and my family, and the changes I was making were resulting in exactly that.

CHAPTER 57

A FATEFUL TRIP TO THAILAND

One Monday at training in late November 2008 Stan told me I had a fight coming up in nine weeks. Butterflies instantly flapped in my stomach but I gave a brave response.

'Fuck, yeah.' Inside, I was extremely nervous. I was training hard and not partying but it was tough. I'd become completely obsessed with diet and training to the point where they dominated my thoughts. I had the fight coming up then after that I'd be joining the navy, so I wanted a breather in between.

I was riding my pushbike down a steep hill to work when a car reversed out of a driveway. The driver saw me just in time and stopped. *Imagine if I had been hit and broken a bone,* I thought. I could have a rest from all the training and kick back for a couple of months, which would give me the chance to relax my mind for a while.

Ruben called and asked me to go to Thailand with him, an invitation that made me realise we'd definitely developed a stronger bond with each other. As I was such an extremist with my training I was reluctant at first to go, but I managed to get a loan and time off work so we headed off.

Twenty-four hours after arriving in Thailand I woke up in hospital to find Thai nurses and doctors standing around me. I'd broken my hip, pelvis, tibia and fibula and dislocated my jaw. What happened? I'd got blind drunk, snorted cocaine, had a night filled with drama and then decided to hire a motorbike. I wasn't wearing a helmet and had a high-speed crash, impacting with a pick-up truck.

In the brief time I'd been in Thailand I'd done some really stupid things and had nearly ended up in gaol, which had stretched my newly bonded relationship with Ruben. The trip that was supposed to be my last party had almost killed me. Travel insurance didn't cover me, so Dad had to get a $22,000 loan to get us home. Mum and Dad struggled for every cent, and it devastated me that they had to pay for my dumb actions.

My life had been unreal: everything had been working out and my boxing had been going from strength to strength. Taking drugs had been out of the question and I was only drinking every few months, and I was heading to the navy to make everyone, myself included, proud. But now my old life had hooked me back. I could hear the response to my prayers: *you were going well; we gave you good. You wanted to go back to bad? Well, here you go.*

We always think the grass is greener on the other side. When I was training every day and working hard I thought I was missing out on partying with everyone, so I thought I wanted a break from training to get messy. A few weeks later I got very messy and was shown exactly what I was missing out on: absolutely nothing!

Apart from all the drama and violence and coming close to death in Thailand, I had some profound moments there that answered a lot of questions for me. It opened up my eyes and mind to why certain events had happened in my life, and with these realisations the biggest seed had been planted.

When we got back to Sydney we headed straight to the Royal Prince Alfred Hospital, and memories of my previous visits flooded back. I hadn't been there for at least a year and I didn't miss the place. The nurses took one look at me and rushed me into emergency. After a night of scans and drugs to treat an infection, I was informed the operations that had been done in Thailand appeared to be successful.

For $22,000, I certainly hoped so.

I felt pain all over, however, so they scanned the length of my body. My jaw was okay, which came as a surprise because it clicked when I spoke and the pain was getting worse, but who was I to argue with a doctor?

At the time I rarely spoke up or questioned things even if my body, as it did in this case, told me something was up. I'd often find out my gut instinct was right and regret not listening to myself.

I now usually listen to my body and gut and sense energies before anything else, although there are moments when I'm off with my perspective. Those moments don't come close to the amount of times my gut feeling is on point, and even when I'm not right I at least speak up and trust and back myself.

During my teens and early 20s I was in a world where if I read someone or a situation wrong I'd end up with a knife in me or in gaol, so I had to be good at reading people. This has helped me a lot throughout life. I think we all have the ability to smell bullshit, though we often don't speak up or make changes according to our own internal guidance systems. People are so conditioned to trust and believe people in positions of perceived authority that they've forgotten they're human beings who make mistakes, or there are ulterior motives behind their actions and decisions. I say: go with what feels right to you.

As I lay on my hospital bed I heard a voice.

'Babe,' Anne said as she walked into my room. She'd returned to me plenty of times and I wondered why she still stuck by me, but her appearance made me feel instantly better. I'd ended our relationship, but when I'd spoken with her while I was in Thailand I'd realised I still loved her. 'I've set you up a bed at home,' she said, 'and moved all your stuff to my place. You can live with us.' Anne saw this as a chance to get back with me, and I'm glad she did.

Mum came into the room, crying again. I'd come so far and made them proud but it had all turned to shit again. I'd become a new person who impressed people for the positive actions I was taking. There were still doubters who would have been happy to see me trip up, and that was exactly what had happened. I was travelling well and on track but then I stumbled. Would I get back up or stay down and play the victim, which would have been much easier?

Anne had set up the area downstairs at her parents' house. It was as though we had our own place, but I knew her parents didn't really want me there. They knew me as a reckless young man who led a life full of drama and had witnessed me having endless drunken fights with their daughter. They'd also heard stories. I may have had great manners but they knew I had a dark side.

I'd left the hospital and was at Anne's when I received a call from the hospital. They'd reviewed my X-rays and realised my jaw was dislocated, which I'd suspected. I needed to explode the ingrained belief that those in authority were always right.

CHAPTER 58

BACK TO SQUARE ONE

'Punchy, I'll come pick you up.' It was Billz, who was living in the suburb next to Anne's.

'I still can't go anywhere, my leg's buckled. Give it a week.' After Natch had stabbed me my relationship with Billz had been on shaky ground. We still met up from time to time but things weren't the same, and I'd opted to hang out with other boxers and positive people. Apart from Snap and Base, I'd rarely seen the boys over the previous year.

As we were living so close by Billz saw an opportunity to rebuild our relationship. I did enjoy his company as he enjoyed mine, and even though we both had massive egos when it was just the two of us we dropped our guards to chat and laugh.

'Punchy, it's sad. It's not like it used to be.' Billz stopped our laughter one afternoon in his lounge room. 'Everything's changed. I don't see anyone any more.'

'Yeah, things have changed, mate. Everyone's just got their own lives now,' I said.

'Fuck, we ran amok, didn't we?' he said, laughing.

'We sure did, bro.'

* * *

Christmas was just around the corner and Stan was having everybody over to his place for the gym's end of year party. Mark, another of Stan's fighters who was also a writer, picked me up. He was a lean, strong 25 year old who sported a scar on his eyelid, evidence that he was a fighter. In fact, he was a talented fighter both in and out of the ring.

As we drove to the party Mark threw me a pill. I knew my recovery period would be full of temptation and that as I was unable to train or work I could easily spiral back out of control. I'd come so far, but with my positive labels gone my ego needed something to attach itself to. 'Unlucky injured man who's keen on partying' was my new mask.

At Stan's place I sat with my crutches leaned up against the couch. I had another 10 pills and several lines of coke and soon we were all off our faces, although we were trying to hide it from Stan. Day turned to night and people called taxis to go home but Mark, my friend Ben and me weren't keen to stop. There are always a few in a bunch who don't know when to call it quits, opting instead to seek more drugs.

Those who party on for as long as possible often suffer from depression or from a highly active mind – which is pretty much the same thing. The drugs hide the pain for a while, but as they are scared of the comedown and its compounding depressive effects people delay the end as long as possible. On this occasion Mark, Ben and I headed to Ben's house, where we sat for the remainder of the night until the sun was peeping through the windows. Ben had passed out and I was wrecked.

'Let's get out of here, Punchy,' Mark said.

The day was already hot. With the sun scorching the tops of our heads we headed across an open field towards the train station. The effects of copious amounts of mind-altering substances were taking their toll and I had to lie down in the grass. I was exhausted.

'Get up, Punchy. Come on, let's go,' Mark pleaded.

'Leave me alone. I'm chilling here.' The pain from my leg had broken through the effects of the drugs and had crept up on me, growing from a little tingle to a throbbing. I closed my eyes: maybe sleep would save me.

'Sir, sir, relax. You're on your way to hospital.'

I was in the back of an ambulance and it was night time. Not again! I'd fallen asleep in the park and had lain in the summer sun for nearly six hours, my crutches beside me. A concerned walker who had been unable to wake me had called for an ambulance. I had severe sunburn and particularly on my legs, which had copped the full force of the sun and were purple. I was wearing sandals and my feet, which were normally a pasty white, had turned the colour of a black eye after a fight. They were damaged.

When I arrived at hospital I saw that my phone was full of missed calls from my parents. 'You're in hospital again?' Mum had found out when a paramedic answered my phone. I didn't want this. I'd promised myself and them that I wouldn't stuff up again and I'd been confident I could keep my word, but now I was back to square one.

Mark arrived, and his eyes popped out of his head when he saw my burned body.

'Why did you leave me?' I asked.

'Punchy, you stubborn prick, you wouldn't move!'

'Let's get out of here,' I said.

'Brother, you're pretty bad: look at your body!'

I was on a drip, but that wouldn't stop me. I said: 'I'll be okay. Watch this, mate. Arrgghhh, my leg, it's throbbing!' A nurse ran straight over. 'Please, the pain's so bad I feel sick.'

I winked at Mark, who wondered what I was up to.

'I'll get you some tablets to kill the pain,' the nurse said.

'No, it's worse than that. Can I have some morphine please?'

Mark realised I was putting on an act to get some morphine and shook his head in disbelief. The drug was one I'd loved in Thailand and I wanted it now. As the nurse injected me with morphine I sat smirking then as soon as she walked off, I pulled the drip out of my arm.

'Let's get out of here.' I grabbed my crutches and hobbled off.

'Where are you going, sir?' The nurse stood in my way. 'You can't leave, you have to stay under observation.'

'I'm just going outside for a cigarette.' I didn't smoke.

When we got outside we jumped into a taxi and continued the party, and the next two months were a blur of drugs, alcohol and depression.

One afternoon Base asked me over to hang out with the boys. My legs looked like the skin of a fish, the blisters from the burn like sparkly scales. All the boys marvelled at my legs.

'I think you should go to hospital, Punchy,' Base said, worried. 'It doesn't look good.'

'Fuck it, you'll be right, Punchy,' Chad butted in. He wanted my company even if it meant losing one or both of my legs, one of which was worse than the other. It was purple and sparkly and the blisters would pop, causing liquid to run out and down.

'I fucked up, brother,' I confided to Base, who was sitting beside me on the floor. 'Do you think the navy will still take me?'

'Man, if you can get fit again why not?'

'Hope so.' I needed the navy to be my saviour.

Before leaving for Thailand I'd bought a motorbike, and I couldn't wait to recover enough to ride it. One day I was hanging out with Billz, who needed to go to the city. The condition I was in meant I couldn't go, and with our reputation heading to the city would have meant fighting other crews. Instead, Billz took me home.

Anne got me something to drink, hoping I'd stay home with her, but whenever I was drunk or on drugs I wanted to head out with the boys. When Anne fell asleep my never-still mind looked for something to do so I called Billz, who was at the casino.

'I'm coming,' I said. Billz told me to stay home because he knew how crazy I was when drunk, but I hung up on him. How was I going to get to the city when I lived 15 minutes' drive away? I spotted my motorbike keys on top of the cupboard. The last time I had ridden a bike I'd ended up severely injured in a foreign country but, like a big bully picking on a small child in a playground, alcohol stood over my doubts.

I didn't want to wake Anne so I quietly picked up the keys and used my crutches to get outside. For a second I thought about the stupidity of what I was doing. *How could I take my crutches with me?* I put them on the ground and jumped on my bike. The bully had won again. As I sped through the streets I kept the visor on my helmet open so I could feel the air on my face. It saddens me now to think back to that poor soul.

When I arrived at the casino I parked and limped inside. Even through the alcohol haze I could feel the pain. Billz was nowhere to be found, so I sat by myself drinking then eventually I hobbled back out to my motorbike.

The next morning I woke with a groan. As I raised my leg I felt the weirdest sensation, as though my foot was still on the bed. I lifted the blanket and was met by a sickening sight: the plate that held my bones together to repair my leg had snapped, pierced the skin and forced the separation of my shin. Hours later I was back in hospital.

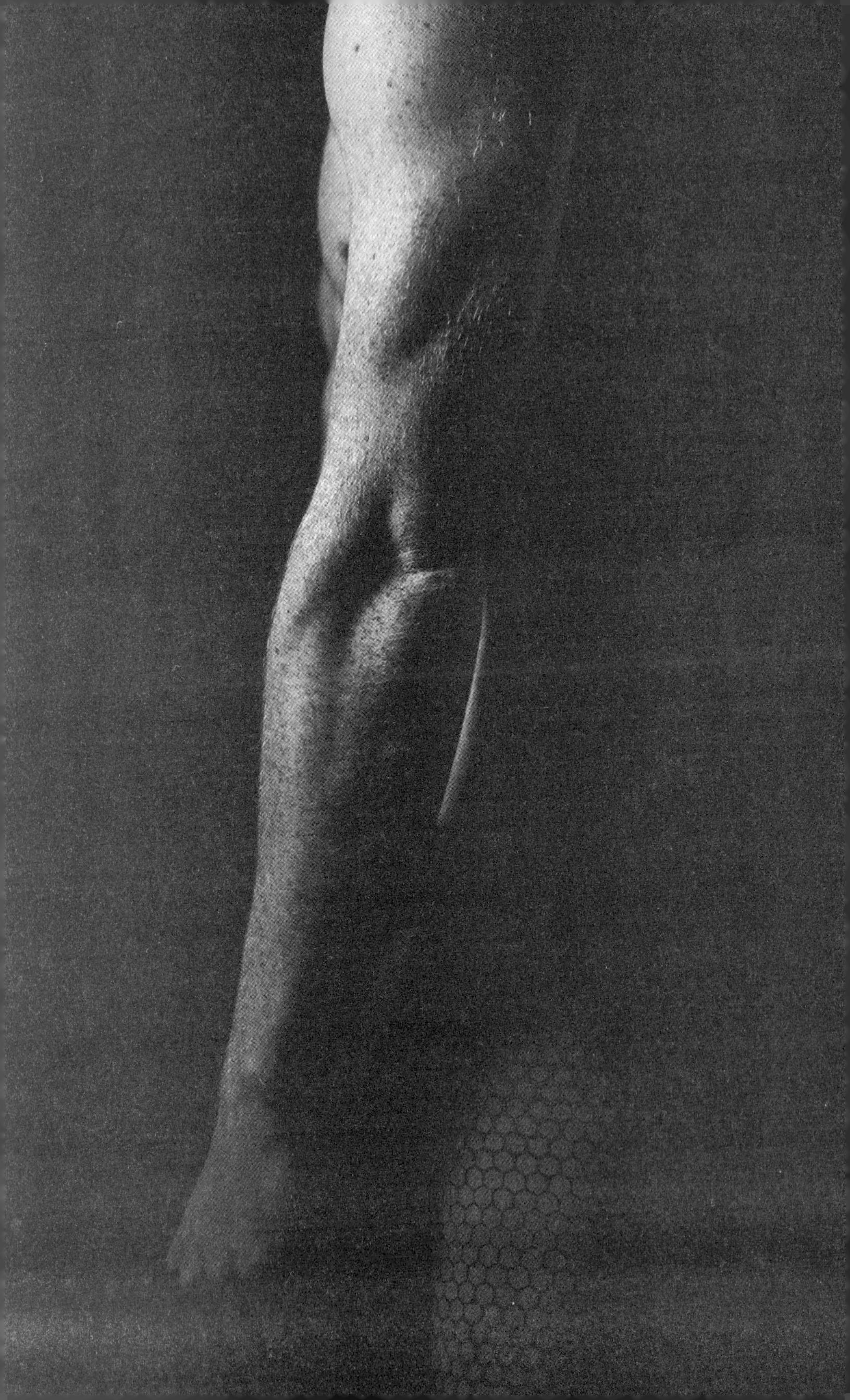

CHAPTER 59

HE'S BACK

After three months of recovery I was back at the start, needing an operation to replace the plate. The look on my parents' faces when they heard the news was a look I'd seen years earlier: utter worry. It seemed that the solid brick wall I'd been building had fallen apart, but what I didn't realise then was that these extreme experiences were actually adding to its strength.

A visit to the physiotherapist convinced me I'd still be able to join the navy. 'You're getting stronger,' he said. 'Start swimming. It'll help even more.'

I hadn't swum in years. When I was overweight I stayed clear of swimming because I didn't want to expose my obese body, and when I was skinny I didn't have the time. Now, like a man possessed, I headed straight for the swimming pool. I was confident of my swimming ability because as a child I'd defeated Ruben in all our races, although that had been 15 years earlier.

I watched as a man in his late 80s dived in and began doing laps. He was going so slowly he might as well have been going backwards. I giggled at his snail's progress and dived in, setting off at a very rapid pace. As I kicked and flailed my arms I glanced to my left to see the elderly man cruise past me.

Spending a few hours in the pool allowed me to justify my drinking, and before I knew it I'd gained 20 kilos. When I looked in the mirror each day I could see my stomach muscles slowly disappearing. I'd worked so hard, but the miserable fat man was back.

* * *

'Hey, Punchy!' Stan said. 'He's back, boys!'

I hadn't been to the gym since the accident. I hugged Stan and all the other fighters; it felt good to be back. The smell in a boxing gym is like nowhere else, as the sweat comes from deep within the body and is brought to the surface only by utter effort and determination.

'So you're back, Punchy?' Stan stood back and checked out my leg.

'Yeah, it's still not one hundred per cent but I need this.'

Over the following few weeks I slowly got back into training, which at least kept me off alcohol for a few hours. I was also scheduled to start back at work and was elated at the thought of getting back into my routine and getting off the alcohol while I waited to hear from the navy. Joining the navy had turned into my dream: it would be my complete escape from everything, a world away from the boys and any chance of messing up, a world where there'd be no temptation. It would be a fresh start, a new me.

I'd promised Mum I'd give up drinking for good and she was desperate to believe again, but her hopes had come crashing down after the accident. 'You watch, Mum,' I told her. All I wanted was for my parents to be happy and relaxed because they'd done so much for me – and they always will. They were still paying off the loan from my accident so I couldn't wait to start working again, but my employer called with some news.

'Luke, your position was filled. We'd love to bring you back on but all we have is a spot on the graveyard shift.' The graveyard shift went from midnight until 6 am from Monday to Thursday, then from 1 am until 10 am on Sunday mornings. It would be a tough gig, but at least it would steer me away from partying. Although I was back training and working I still had to crawl out of that hole I frequented too often.

The first week back at work was tough, but once I got into a routine it worked out well for training. The other boys at the gym had to work all day before training whereas I'd work all night, sleep all day then arrive fresh at the gym.

I found out Anne had cheated on me but, funnily enough, hearing the news was like receiving a big hug – I needed it to break out of once and for all what had become a bad relationship. Anne and I had met when we were only kids, and we'd hung on to each other through some tough times because it was all we had. She'd always stuck by me, but even though I still loved her it was time to end it. I didn't look at it as a lost opportunity; I looked ahead to what I could achieve.

Base let me stay at his place while he was away with the army. I was excited, as it meant I could be alone to get back into my own routine. I thought about how people would react at seeing me fight back and I relished the challenge.

CHAPTER 60

SEARCHING FOR A SILENT MIND

My sister Sarah had a second daughter, Mia. Sarah always makes me smile, and I'd never seen Mum, Dad or Ruben happier than when they were with the girls. Sarah's two precious daughters were a gift to our family.

On one occasion when I went to Sarah's place I'd been drinking, and that night I had a dream in which I won a fight in the ring and the referee handed me the trophy. Before getting out of the ring a man with a white aura around his cloaked body came over and shook my hand, then he leant in and whispered: 'You need to stop drinking.' When I woke up the man's words were ringing in my ears, and I felt as though any decision I made about drinking could be a matter of life or death.

'I'm never going to drink again,' I told Dad when I saw him that morning. Dad nodded his head, just as he'd done all the previous times I'd promised to stay alcohol free and had failed. 'I promise you.' I wanted him to believe it because I did.

'You'd make me the happiest man alive, Luke. There's nothing better than being free of it; my regrets are gone,' Dad said. He'd given up alcohol a couple of years previously. He'd been a terrible drunk, as all of us Kennedys were. When Dad decided to quit no one believed he could, but he managed to achieve it.

During Dad's heavy drinking days he'd often beg me to stop drinking because he knew what it was doing to my life. I'd laugh and say, 'What do you mean? You're getting blind drunk all the time.' He would stop talking and look incredibly disappointed. When he quit alcohol after finding Jesus he led by example, which gave me hope.

Throughout life we often want to help those close to us; however, it's almost impossible to change other people. Sure, we can plant seeds of hope and give tools and advice, but you can't change people unless they want to change. The most important thing we can do to inspire change is to lead by example, to illustrate how great life can be when we've made positive changes ourselves. Often those around us will be influenced by the changes and will make moves in their own lives. If they don't, it's their choice.

Leading by example doesn't mean we have to be perfect, as none of us are. I still make mistakes, but how I learn from and adjust to those mistakes is what counts. We're human and we all mess up, but if you master your fuck-ups you're a step ahead. You can't and shouldn't want to avoid making mistakes and fucking up, because mastery comes from sitting in the mistake, feeling it, dissecting it, observing it and not distracting yourself from the impact or blaming others. Mastery comes from what you learn from mistakes and from noticing the lengths between the messings up and seeing that they are getting further apart. There's definitely mastery to be had in fuck-ups.

I went through some testing times at parties when I had to refuse drinks that were being offered to me. These parties were places in which I'd normally shine, because drinking and having a laugh with the boys were what my ego loved, but my new life was beginning to offer true love for *myself*.

For three hard months I went without alcohol, and after a while the boys finally gave up trying to convince me to drink. Unfortunately, the chatter in my mind was still there but then I remembered my trip to Thailand. A lot of deep moments happened while I was there and a few things in particular really opened me up.

One day after drinking heavily I listened in on a monk who was shepherding a tour and heard him mention something called the 'silent mind'. Even in my intoxicated state, when I heard those words I experienced a feeling of warmth wash over me and I felt as though the words were a part of me. It sounded majestic.

I thought such a thing as a silent mind was beyond my reach but the monk's words stayed with me, so I began to do some research. I picked up Tolle's book *The Power of Now* that Lucas had given me and attempted to read it again. When I'd tried to read it the first time I'd been disheartened; perhaps now would be the right time? However, after reading a few pages I gave up again, as just attempting to understand it gave me a headache. I tried to get a grip on the idea of stillness and awareness but my mind still couldn't – or wouldn't – understand.

I threw the book back into my cupboard and kept searching for answers. I read some more on meditation, peace and love, which I'd grown up believing were things only hippies or people off their heads on acid talked about. I'd tried meditation after seeing the man meditating in peace in the hostel in Melbourne and I'd attempted it in the interview room after getting charged but had never tried it again.

I so wanted to be free of my habitual, frantic thought processes that I continued to search. I found a book on meditation for beginners that said the idea was to sit still and concentrate on breathing. *Sounds easy enough,* I thought.

The first couple of weeks of meditating were frustrating. I'd get angry when I caught myself thinking about other things instead of my breathing or I'd just fall asleep, but I had read that becoming aware of thoughts is a massive step towards being free of them. I stuck with it, and after a while my breathing slowed and so, too, did my thoughts. *Is it working?* I'd catch myself thinking during meditation. A little grin would cross my face as I realised my thoughts were trying to take over, so I would go back to concentrating on my breathing and the grin would remain but the thoughts would disappear.

The books were starting to make a lot more sense to me: I could appreciate what I was reading and how the mind attempts to take over. I only meditated for 10 minutes each day, which was all I needed. Sometimes I'd start feeling tingly all over before a feeling of ultimate warmth surrounded my entire body. I kept my meditation to myself, because although I was making inroads I still wasn't free of the worry about what others would think of me. Sometimes when Base was home and opened the door to my room while I was meditating I'd pretend I was doing stretches.

I speak to people now about meditation, and they tell me they can't meditate because their thoughts don't stop. 'Perfect,' I respond. 'Realising that is the first step.'

Without realising you *have* a thought you *are* the thought – you are the voice in your head. When you separate yourself from it and can see it as something similar to a passing cloud, you can observe the thought then release it by coming back to your breath. The more you do that the more presence comes into your life. The thought really isn't the issue; it's the attachment and emotions that you have to the thought that are the issue.

Some people don't like to meditate because it goes against their religious beliefs. Well, don't meditate – call it 'chilling out and breathing for 10 minutes'. Everyone can do that.

What was going to happen from here? For years I'd been a heartless thug doing wrong by everybody, and now I was trying hard to turn it around again and discover a new life away from the scary, clouded mind of an anxious young man. My leg was almost 100 per cent better, and I put it through some heavy tests to make sure. Besides the occasional sharp pain I was good to go. Joining the navy would complete my total transformation: physically, mentally and emotionally.

CHAPTER 61

NEW PRESSURES

A letter arrived with the Australian Defence Force stamp on the front. *It's about time,* I thought. I'd been ringing and sending letters to ask when I was due to start, but the letter crushed all my hopes. Because of the injuries I'd sustained in Thailand my application had been rejected.

I contested the decision and spent weeks proving my fitness. I had to get new scans on my legs and also a lung-capacity test due to the punctured lung I'd received from my good friend Links's blade. I passed every test, but at the end of it all I was informed that due to the metal plates in my hip and leg I couldn't join.

When the man I spoke with on the phone told me the decision was final I instantly became angry. I was fuming, my mind running through different scenarios. *Fuck this life – I don't need a job. All my mates sell drugs and they have more money than me! Fuck working! Is all this 'doing good' shit worth it? Being the bad boy was more fun. I keep getting bit on the arse trying to do good. Fuck it all!*

I stopped myself. There was a time when I would have headed straight out on a bender, but this time I went for a three-hour run. I still had the dream that had told me to stop drinking firmly embedded in my mind, and I wanted to keep my promise to Dad. As I ran I thought about my life, and in the end I concluded that something good would come out of this.

Where had these positive thoughts come from? Had I always had them but never given them a chance, drowning them instead with substance abuse, or had the meditation opened doors in my soul and shown me that anything is possible if you allow it to be? I didn't know where the positivity came from, but it felt good.

I went to see Mum and Dad to tell them the news in person.

'But I thought you proved you were okay?' Dad said. I could see the optimism on his face.

'Apparently, if you have a plate in your body it's a risk, so they can't take me,' I explained.

'Yeah, but you'd be fitter and stronger than all of them. This is what you wanted, mate. Are you going to fight the decision?'

'I already have; the decision's final,' I said a little more sternly, so he got my point.

Dad was really keen on me joining because he knew how much I wanted it and knew also it could well determine the kind of person I'd become. I'd promised him time and again that I was changing, but something would happen that dragged me back down. It had been more than six months since I'd had a drink or an argument or even eaten sugar. I'd completely changed every aspect of my life, detoxing my body and mind, but Dad knew the temptations a young man faced and had hoped that joining the navy would help me to avoid them.

'Who cares about the navy: you don't need them. It's rubbish, anyway.' Dad always knew when it was a good time to change his mind on something. He'd talked the navy up to everybody, saying what an honourable position it was, but the moment he found out I couldn't go it became the crappiest job going. 'You don't need them,' he repeated. 'You can do whatever you want in life, Luke.'

'Except join the navy,' I said, laughing.

Dad laughed too. 'Well, yeah, except that.'

* * *

'Never mind, Punchy, you're my next champ anyway,' Stan said when I told him the news. 'The state titles are coming up: I think we're in with a chance.'

'For sure, mate, easy done,' I said, smirking.

'I'm putting your name down for them. You've got this, Punchy.'

The state titles ran over a few days. If you won your match you fought again the next day, and if you lost your match it was contest over. I was used to fighting once every couple of months, but for this I'd have to fight for a few days in a row. If it all went to plan, that was. When I told Dad and Ruben that Stan was entering me in the state titles they were pretty excited.

'You know we won that,' Ruben said. It was true – both Dad and Ruben had won state titles in the past. 'Yeah, so make sure you win it. Don't ruin the Kennedy name,' he teased.

'Yeah, no pressure,' Dad joked.

I laughed too. *Imagine that – all three of us winning the same title!* I thought to myself. *It would be incredible! I have to win!* But the pressure felt huge.

I directed all my attention back to boxing. One day when I arrived at training Stan sat me down. 'I found out some information about our competition,' he said. 'A couple of them are going to be easy and another couple have good records, but the one person we have to worry about is Adam.'

Adam was from a reputable fighting gym, and just weeks earlier I'd witnessed him knock out an opponent with a sickening punch. We were the same weight and were both undefeated after four fights. Stan knew Adam's trainer and I think both trainers were hoping to avoid the bout, but in the state titles we would surely come up against each other.

I started training extra hard because I desperately wanted to win the title. I so wanted to live up to the Kennedy name and defeat a hard opponent. *Hopefully he gets beaten before the final,* I caught myself thinking one night before bed. *Don't be a bitch – you got this,* I thought to straighten myself out.

I was warming up at the gym one day when Jake, one of Stan's best fighters, called out to me. 'Hey, Punchy! Adam's trainer bet me a hundred bucks they'd knock you out. I took the bet. I put a hundred bucks on you knocking *him* out.'

'I want half,' I said, laughing, but I had doubts and I was worried. My mind swung between visions of me raising my arms in victory and me raising my head after being knocked out. I couldn't wait for it all to be over.

As I waited for the weigh-in with Ruben on the first day of the titles I spotted Adam across the other side of the room. He looked over at me and I pretended to laugh, trying to look relaxed. When the card was released for the first bouts I eagerly grabbed it to see who I was fighting: not Adam. I won my first fight easily, as did Adam.

On the second day I scrolled through the schedule of fights to see who I was fighting: not Adam. I won again, as did Adam. The next day we were both fighting the semi-finals, so if both of us won the stage would be set for a blockbuster of a final.

'This title is ours,' Stan said, giving me a hug just before the bell rang to signal the start of my semi-final.

It was a tough start to the round, then I landed a strong right hand that knocked out my opponent towards the end of the first round. I didn't celebrate, because I was already thinking of the final. As I walked out of the ring I saw Adam seated and watching with his trainer. Adam also won his semi-final by knockout in the first round.

I was undefeated. So was Adam.

I was in the final. So was Adam.

CHAPTER 62

THE FIGHT OF MY LIFE

The finals were to be held two weeks later and for those two weeks I trained like a machine, leaving nothing to chance. There was a buzz at the gym and I loved being the centre of attention, which at least was for something good this time.

'Am I going to win this bet or what, Punchy?' Jake hollered as I thumped punches into Stan's pads.

I laughed and continued punching, but Stan seemed a little different. 'You okay?' I asked.

'Speak after the session.'

After I finished stretching Stan called me outside. 'Punchy, mate, I'm sorry: I can't be there for the final.' I looked at Stan blank-faced. 'My work's sending me away for a week and if I don't go I'll lose my job. Fuck, Punchy, it means the world to me to see you win but I have to go.'

'It's okay, I understand,' I said. 'Who's going to be in my corner?'

'I've already spoken to Ruben and Jake. They have it covered.'

In the dressing room on the night of the fight I got busy with my own routine preparation. I always wore the same red underwear for each fight and also started with wrapping my left hand first. I was incredibly superstitious at the time. My mind had to know all was well before agreeing I would win.

I heard the door creak open to reveal Ruben and Dad.

'How're you feeling?' Dad asked. He looked concerned.

'Dynamite,' I replied. Dad started massaging my shoulders as Ruben filled a water bottle.

'Boys,' Dad said, gaining our attention. 'Look at what we're doing: we're together preparing for a fight. Seeing my two boys like this, one fighting and the other in the corner, is something I'll remember forever. We've already won, but soon all three of us will have held the same title.'

I looked over at Ruben then back at Dad. He was right: what more could we ask for? I was thankful, and Ruben also looked happy. Now all I had to do was win the title.

As we walked out of the dressing room Jake yelled out to Adam and his trainer, 'Hope you guys are ready: our boy's got this!'

'Yeah, not long now to see who the real champ is,' they shouted back.

I was pumped as I entered the arena. Loud music was blaring and smoke from a smoke machine filled the air. As I walked past Dad he winked at me and nodded his head. I climbed the steps to the canvas, then stopped for a second to look around the arena as I wanted to feel the experience on a deep level. My mind felt clear and I was happy.

'Let's go!' Ruben said, tapping me on the shoulder before spreading the ropes for me to go through.

I did my routine warm up – a few bounces of the feet and some flailing of my arms – as the announcer called out my name. There was a huge cheer from the crowd and an equally loud cheer for Adam. The referee called us to centre ring. I strolled over, reaching the referee just as Adam did. We both stared into each other's soul; it was the first real look at him I'd had. On other occasions I hadn't wanted him to know I was looking at him so I had avoided eye contact, but now he was just centimetres from my face. His eyes were dark brown and he looked confident as a bead of sweat rolled down his cheek.

'Touch gloves.' The ref broke our stare. I turned and walked back to Ruben and Jake, who were standing on the canvas outside the ropes. Ruben siphoned water into my mouth.

'Let's get this hundred bucks,' I mumbled through my mouthguard to a smiling Jake. Both boys punched my glove, wishing me luck.

Ding! Presence.

I walked towards Adam, and we exchanged a couple of punches before getting tangled up in each other. We wrestled a little and I attempted to push him away, but he stood firm and pushed me back before the ref separated us. Adam's strength shocked me: he was a lot stronger than anyone I'd come up against before.

Whack! He landed a good right hand that had my left ear ringing. *Fuck, I'm going to lose.* As my mind started to give in I landed a couple of good shots myself, and the doubting thoughts disappeared. It was only the first round, but the tide changed a few times; it was tough. The bell rang for the end of the round.

'I think he won that one,' Ruben said as he pulled my mouthguard out to give me a breather. As I listened to Ruben I remained standing: I didn't like to sit down on the stool between rounds out of superstition. In one of my fights there'd been no stool available so I'd decided I shouldn't sit in any fights.

Ruben was right: Adam had won the first round. There were two rounds to go, so whoever won two out of three would win the title.

'How you feeling?' Ruben continued.

I kept my eyes on Adam, seated on the other side of the ring. 'Yeah, sweet.' I gasped a little for air. Regardless of the amount of training you do a hard round still buckles you.

'Go to the body more this round,' Ruben said. 'We have to slow him down a bit.' He shoved the mouthguard back in my mouth as I punched my hands together. The bell sounded. 'Go to the body!' Ruben hollered again as I crept forward. An invisible, violent, magnetic force seemed to pull us two fighters together.

The first half of the second round was even. Adam's strength wasn't wavering and he kept coming forward, as did I.

'Body, Luke!' I heard Ruben yell as the ref broke us up after we got tangled.

I faked a shot to Adam's head, which brought his hands up a little, then I bent down and threw a right rip to his body. I felt my fist go deep into his organs and his body tense up, and for a split second he was frozen. For the first time in the fight he retreated so I went forward. The crowd saw me do that and roared, which gave me a skip in my step. Whenever I had a street fight I'd notice my legs skip a little, wanting to hurry up and get the fight over with. Back then I hoped to be victorious so I would win the respect of my crew and gain notoriety in the graffiti world. Now, as I felt Adam give in a little I skipped forward, hoping to make my father proud as he sat watching both his boys in the same team trying to win the title he'd won.

This fight meant more to me than any victory in the street, any train I'd painted, any recognition gained from what I'd done in the past. This fight was my fight to feel good about myself for doing the right thing.

Confidently I steamed ahead. *I've got this!* I thought. The crowd's cheers were deafening. Adam backed up onto the ropes as I went in for the kill. Whack! I felt his hard fist crash into my nose. He'd thrown a huge right hand in the hope it would land so he could get off the ropes. It did. The sound of a branch snapping told me my nose was again broken. My head trembled and I tasted blood. Everything went quiet and I couldn't see. *Am I knocked out?* I wondered.

I shook my head a little and then the sound of the screaming crowd was back – I could hear again. This time, though, they were cheering for Adam's efforts. I felt my legs under me. *I'm not knocked out. Put your hands up,* I thought to myself. I must have been momentarily knocked out while still standing. I threw some punches then we went blow for blow, until I felt the ref's arms come between us to put a halt to the battle. We both looked questioningly at the ref.

'Time out!' the ref said, looking out of the ring at the timer. 'Gotta get rid of that blood.' He put his arm around my shoulder and escorted me over to Ruben, who was already standing up on the canvas with a white towel. Ruben wiped my face clean and pinched my nose a little in an effort to stop the bleeding.

'Besides that shot you're winning this round. Finish strong,' Ruben said, pushing me back out to continue.

Adam headed quickly over to me, thinking I was hurt. I threw a good left–right that rocked him, then he returned with his own. Ding! It was the end of round two; one round to go. I couldn't breathe as I walked back to the corner.

Ruben was smiling. 'I think we won that round.' He pulled the guard out of my mouth. I leant against the ropes, my lungs feeling like they had years earlier when I was pepper sprayed. I felt my stomach cramping – every organ was working overtime to keep me going.

'Ahhh, ahhh,' I gasped, blood pouring down my face.

'Luke!' Ruben yelled. I didn't want to answer as I didn't want to waste valuable breath, but I looked into Ruben's eyes to let him know I was paying attention. 'Man, we gotta dig deep!' he said as he grabbed hold of my shoulders. 'We need to win this round. We might even have to knock him out to win. Do you want to fucking win this shit? Do you?'

'Yeah!' I shouted.

'Well, come on, bro, please!' I could hear the passion in his voice. Ruben was right there with me; my brother was dying to see me win. The bell sounded and I felt Ruben's arms push me forward.

Adam and I exchanged a few more punches each. He was still very strong and was leaning up against the ropes, and I was leaning up against him. His sweaty body shifted to my left a little as he threw an uppercut before trying to throw a left hook. I blocked his hook and threw my own uppercut then we got tangled up, and again I felt the ref's arms come between us to pull us apart.

'Finish strong, Luke!' I heard Dad's unmistakable voice call out over the top of everybody else's.

The ref moved out of the way so the fight could continue. I threw a straight right to Adam's body that dropped his hands down slightly. I brought my right arm back up after the body shot and reloaded it, this time aiming at his unprotected head.

'Sometimes, when you land a shot your arm jars or you hurt your hand, but when you land a flush shot you get a tingle up your arm and it feels as though your arm is weightless. There's nothing like it,' Dad had once told me when we were training in the garage.

I hadn't yet felt that effect, but as my right fist speared into Adam's head I felt my whole arm tingle in pleasure. Adam dropped to my feet as though his legs had been cut out from under him. A deafening roar from the crowd that hadn't registered at first made me realise I'd dropped him.

The ref grabbed hold of me and pushed me towards the corner to start the count on Adam. I wiped the blood clear of my nose and bounced to the opposite corner, a new-found energy buzzing through me.

Adam pulled himself up to one knee. *Stay down, stay down!* I thought, looking over at him. If he managed to last out the round out he could still win. *Stay down.*

'Seven . . . eight . . .' the ref continued.

Adam looked over at his corner and, gaining some strength from his watching trainer, he got up to his feet. *Here we go again.* The ref checked him over, looking into his eyes and making sure he was steady on his feet. The strong bastard was. The ref wiped his gloves clean and stood out of the way to allow the fight to continue.

I have no idea where it came from but Adam fought back, landing some shots. With the round almost over the ref separated us for the last time.

'Almost home, boys,' he said.

Adam and I headed towards each other. Both of us had almost nothing left, but I bit down on my mouthguard and threw an overhand right. The crashing sound of my punch landing on Adam's face silenced the crowd, and his eyes rolled into the back of his head and his legs wobbled. He was falling to the canvas but grabbed hold of me to hold himself up.

I was about to throw an uppercut to finish him off. 'Stop!' the ref yelled, pulling me away from Adam. 'He's had enough!' The ref waved his arms to call a halt to the fight.

What happened? I thought. I looked at the ref's face, and he gave me a little grin and nodded his head. He was congratulating me. I'd won! The ref stopped the fight and I'd won!

'Yeah!' I shouted out very loudly. I threw my mouthguard away and ran over to Ruben, who was yelling out just as loudly. I hugged him, and it was the first time he'd ever hugged me back.

'You did it, bro!' he said.

I turned around and with my arms in the air looked up to the darkened ceiling. It was my own little bit of alone time, just me and the darkness. I felt pure.

'And the winner of the New South Wales amateur title by TKO – Luke Kennedy!' the announcer called as the ref raised my right arm.

I raised my left by myself as I again looked up to the ceiling, wanting to feel every bit of the experience. Dad was standing with outstretched arms by the stairs up to the ring. His clean white jumper soon had my blood smeared across it but he didn't let me go. I felt tears in my eyes and was glad he wasn't talking because I would have cried. Cradled in my dad's arms, I felt his complete love. That's life.

CHAPTER 63

A NEW PATH

Eight months later I was still undefeated in the ring, but something was missing. One afternoon as Stan drove me home he noticed me staring out the window.

'What's going on, mate?' he asked.

I turned my head to look at him. 'I don't know. I don't know what to do with myself.'

'You're kicking arse! You haven't lost a fight!' he said, a little confused.

'I know and I love that, but I need something more.'

'You still down about the navy?'

'Yeah, I think so. Don't get me wrong, I love the boxing, but I don't want to just have the label of a fighter my whole life.' He stopped talking and continued driving. I stopped talking too.

I'd learned about beliefs and the labels we place on ourselves in the books I was reading but I'd never talked about them before, and now it was coming out in my language. I realised as I was sitting in that car that we all live by the labels we create in our minds and these labels keep us away from our true unlimited self.

I looked over at Stan. His label was 'trainer', so he acted and thought like a trainer. Whenever anybody asked 'Who's Stan?', the response was: 'You know, he's that boxing trainer.' *It's shaped his whole life,* I thought, as I looked at him. The labels we place on ourselves – where we work, what we're studying, how old we are, what we wear, even whether we're male or female – shape our actions. Stan was proud of his position and loved helping out fighters. *If I took that label away from him who is he?* I thought. *Who are any of us? Who are we without our labels?*

'Punchy.' Stan broke my thoughts. 'You love helping me out at the gym with the boys, so why don't you become a personal trainer?'

I felt proud that Stan had noticed that about me, because I did like helping. Whenever Stan had too many people to look after in one afternoon I'd get the pads on and call out combinations to an eager fighter looking to hit them. I enjoyed it and got as much of a buzz out of it as when I was just training myself.

'You reckon?' I'd never thought about training people as a career, but now the thought excited me.

'Yeah, for sure. They make good money, too.'

'How do I do it?' I asked.

'One of the boys at the gym did a course last year. I don't know where, though.'

As soon as Stan dropped me home I searched online for personal trainer courses. I called the first one I clicked on to and organised to visit them the next day to discuss the program. That night I was extremely nervous, because I hated meeting new people and imagined a college full of buff, good-looking people waiting to ridicule me. As I sat eating breakfast the next morning I was ready to pull the pin. *Do you really want to do this?* I thought. But something made me go through with it.

At the college I was greeted by a professional young woman who instantly made me feel comfortable. With her I could be completely open about everything, and I told her of my worries about the program and my anxiety about meeting new people. 'Do you really think this is the right industry for me?' I asked.

'You seem like you have a passion for training and helping people, and that's all that's needed. We help with the rest. You'll be confident in no time. I was sitting where you are last year with exactly the same worries, and look at me now.' She smiled a sure smile.

My other concern was time: I had a full-time job and was also training for fights. *How could I study as well?* I thought. It turned out the course was only two nights during the week plus all day on Saturday. I was keen to go.

'You won't regret it,' the woman said as she shook my hand. She was right – I wouldn't.

* * *

'What: six thousand dollars! Mate, you're getting ripped off!' Dad said. 'You sure you want to do this?'

'Yeah, Dad. Don't worry, I'll make the money back easy.' As soon as I walked away, though, I started doubting my decision. Was I kidding myself? On the first day I sat by myself watching the other students chat. I'd expected a class full of young, perfect-bodied and pretentious people but I couldn't have been further off the mark. There were people of all ages, weights and personalities; nevertheless, I'd tense up when I saw someone heading my way and would pretend to be on my phone to avoid a conversation. I hated small talk.

I'd only trained in a boxing gym and mucked around with weights at home, and in the personal training course I learned a heap of new information. It was a massive eye-opener.

One Saturday I was sitting by myself eating my lunch of chicken and vegetables when a lady with a mane of blonde hair surrounding her striking face walked out of the kitchen area. She resembled a lioness. As she made her way into class she glanced back at me: studying suddenly seemed a lot more fun. Her name was Jade, and occasionally she'd catch me staring at her and she'd look away with a slight grin. One Saturday at lunchtime she walked into the kitchen. My body froze a little and I tried to look relaxed.

'Hi,' she said, sitting down next to me.

Because of her looks I was surprised that Jade wanted to sit with me. I had been a fat guy for so long it was taking a while to believe I was anything but that. We ended up laughing and joking for half an hour. I thought she was really cool and cool and sexy were hard to find, so I sat, amazed.

'I used to be overweight. I've lost over sixteen kilos.' She showed me an old photo. I thought she still incredible even then. 'What's your story?' she asked.

'Umm, not much.' What could I tell her? 'I'm a boxer. I love my boxing.'

I still liked to boast about boxing, hoping to impress.

'Ah, I'm not really a fan of fighting. I don't like violence,' she said. I smiled.

We walked back to college together and on the way I threw my rubbish on the ground. Jade bent down to pick it up and I laughed at her disappointed look. 'What's the big deal? Why are you picking it up?'

'It's for the greater good,' she said.

'What do you mean?' I asked.

'It means doing something good for the universe, not the individual,' she said quietly. 'It may not benefit you personally but it may benefit the human race as a whole.' I had never heard of such a thing: most people I dealt with did everything for their own gain. When I heard this girl say that picking up rubbish helped the world I thought she was like a saint. 'It isn't why I do it, but if you do good things for others it will come back to you,' she continued.

I haven't dropped a piece of rubbish on the ground since.

That night I searched Jade's Facebook and 'Liked' some of her photos. She did the same to mine.

'Brother, check out this chick! She's liking my photos! She's keen as!' I said to Base.

'Fuck, she's hectic!' he said.

'Yeah, I reckon so too.'

A test was coming up at college in which I would have to instruct another student in front of the class on how to do an exercise, but the thought of having to stand up in front of people smashed my face with sweat. I couldn't handle it. When I was out of my comfort zone in new group situations and without the confidence of being a crew leader or in the gym as one of the main fighters, I couldn't breathe. I'd stutter and forget what I was talking about. I studied the exercise endlessly, but nothing registered in my brain because my thoughts were stuck on being in front of a whole bunch of people talking.

On the night of the test Jade noticed my nervousness and gave me some much-needed advice. Then we split up into small groups and soon it was my turn. With four students and the teacher watching, I walked over to the machine. For the next three minutes my head felt as though it was steaming hot as I stuttered and mumbled my way through the worst exercise instruction possible.

'Luke, you need to come back tomorrow night to give it another go,' the teacher said afterwards. I'd failed! I felt incredibly embarrassed.

That night I spoke to Jade. 'I'm finishing. I don't think this is for me,' I announced.

'What do you mean: you love your training! Why not get paid for doing it?' Jade shot back.

I tried to excuse my quitting attitude. 'I can't even show a classmate how to do an exercise without almost dying of nerves. How can I do it with a client in a gym?'

'Give it a shot, you can't stop now. Besides, who would I hang out with?' Jade knew how to get me.

The next night I reluctantly arrived at college to give the test one last try. The teacher who'd failed me the night before gave me some tips so I felt that I was ready this time. I aced it! Practice and failures make perfect.

'Hey, I passed!' I excitedly told Jade over the phone that night.

'I knew you would,' she said.

'I'm glad you convinced me to stay. I owe you one, so let me take you out for dinner,' I blurted out.

Jade was silent for a moment. 'I'd love to,' she said, finally. I'd asked Jade out and she'd accepted! Once I knew a woman was interested in me I radiated confidence.

On the night of our date I stood in front of my bathroom mirror. I slipped on my collared polo shirt. Usually, I'd pop the collar and convince myself I was looking sharp, but this time the collar stayed down. *I'm a new person,* I thought as I stared at my trim, respectable-looking reflection.

'Look at you, my man!' Base said when I walked into the lounge room.

'Yeah, looking all right?' I asked.

'No wonder she's keen on you, mate.' He put his arm around my shoulder.

Jade was going to pick me up in her car. As I had been an alcoholic for most of my teens and early manhood I never got a driver's licence. It was probably the smartest thing I did during those times; I just didn't trust myself with one.

'You look great,' I said, kissing her on her cheek after climbing into the passenger seat. Her white dress revealed just enough leg to tease me. *What's she doing with a fat thug like me?* I wondered again. It would take some time to be free of my old self-image.

As we drove I watched as Jade's beautiful face was illuminated by passing street lights. I'd been nervous leading up to this dinner. *What if it gets awkward?* I wondered. *I better take some mints – I don't want my breath to smell. I hope she thinks I'm smart. I don't want to look like an idiot.* My mind was at it again. *Maybe I should have just one drink to take the edge off. Nah, don't be stupid!*

It had been more than a year since I'd had a single drop of alcohol and I didn't want to break that, and I found that as I sat across from Jade in a Thai restaurant in Newtown I soon felt perfectly relaxed. Our conversation didn't stop – it was amazing. I felt as though I was catching up with an old friend: a sexy old friend. I looked past her at the pub across the road, the same pub Billz and I had had the fight out the front of only a few years earlier. I couldn't have been further from the person I was then.

On the night of our first date we kissed. Jade's soft, gentle lips left me warm for days and from then on I started spending more time her. Some nights I'd head back to her house in Bronte, where we'd chill out before she drove me to work. I felt at peace at her place and often stayed there on weekends.

'I love it here,' I told her one Sunday.

'I love having you here.' She smiled her gorgeous smile.

'I just feel different when I'm out these ways. When I'm back in my area I have too many old memories. I walk past places where I had a fight or something and it just brings back old feelings. I get a bad energy.' I'd told Jade about my past. At first she'd found it all hard to believe, but after running into some of the boys she realised I was indeed a different person compared with who I was now.

'Why don't you move here, then?' she asked.

'Really?'

'Yeah.'

'Umm . . .' I laughed. Jade giggled and tensed up with excitement, then she gave me a hug. 'Let's see what happens,' I said.

CHAPTER 64

YOU ARE YOUR ENVIRONMENT

A full-time job, studying and training were keeping me busy. I liked the discipline and was spot on with my routine, and the graveyard shift worked in my favour big time. Not that I would have ventured out anyway, but it was another reason I couldn't go out. I worked from midnight until 6 am then slept until 3 pm. After I woke up I'd head to training with Stan at 4 pm. I'd finish at the gym at 6 pm and would ride my pushbike home and relax before doing it all over again. I'd sold my brand new motorbike to help pay for some of the loan Mum and Dad had had to get to sort out my Thailand disaster.

One night at work I heard a crashing noise: a delivery driver who'd just dropped off a container full of equipment had tripped and fallen down the stairs. He was lying on his back staring at the ceiling as I rushed down the stairs to his aid. His eyes were wide open and his top lip was perked up as though he was about to say something. He looked as though he was wondering where he was, and blood trickled from his nose as his eyes continued to look into mine.

With a calm release of breath his perked lips rested. He stared right through me with his dead eyes. He had just had his questions answered; his cadaverous face knew more than my lively one. Someone had already called for an ambulance when a co-worker broke up our somewhat romantic interlude.

'They're asking if he has a pulse.' I touched the driver's already cool neck, feeling for a little thump through his skin, but I knew that he'd departed on a one-way ticket.

'No,' I said.

My co-worker had a phone to his ear. 'They said to take him off the stairs and lie him flat.'

I picked up the driver's limp arms and started dragging his lifeless body off the stairs, still looking at his face. His soulless eyes continued to speak to me, the emptiness of them telling me he had now left this world. I knelt down; I couldn't stop looking into his eyes. He was gone. *Where?* I'd always questioned death, often asking people what they believed happened when we died. As I was searching for the answer myself I liked to hear people's ideas on the subject, hoping that by asking often enough I'd find the answer. I still ask those questions and continue my search.

That morning after getting home I felt good. I didn't have any bad feelings, but when I realised this I got angry with myself. *A guy just died! Do you even care? Of course I care, but it doesn't have to get to me,* I argued with myself. I'd often question my empathy and get annoyed if I felt as though I didn't care. *Relax. You do care. You just don't let things get to you,* I'd try to reason, which would make me feel better.

I'd hoped that as I cradled that man, just as I'd cradled my young friend Deny, he'd come back just as Deny had come back despite losing his arm. Deny had been lucky: he had survived and gone on to live a normal life, eventually opening up his own graffiti and hip-hop store out west. We'd catch up from time to time, and he always thanked me for saving his life. I'd feel like a fraud when he did, because I had been the reason he'd been there in the first place.

When I told Jade the news she was shocked. 'Oh my god, babe, that's terrible! Are you okay?'

'Yeah, I'm fine. Really, I'm okay.'

'Far out, I don't know how I'd handle that. I've never seen a dead body,' she said, in a scared voice.

'I have. That doesn't really scare me. What scares me is thinking about dying.'

'What do you mean?' she asked.

'I mean, I don't really think about what I saw, but I do think about dying a lot.'

'You mean your own death?'

'Well, yeah, that, and also what happens after we die. I mean, does everything just stop? Now that scares me.'

'I think you should go see someone,' Jade said, with a concerned look on her face.

I laughed. 'Relax, I'm fine. Seriously, it doesn't bother me. I've seen this kind of shit my whole life.' The week after the accident my employer also suggested I see a counsellor to talk it over. After thinking about it more I was excited by the prospect: perhaps I'd get some answers.

After a bit of a chat the counsellor asked me about my life and I gave him a brief outline. He just nodded his head. It felt great to talk about my life with a person who was there to listen. Usually when talking about myself I'd speak really fast and mumble, because growing up I'd sometimes hear from Dad about someone: 'All that guy does is talk about himself. He's just a big noter,' so when I spoke about myself I thought I was being judged and would get my words out quickly. With the counsellor I was at a place where I was meant to talk about myself, and it felt good to get some things out.

He asked me what I wanted from life, a question I thought I knew the answer to although I had to think for a while. 'I want a relaxed life away from all the drama.'

'What does that mean for you?' the counsellor asked, wanting me to elaborate.

'Even though I have changed my life around I still get caught up every now and again.'

'How do you mean?' he asked.

'Well, even though I've changed it's hard, because I still see all the old crew on a weekly basis and the temptations are always there.'

'How have you changed?'

This guy is good, I thought. 'I still have the same terrible thoughts about fighting and other bad things but they are lessening. Also, I don't act out on them any more.'

'So you're suppressing your anger?'

'No, I don't think so. The anger is nearly gone but the thoughts are still there. You get me?' He didn't say anything. 'I mean, the thoughts spring up but my automatic attack response is going.'

'Going?' he asked.

'Yeah, going. It's nearly gone, but I still have to fight it. I've been meditating and it helps big time.'

'Why do you think it helps?' he asked.

'I concentrate on my breathing when I meditate and it relaxes me. When I feel the bad thoughts or anger come on I look for my breath and it instantly calms me down.'

'So you still see your old crew? You know how important your environment is, don't you?'

'Um, I don't understand.'

'If you're hanging with a bad element you're going to pick up on its energy and it'll make it harder for your new thought processes to flourish.' He was right – when I hung out with the boys even my language changed. 'Can you move away?' he asked.

'What: to another state?'

'No, just out of the area,' he said, as though it was a simple task.

I sat and thought for a while. *Just out of the area? Where to?* Then it hit me. 'You know, I'm seeing this girl from the Eastern Suburbs. She wants me to move in with her.'

'Is she different from those you hang around?'

I told him the greater good story. Judging by his nodding head I think he was happy.

* * *

'I'm moving in,' I told Jade over the phone.

'Yay!' she said.

When I went over to Mum and Dad's to tell them they were both really happy for me. 'That's great, mate,' Dad said. 'I can help you move your stuff if you like.' Mum and Dad thought Jade was perfect, and they were right.

When I first started going out with Jade I hadn't wanted her to meet them. Family is everything to me, and if they didn't like her it would have devastated me. I also wanted to avoid being embarrassed, as Dad would crack jokes and carry on and I didn't know how Jade would take it. As it turned out Jade got on with Mum and Dad from the second they met, and I knew there and then she'd be the girl I would marry.

CHAPTER 65

NEW CAREER

I was still nervous when I had to demonstrate exercises in front of people, but the more I did it the easier it became.

'What do you want to do when we finish college?' Jade asked me one day.

'I just want to train enough people to be able to quit work.' In my full-time job I was clearing $550 for a 40-hour week, and there were 15 hours of travel. I was looking forward to getting away from that.

'That's it?' Jade asked, a little surprised.

'Yeah. I mean, I want to make more money – that's what I want to do first.' I realised straight away it was a limited goal. I had known Jade for a few months and I could see how much of a go-getter she was. She'd listen to personal development audio tapes by motivational speakers such as Tony Robbins, then she'd call me with different plans she had for success.

'Babe, you have to listen to this stuff. It changes lives,' she'd say.

One day I listened to one for a few minutes then switched it off. 'What a load of shit that is,' I said. Jade just smiled.

College was due to finish soon, so I began to think seriously about what I wanted to do with my qualifications. I called a friend who was a personal trainer at a gym nearby. 'Bro, I make close to three thousand a week. I can get you a job here,' he said.

However, when I told Jade I had an interview at the gym she didn't seem so excited. 'I thought you wanted to do it on your own?' she said.

'I do, but where can I start? I mean, where will I do it?'

'If you want to do it alone we'll make it happen.'

I was a little disappointed she didn't like my decision to work at a gym, where I'd have been making more than four times the money I was on at the factory and for fewer hours, but Jade knew our power together was unlimited and that I just needed to believe it.

I went to the interview and was proud of how I handled myself. They called later to say I had the job and that there'd be an upfront payment of a few thousand dollars to get me started. *Where would I find that kind of money?* I thought. Nowhere, that's where. It was impossible for me because I didn't have a cent to my name and couldn't borrow it. I was crushed.

I probably would have been able to find the money somewhere, but I suppose deep down I knew I shouldn't work there. That decision – not working for someone else – opened my life to unfathomable amounts of growth, challenges, successes, failures and beautiful relationships.

'Don't worry, babe,' Jade said. 'Everything happens for a reason.'

I told Stan what had happened. 'Hey, you can use the gloves room to train your clients in,' he said. The gloves room was where all the boxing gloves were stored; it was no bigger than a prison cell.

'Thanks, mate. I appreciate the offer but I don't think it's big enough,' I said.

'Mate, it'll be okay. Anyway, it's there if you need it.'

Not long after a colleague approached me at work. 'I hear you're a trainer. Can you train me?' he asked.

'Sure. Come in for a free consultation and we can have a chat,' I said, copying some of what I'd heard at college.

'Cool. Where?'

'I have my own studio at the gym where I box.' I guess I was taking Stan up on his offer.

Jade was just as excited as I was that I had my first client. Together, we spent hours clearing out the gloves and cleaning up the room, and when we were done I looked over my new studio. There was no real equipment and no ventilation and I had no confidence that people would want to train in it. What it did have was stained carpet, a set of boxing gloves and pads, a mirror and a portable radio to at least make it sound like a studio.

The night before my first consultation I couldn't sleep because I was sick with nerves. *He's smart. He'll find out that I don't know what I'm doing.* If the other person was older than me or I thought they were smarter my confidence would plummet. I'd be inside my head the whole time, hoping they didn't think I was stupid.

I got to my gaol cell–sized studio two hours early to rehearse the session and paced the room, so much so my legs got tired. When my victim arrived I got him to fill out an exercise questionnaire. He looked around the room, confused, before sitting down. He seemed keen to get into the training – until I started the session. My theory was that people love to see themselves progress in training, and with that in mind I decided to do a whole range of awkward jump and timing tests. The first exercise was a long jump from a standing start, but as my client wasn't warmed up he didn't jump too far.

I pulled out a tape measure to check the distance, but the tape wasn't long enough so I needed my client's help to hold onto one end. Next was a vertical leap test for which he had to jump up and touch a spot high on a wall. He jumped pretty high, so high I couldn't reach, so I had to leave the room to find a step ladder. The whole session was filled with awkwardness and he left without breaking a sweat. I, however, was sweating up a storm with embarrassment. Needless to say, I never trained him again.

Jade laughed uncontrollably when I told her, and we both decided that I'd practise training her first. I got a friend to take a photo of me training Jade and posted it on Facebook with the heading 'Jade training hard, getting super fit'. Jade *is* fit and toned, and I soon got three inbox messages from people asking if I could help make them look like Jade.

'Jade, it's all happening! Heaps of people want me to train them,' I told her, exaggerating.

'Of course they do, babe! You're inspirational. Look what you've done with your life!'

We spoke for a few minutes more, but even after I'd hung up the phone her words stuck with me. 'Look what you've done with your life!' I laughed. *What have I done?* I thought. *I lost weight – big deal!* My mind cut me down. *You've changed your whole life around; you help people now. This is what you asked for! You're going to be successful.*

'You're going to be successful! I shouted into the mirror. Wow: that made me feel good!

I called Jade back. 'I need a business name.'

'What do you want to call it?'

'Punchys PT,' I said, proudly.

'But isn't Punchy known for the wrong reasons?' I could tell Jade didn't think it was a good idea.

'Yeah, but I want to change that. I want Punchy to be known for being positive. I know that it'll work: I have power.' I laughed. 'Seriously, babe, I know it'll work.'

That weekend Jade helped me make a logo, then we put together a business card. When the cards were printed I was in awe. 'Punchy' was on a business card. 'Punchy' was now turning into something that helped. I quickly got so busy training people my own training had to take a back seat.

'Luke, this is your new career. Take time off your boxing and get into it,' Dad said. He was right: I was running myself into the ground with everything and some time away from fighting was needed.

I knew that if I held a boxing class I could get a large amount of people to attend. I searched for a hall to hire and found one in Penshurst, then I saved for weeks to get enough gloves and pads for 50 people to attend. I set my goals high from the start. As in the graffiti game I wanted to be everywhere, so I spent any spare time I had handing out business cards and a new brochure we had had designed and printed.

I couldn't leave my equipment at the hall I was hiring and I still didn't have a driver's licence, but luckily Kon lived quite close by.

'Of course you can leave your stuff here,' he said. I hadn't seen him for at least a year and it was great to catch up. Even though growing up together we'd had our moments when we came close to literally killing each other we were still close, and now with my guard down and not trying to outdo him we grew even closer. Whenever he was with others and discussing crime I kept my distance, but when we spent hours together chatting over lunch Kon could be pretty deep and I enjoyed our conversations.

In return I offered to train him. I knew that, for me, training kept me disciplined and positive and I hoped it would do the same for him.

'Yeah, sweet, Punchy. Train me in boxing, then I might be able to get revenge for you bashing me that time in the park.' We both laughed.

I called all the boys, because I wanted Stintz, Chad, Mick, Base, Snap, Kon and everybody else I knew to come for the launch of my boxing session. In fact, I begged everyone I knew to attend. Scared doesn't describe how absolutely petrified I was. I was someone who felt sick at the thought of talking in front of a couple of people and now I would be instructing a whole room full. *What have I gotten myself into?* I'd never forgotten totally screwing up at college, and I had my doubts.

'Relax, babe, you'll be fine,' Jade said.

On the day of the launch Jade left work early so she could help me set up – I actually think she wanted to make sure I didn't take off running – then the first couple of people arrived. Nervously, I showed them to a table to fill out forms. Pretty soon the hall was jam-packed: I had 44 people at my first group training session. All the boys were there.

'Okay, guys, we're warming up with some upper cuts.' With that, the session started. For the next 50 minutes I felt pumped up with energy. When I noticed people struggling to keep going I jumped in to push them a little harder. People were laughing and having a good time and I was on cloud nine.

'And done.' With those words, I heard a collective sigh of relief. People rolled on the floor in exhaustion because of my efforts!

'That was great, Punchy!' Base said afterwards. Numerous other people came up to say it had been the best routine they'd ever done. You couldn't wipe the smile from my face for days.

CHAPTER 66

OUT OF MY COMFORT ZONE

I was training people full time so I quit my full-time job. I was still without a car and travelled everywhere by bus and train. My gaol cell/training room was a fair distance from the train station and my late sessions would go past bus running times. If I couldn't get a lift from my last session I had a 45-minute walk ahead of me, which was crushing after a long day. Two days a week I'd head to the hall where my group session was held, then take three trips back and forth to Kon's house to gather all of the gear. That took more than an hour. After the boxing session I had to repeat the three trips to take the stuff back. I worked hard.

I was meeting new people on a daily basis, which helped with my awkwardness in fresh situations. I was confronting and changing all of my limiting beliefs from the past. Jade had advised from the get-go that I needed to work on my personal development to overcome my nerves, and she gave me some more audio tapes to listen to. 'These changed my life,' she said, as she downloaded some Tony Robbins onto my phone. However, I couldn't get my head around how the things being said related to my situation, although I now realise it all relates. One Tony Robbins audio tape I heard on confidence did actually help me.

I confessed to Jade one day that I hadn't put any brochures in shops because I was worried about how I'd look. I didn't want people to think I was a nuisance or, worse, a salesman. 'Fucking salesman, they're all con artists,' Dad would say when I was growing up. I didn't want to be known as a con artist.

'Let's make a plan, then,' Jade suggested. We decided I'd approach just a few shops in a local shopping centre so the next day I sat in the food court listening to my audio tapes in an attempt to psyche myself up. 'Okay, let's do this,' I grunted to myself.

I walked past my first target in an attempt to scope it out. An employee stood behind the counter as a customer browsed the shelves. The lady behind the counter noticed me looking in her store as I walked past. *Cover blown*, I thought. I'd come up with any excuse not to go in, justifying it by thinking I'd go in next week.

With my first opportunity blown I went back to listen to the audio tapes before attempting again. In this particular audio there was some great advice and information on caring less about what people think. It was this: when it all boils down to it, we live just once. Do you want to worry about other people's perspectives for your whole life and never live in the moment? After listening, I was ready!

I decided to not think about what I was doing and just walk straight into the next store, which sold health foods. With brochures in hand and backpack on, I darted straight in without giving it a thought. My quick moves turned into a light stroll as two employees stopped what they were doing to stare at me. I smiled an unsure smile. They were looking at my brochures.

'Fucking salesmen.' I could hear Dad's words in my head. My face boiled and I gulped what little saliva I had down my dry throat. I stood for a few seconds without saying anything, hoping I'd wake up from this nightmare.

'Um, do you have the little cherry-flavoured protein bars?' The shop staff looked at my brochures then back at me.

'Yep, they're just under the counter in front of you,' one said.

I grabbed a protein bar, but my hand was shaking and I dropped it. I bent down to pick it up and put it on the counter. It felt like I wasn't breathing. 'Just this, thanks.' My voice was shaky.

The shop staff looked as though they were waiting to hear the real reason I was in there. They handed me my change and I turned to walk out of the store. 'Oh, is it okay if I leave these here on the counter?'

They both cracked a smile. 'Sure, that's not a problem. We'd love to help.'

I couldn't give them the brochures fast enough before disappearing out the door; I felt like an absolute idiot. When I called Jade to tell her what had happened she laughed for what seemed like 5 minutes before she was able to compose herself. I chuckled along with her. 'I'm proud of you,' she said. 'I know how hard that was for you to do.'

I've since learned that with anything I worry about doing I need to just do it. My mind now finds it tough to make up stupid excuses and scenarios, and once the task is over I feel amazing. My pure self, which knew better, was starting to shine.

CHAPTER 67

TESTED

I was excited about how things were going: I'd met the most inspiring lady and she loved me, and I had my own business that helped people. However, although I didn't know it my new outlook was about to be tested and my new life threatened.

I was eating lunch with Chad and Stintz in the same food court where days earlier I'd listened to motivational audio tapes before entering the health store to ask if they'd take my brochures. I was telling the boys how hooked I was on Jade, and as they could see how keen I was on her they were happy for me.

'She's a life changer,' I said.

'Settle, Punchy. You've only been with her for five months,' Chad said, laughing. His womanising ways always had him doubting relationships.

Eventually, we stood up to leave. I grinned – I was the only one who'd picked my rubbish up from the table. We walked through the food court, and out of the corner of my eye I saw somebody I recognised. As we passed him he turned away so I couldn't see his face, but I knew who it was.

'Links!' Chad said, quickly.

'I know, keep it down,' I said, heading in Links's direction. If I'd been by myself I'd have kept walking. I didn't want this, but being with the boys meant I felt compelled to show force and get the revenge I'd promised for years I would get.

Links walked over to a table where a man and woman who were probably his parents were seated. I ran behind a pillar.

'Come here, boys,' I whispered. For the first time in a long time my body seized up and I felt the sickening nerves I always had before a street fight. We were in the middle of a food court, and there were shoppers and security cameras everywhere to witness the upcoming mauling.

'You want me to jump in too?' Stintz asked.

'No, leave it. I want him for myself.'

'You think he saw you?' Chad queried.

'I don't know. Let's just wait until he finishes eating and walks past,' I said. I was breathing deeply, readying myself for a ruthless attack. I envisaged being locked up and Jade deserting me, but I couldn't bitch it. If I didn't get Links after talking about it for so long imagine what all the boys would say.

When I look back at the incident it astonishes me that I was about to jeopardise a peaceful life with Jade just so people wouldn't think I was a coward. I know now that other people's thoughts about you shouldn't determine your actions, and that when we realise this and fully allow it to be we are free. However, there I was standing behind a pillar about to throw my life away, a life that was shaping into something special.

'He's walking over,' Chad said, peeking around the pillar.

I took off my backpack. It was as though my bag, which was filled with brochures about my first business, represented my new, honoured life. I didn't want it to get mixed up in this shit. I looked at the bag and felt embarrassed for what I was about to do; it was weird. I looked up at the boys and waited for my gaol sentence to reach us. I waited and I waited, my mind buzzing with tense energy and my fists clenched.

'Have a look: see if he's coming,' I whispered to Chad.

'Fuck, he's gone.' Chad cried out. Links had seen us behind the pillar and had feigned heading in our direction before making a quick escape while we were hiding. If Links had stayed it would have meant death for him, and it would have killed my life. My heart smiled and my body relaxed. This would be a turning point, I decided. I would never let another person's opinion control my actions.

I called Jade straight after and headed to her house, where I felt safe. I just needed to be with her, as her innocence about violence and conflict calmed me down.

'What would you have done if he had walked over?' she asked.

I didn't want to answer, and I didn't want to lie to her. In the past I'd been in relationships that were built on nothing but lies, so I had promised myself I'd be totally honest in any situation with Jade. 'I wouldn't have stopped.' I sat with my head down, not wanting to look up and knowing my answer didn't represent who I was now.

Jade hugged me tightly. 'That's not you.'

It wasn't me; I knew that. Even though I was in the process of releasing the labels that nearly ruined my life, being so attached to them and having no time to contemplate my actions meant I'd been ready again for battle, ready to risk my freedom, my new career path, my new life-saving girlfriend and my family's sanity just because my mind felt threatened. But it was all made up! To any readers who might be sitting in a gaol cell or thinking of doing a crime, I ask why? Is it because you are worried about the thoughts of other people? Did you beat someone down because they made you look bad?

Most if not all crimes occur because a person's mind makes things out to be worse than they actually are. Nothing is wrong except those things their mind makes up. If someone has made you look bad, who cares? Only the mind does. It's an illusion the mind creates so it feels alive, but the pure soul knows different. The pure soul feels the warmth of love. That's what life is.

Do you feel safer or happier when you're being hugged or talking about something you love? That's the soul at work. It will get beaten down time and again by an incessant mind and have you doubting things, but if you're aware of the mind taking over you can smile and be happy in knowing your awareness will soon lessen the insane mind's power.

Jade gave me a hug that wished my spirit greatness. I opened the cupboard in my room to hang up my jacket, and as I tried to close the messy cupboard something got stuck in the door. I looked down: *The Power of Now* was holding the door open as though it was calling to be noticed. I opened the book and started reading and didn't put it down for three hours. With each page I turned I felt lighter. My mind, which had written the book off on previous occasions, took a back seat to my quest for answers. It was not for my mind to understand but for my heart to feel.

When I eventually put the book down I looked around the room, taking the time to further feel what I'd read. My mind had been either regretting something in the past or worried or excited about something in the future for so long I had never truly lived a moment. To live in the moment is to live life. Seeing with my mind's perspective for so long meant I saw things the way it wanted to rather than the way things actually were. I'd been anxious or depressed for years because of incessant thinking about the past or the future, what people had done or thought and what people would do or think. When I looked around the room that day I became aware that the present moment was the only thing that was real.

CHAPTER 68

FREE FROM THE FIGHTER'S LABEL

I started reading anything by Eckhart Tolle and watched a heap of his YouTube clips, and could feel my mind relaxing with every word. I also started to make more changes in my life, forgiveness being the first step. I never felt so restful and calm as the day I let go of my angst towards all those who had harmed me. They were battling their demons just as I was, and now I was aware of it.

I saw it as being my responsibility to start the shift towards self-awareness within my group. The first thing I needed was to be freed from the violent fighter's label, so I searched for Links – this time to forgive him. I found his profile on Facebook and sent a private message to him: 'Hi, mate, how have you been?' I just hoped he'd respond, because I'd been hunting him down for years and knew he'd be hesitant.

'Hi,' came his reply.

'How have you been?' I asked again. The sound of my finger hitting the enter key signalled the start of a whole new path into my true self. I was ridding myself of the fighter persona and felt serene in the fact that I didn't have to defend a false ego that had been conjured up by my mind.

'Yeah, good. I know you can't forget about what I did to you but it was self-defence. What else could I do?' he messaged back.

'Mate, I'm sorry. All is forgiven.' I didn't get a response.

After forgiving Links I imagined him showing the KS boys the message, which made me feel even better. Before my anxiety would have had me tensing up, stiff with worry that they'd think I'd backed down, but now I felt light as a feather. I'd been desperate for retribution for so long I had no way of being at peace. I had always looked forward, thinking I'd only feel fulfilled after I paid my enemy back. With no pressure of backing my fighting name the pearly white gates were opened and my heart streamed with total pleasure. I looked around the room. I was calm and didn't have a worry in the world.

I was sitting at home relaxing with Jade one Saturday when my phone rang. 'Hey, brother.' It was Stintz.

'My boy! How you doing, mate?'

'Hear about Chad?'

'What do you mean?' I asked. I could tell something big was up.

'His house got raided by police.'

'Ah, no way! How big?'

'The biggest, brother.'

'What happened?'

'Murder.' Chad had been charged with shooting someone in the head and killing them. I was silent. 'You there?' Stintz said.

'Stintz.' I broke my silence. 'This is why you've got to keep up with your training. You need to stay out of all that shit. You can take your boxing to the next level. You've got it, brother!' I'd been training Stintz: he had won his first fight convincingly and also won fighter of the night, and I knew that if he were disciplined he could have the world at his feet. He was talented and strong, but sometimes he'd go off doing the wrong thing and miss training for weeks.

'You're right, Punchy.'

As I hung up the phone I remembered back to when Stintz went to gaol after being pulled out of the roof following the break and enter. I recalled Chad's words when he noticed my sad look: 'Don't sweat, Punchy. It's going to happen to all of us anyway.'

Chad, the young, blond pretty boy I'd been so close to, is serving a life sentence.

* * *

After winning the state title in 2009 I had been awarded Amateur Boxer of the Year in 2010. I'd stopped fighting when the business started to take up most my time, but because I was so close to all of my clients they knew of my success in the boxing ring even though they hadn't seen me fight. With my clients I had the tough-guy fighter's image as well as being known as a good person, but it seemed God knew that for the greater good and for my own benefit I needed to lose the fighter's label once and for all.

I eventually started boxing training again, and when it was time for my first fight many at the gym were excited to come and watch me. The stage was set for me to show off and reign victorious. Before the fight as I was warming up in the dressing room I felt out of place – it wasn't for me any more. I walked out into the ring to loud applause and saw all my friends and clients there with expectant faces, ready to finally witness my fighting ability.

To cut a long story short, I got beaten. Not only did I lose the fight, but I fought terribly – I looked like a complete novice. After the fight I didn't want to leave the dressing room to see all the disappointed faces. Reluctantly, after an hour, I walked out. My friends couldn't have been happier for me; the fight didn't matter to them.

On the way home with Jade I was a mess of anxiety as I imagined what everybody thought of me. I felt like an utter fraud. I'd been talked about as a fighter, and in the first fight they saw I could barely hold my hands up in defence. For the next week I couldn't sleep. I stared at the ceiling, reliving every moment of the fight and hearing the voices of those watching. I thought they no longer respected me. Any time boxing came on television or came up in conversation I'd change the channel or talk about something else.

My association with it had changed: I loathed it because it reminded me that other people would think I was a failure. I'd stopped meditating for a couple of weeks before the fight as my training took priority in the mornings but now, needing meditation more than ever, I sat with my eyes closed. All I could see were my opponent's hands in the air as he was awarded the win. I had glimpses of stillness, though. It was all I needed.

One night in bed as I stared at the ceiling I had an awakening: losing the fight was what I had needed to enable me to step back to purity. God was telling me to let go, that I could finally be completely free of the macho image. What felt at the time to be an embarrassing, devastating event was actually a supportive release to my true and pure self. This fight, although extremely tough at the time, turned out to be another step towards the true me. It helped me detach even further from the worries about what other people think of me, and I am happier because of it.

CHAPTER 69

NEW GOALS

I organised to have lunch with my two main men, Base and Snap. 'I'm asking Jade to marry me, boys,' I announced.

They both stood up with smiles on their mature faces and gave me a hug. 'We love you, Punchy. We're so proud of you.'

For the next few months I secretly saved money to pay for an engagement ring.

'Okay, time for some goal setting,' Jade said one day, excitedly. We were sitting on a grass patch near Coogee beach, and Jade had come prepared with cardboard and markers. I smiled at how cute she was as she carefully wrote 'Goals' at the top of the large white piece of cardboard. I leant back and took in the sun. Jade noticed my relaxed approach to it all and said a little sternly, 'Luke, this is important. Sit up. Okay, what's your ultimate goal?' she asked as I giggled and succumbed to her sweet, threatening tone.

I sat up and looked at the beach; I really didn't know. 'I want to make ten thousand dollars a week,' I said to break the silence. I laughed, but she didn't.

'And what does that mean for you?' she pressed. I had always wanted to help my parents out of financial stress because they'd been there for me my whole life and supported me through some really tough times.

Jade and I worked on our goals for nearly two hours, and by the end of it I could see the impressed look on her face. Afterwards I felt really light, as though putting those goals down on paper meant they were actually going to happen. One of my main goals was to find my own premises. I'd outgrown the small room Stan had let me use and needed a bigger spot with equipment. It would also help solve another problem, which was the fact that I was an absolute wreck from exhaustion.

Now that I was living further away I was waking up at 3.50 am to get to the studio in time for four or five one-hour sessions in the morning, then I'd head out by bus, train and on foot to distribute my brochures. My back was forever in pain from carrying the brochures. After spending a few hours marketing myself I'd return to the studio to do my evening sessions, hoping my last session would give me a lift to the station. Two nights a week I'd get the train to the next stop for the boxing session. This had gone on for over a year until I finally got my licence, which was like receiving a vehicle sent from the heavens. I couldn't believe the freedom! *Now I can rest more,* I thought. Nope: I just headed further away to spread my name and rested less.

After seeing how tired I was Jade reminded me of our goals. 'We have to find you a different studio, one that's more professional and comfortable for you. Imagine if you had a spot where you could rest between sessions?'

We sat down again to look over the goals and how we were tracking. The two months we'd set ourselves to find new premises was just about up then, as though looking over our goals again was a cue for it to happen, the very next day something popped up. In fact, I believe that by setting goals you radiate what you want. Emanating an energy that others can pick up on makes things happen: ask, and you shall receive. Usually after leaving the makeshift studio I'd drive straight home, but one time I stopped to get something to eat. It was a decision that changed my life. I ordered and stood, waiting. After putting my order on a plate, the older Greek man behind the counter turned to me.

'How you been?' he asked.

'Yeah, good thanks. Very busy,' I said.

'Yes, you do the training,' he said, in his broken English.

'That's right, mate. I have a studio,' I said.

'Have you thinking about moving?' He shocked me out of my daydream.

'I am, actually. Why do you ask?'

'Around the corner, above supermarket. It hasn't been taken for long time, very big.' He didn't realise the power of those words.

I grabbed my piece of fish and walked around the corner. Above the supermarket was a 'For lease' sign. This building where I would soon create something huge in a positive way stood only metres from a wall where I had started a career that involved violence, crime, drugs and death: same setting, same person, different mindset; quantum difference in outcomes. A change of mind was all it was. We all have the power to create anything we want, and all we have to do is decide to change things and keep making steps towards it. Changing my mind would show me what life was really about.

I rang Jade. 'Babe, I've found the perfect spot, but it's nearly eight hundred dollars a week. I think we can do it, though. It's big, it's in the best spot . . .'

'Ring the real estate agent and organise an inspection,' she said.

That weekend we met up with the real estate agent and had our first look inside. The place had previously been a ladies' gym and had dark purple and pink walls. Minus the colours it was absolutely incredible. Before walking in Jade had told me not to act too excited if we liked it so we played it cool, but once the agent left we leapt into each other's arms and screamed in excitement. 'It's ours! Let's do it!'

Jade had been doing endless work for Punchys PT on top of her full-time job. She'd work on my marketing and promotional material and I'd get her to call around places to find out information for me. Even though I'd been undertaking training for some time I still got nervous talking on the phone, whereas Jade didn't. We talked about the possibility of her coming into the business full time, which I knew would catapult our success. However, it was a huge risk.

Jade was renting her own apartment and had debt up to her eyeballs. If she quit her job the business would not only have to support my life and outgoings but would have to take on Jade's. It was a risk we were willing to take, especially considering the amount of work she did for the business. First, though, we decided to speak to our accountant about it.

'That's just silly, guys,' he said. 'Jade's making a hundred K per year and still isn't on top of her debts. Where are you going to find this extra hundred K in Punchys PT?'

Well, shit, when you put it like that maybe it wasn't the best idea after all.

'Screw him, babe! We'll show him,' Jade said, as we exited the building. That was Jade – she liked to take a chance on things and didn't appreciate people telling her she couldn't do something.

I loved her take on the world attitude and agreed, but I had butterflies in my stomach. Nevertheless, Jade quit her job and came into Punchys PT full time. It's amazing what a little bit of fear can do to your enthusiasm, but with Jade at the gym working on getting things running properly, I could see us going places. When Jade met people or spoke to them she radiated confidence, and I hoped one day I could have confidence like hers.

The first thing Jade wanted to do was some rebranding, as she felt my old logo was too macho and wouldn't attract ladies. She lined up a meeting with a designer, who asked us a bunch of questions to get a sense of the business and our message. The way he spoke mesmerised me: he talked about how different colours generate different emotions and how colours we like may be seen differently by our target market. I looked over the colour chart and suggested my own colour combinations.

'Wow, you know your colours! Have you done design before?' he asked.

'I guess you could say that.'

'Okay, so what does Punchys represent?' he asked. I chuckled to myself as I looked out of our windows over to the wall. If he'd asked that question a few years earlier it would have been a different answer. In the end we dropped the PT and renamed the business Punchys Training and Nutrition.

When I set out on my personal training career all I wanted to do was help people and have fun doing it. As I had been overweight as a child and teenager I knew how limiting it could be. Life for me was now about having a laugh with good, fun people, and without knowing it I was setting up an environment that would change countless people's lives. By radiating positivity and happiness we attracted like-minded people to the gym, and Punchys soon felt like a family. Some of my best friends now are people who were first clients.

CHAPTER 70

LIFE

I married Jade at the most breathtaking wedding in the beautiful town of Berry on the south coast of New South Wales. The night before the wedding I stayed at a house with all my main boys. Stintz could only come for the ceremony the next day; due to his bail conditions he'd have to leave before the reception.

My main boys, Base and Snap, stood by my side at the altar. As I waited for Jade I looked around the church. Mum and Dad sat side by side, and as Mum glanced around at everybody her smile stood out. She looked beautiful. I had five of my closest boys in the wedding party: Base, Snap, Ruben, Lucas and my childhood friend Ivan. When the music started I looked back down the aisle. There were the flower girls and page boys – my two nieces, Jade's nephew and Snap's young boy. Then I saw her standing at the back, waiting – my angel. Time stood still as she walked towards me.

'You've done well, brother,' I heard Base whisper into my ear.

I shook my head a little, unable to believe the woman of my dreams was walking towards me. Once I would have gotten off on someone like Jade even just saying 'Hello' or looking at me. How life can change if you want it enough. Suddenly, I felt a rush of ecstasy. I felt weightless, totally present. I caught myself in the moment, and for the first time I knew I was living.

'Wow!' I said as Jade reached me. I couldn't take my eyes off her for the entire ceremony, enthralled that this perfect person wanted to be my wife. By marrying Jade I'd not only affirmed my relationship with the woman

I loved but also married my new life. One of the best things about our wedding day was seeing my parents enjoying themselves, happy that their troublesome son had turned his life around.

Our lavish wedding was paid for by the business I had started with my new wife. That business, Punchys Training and Nutrition, went on to win best start-up in the Asia/Pacific Business Excellence Awards and was a finalist in the best customer service category. The award ceremony was a black-tie event at Darling Harbour's Exhibition Centre. I bought my first suit an hour before the event, and Jade laughed as I watched videos on my phone to learn how to put on my tie.

The success of our business lay in the fact that both Jade and I were on an authentic quest to help people both physically and emotionally. The environment we had set at our gym was one of support and happiness and the results we achieved were close to remarkable. Those training with us appreciated that we'd walked on the same weight-loss road. The feeling I got from seeing people's lives change for the better because of our efforts was something I couldn't explain in words. But, then, why would I want to label it anyway?

EPILOGUE

SO, WHAT NOW?

It's been over a decade since we started the gym and there have been many changes in my life – some of which are still hard to believe, but they were meant to be. As I prayed every night during the heavy times I felt as though I was being looked after. I should have been dead or ended up in gaol many times, but it was as though a guiding hand was detouring me around and splitting me apart from what wasn't serving my purpose for being here. It seems that the heavy changes of the past 10 years were an extension of that: at the time they were tough but, again, it was a guiding hand at work.

The battle through my past – surviving two stabbings, one puncturing my lung and the other scarring my head forever, drug and alcohol abuse, obesity, deaths and almost killing people myself – all of that was the easy part. Sure, it was heavy times, but I was numb to it all. There wasn't the tiniest bit of empathy in my body: I was a wrecking ball and really wouldn't let much get in the way. The stabbings were fair enough; it was my fault anyway, but as mentioned that was the easy part. Nothing, absolutely nothing, comes close to the heart-wrenching tearing of soul: the tears, failures and mistakes and the yearning for understanding in my day-to-day dedication to spiritual seeking, self-discovery and betterment of self in every area. This was where the true battle of life was. The gang shit wasn't in the same dimension of heaviness that I've been through to find myself, to understand why I'm here.

The journey of self-discovery came at a big cost, but I wouldn't change the outcome for anything. It was all worth it. I had to literally break away nearly 20 years from an ego that had its filthy fingernails dug tightly around my soul. I chiselled one claw away at a time only for it to return even more deeply. Without dedication to a pain that felt like death – the pain of losing a mind-made self, of detaching from labels, beliefs and a closely held self-image – I wouldn't be where I am now. I've made many mistakes and while I'm still alive mistakes will continue to be made, although I will never allow those claws to return around me.

Growth doesn't come easily, but mediocrity does. The hard growth is worth it.

* * *

Jade and I are no longer together although we are the closest of friends. She means the world to me and I'm super proud of her. So many things happened during our time together and we always had each other's backs. Starting Punchys came out of our passion to help people after going through our own weight-loss processes, but with the stresses of running a financially struggling business and many other things going on our passion for each other left us. We tried everything to get it back, but it turned into more of a friendship than anything else. I believe from the outset we were meant to be together, but together doesn't have to mean intimacy. The growth Jade introduced to my life is something I'll thank her for forever, and if you ask her I think she'll say the same about me.

Society's bullshit rules supreme. Worrying about what other people think and ego all tell you you can't be friends with your exes, let alone ex-wives. It's lucky I don't follow those types of rules, as many of society's rules hinder unimaginable amounts of happiness and prevent lasting relationships. I'm often asked why I'm not jealous when I see this amazing woman speaking to another guy, and I tell people that jealousy comes from attachment. Attachment is the root cause of any pain:

- Attachment to life: you're scared of death.
- Attachment to relationships: you're in pain when you're separating or are worried about being alone.

- Attachment to possessions/money: you have anxiety about making money and get depressed if you lose something.

All pain comes from attachment. If you release attachment to outcomes you can be content.

Don't get me wrong: I was wholeheartedly in love with Jade and I still am, but now she's not mine and I'm not hers. I'm not jealous when I see her with another guy because she's her own beautiful spirit. Relationships change; life changes; feelings change. Passion and sparks for each other leave, and there's nothing wrong with that. We tried everything to make it work, but in the end we had to let go.

If I'd cared about what other people had to say when we separated I would've lost one of the most important people in my life. I've been asked what would happen if I met someone and that person wasn't open to me being friends with my ex-wife. I laugh, because I wouldn't have someone like that in my life anyway. Everyone is different and people are triggered by different things, so I respect that it may not be for most people. However, I honour and respect what's aligned with me. We went through so much together and I'm just supposed to toss that connection away? She's my go-to whenever I need anything. Even though she lives in another state we still chat a few times a week. All she does is make me laugh and helps me to be a better person.

Jade is now an online coach, helping women change their bodies and minds with a holistic approach through support, mindset coaching and nutrition and training. I'm not surprised about the results she gets: you just have to look at how much growth she introduced to my life.

* * *

Punchys Gym is gone. The building is now a child-care centre, and when I'm in Sydney and drive past a bunch of memories come flooding back. From the start the business wasn't really profitable, but the energy it gave us – and it took a lot – the lessons learned and relationships formed all made it worth it. Starting and running a struggling business taught me so much about myself and showed me where a lot of my insecurities were still based.

When Jade and I separated there wasn't enough money in the business to support two single lifestyles. I suggested we close up due to what it was doing to our stress levels with zero money left at the end of the week, but she wanted to try to turn it all around. I decided to leave the business but was still involved with helping out from time to time. A lot happened before the final closure, but with debt building up Punchys had to close.

It was a hard process to go through: I had to borrow money to do the right thing by the employees and to close the place. There were also rumours going around that we had done the wrong thing by our members, and after putting 10 years into forming a strong and supportive culture that was tough to hear. People believed that we sold our membership to a nearby gym so we could close up with a profit, but we actually gave our memberships to a nearby gym so they would honour some of the members who had paid upfront. No doubt things could have been done better, but everything happened quickly and decisions had to be made to ensure our members could be moved to another place.

We closed Punchys after 10 years of gut-wrenching effort, in debt and with people believing we did the wrong thing. Even so, it was all worth it.

* * *

I still see Snap from time to time and it's always great to catch up for a couple of hours and chat about life. He's doing incredibly well with his business and enjoys a quiet and simple life with his wife and two kids.

I don't speak to Base any more. We all change or we don't, morals shift and values don't align and that's okay. He was a close brother to me for more than 20 years.

Stintz is doing solid. He's out of gaol and training hard on his physical body and, most importantly, his mind. We catch up for coffee or a training session when I'm in Sydney.

The rest of the crew I see a few times a year, usually at a funeral. Some have gone on to be successful business owners and there's a heap who have become well-known rappers. What I love seeing the most is that many have become incredible family men. Others are just doing their thing and taking each day as it comes.

I went to a funeral recently that a lot of the old crew attended. Looking around was a bit of a trip, seeing the faces of my old friends – once young and not so innocent faces illuminated by a train's lights as we filled it with colour. Now they were mature and had wrinkles and greying hair, but still with the same cheeky laughs and smiles. Like me, all the scars on their bodies told the story of a life once lived that, for some, was still being lived. When I'm with them I can feel a little of the old Punchy coming out to get among the laughs and give each other shit.

* * *

I went to a boxing match one night in the city, and the place was packed with all the old heads and up-and-comers. I sat with the main boys, and it was interesting to observe myself sliding back into the role of being one of the top men. I enjoyed the feeling when people came up to nervously introduce themselves and watched myself flexing by giving a few of the other main men some shit, just to show my strength in position.

'We're proud of you, brother. What you're doing with your life and how you're helping all those kids: it's mad, brother,' one of the boys said as we got some one on one time.

'You'd fuck them up, Punchy,' someone else interrupted from behind after witnessing the boxers in the ring.

I felt the energy of being proud of myself with what I've done with my life, but that was mixed in with a powerful authoritative energy of being known as a man who could still knock you out. The fighter label isn't fully gone, because the feeling of power is all encompassing. It feels good to be powerful, which is why people can't let it go. It's a power over others, though, and although it might feel strong it's the mind-made illusion of strength.

Real strength is spending time alone figuring out who you are and what you want to do with your life: that's strength. Having the ability to spend years bettering yourself: that's strength. Focus and discipline: that's strength.

Understanding traumas and working through them: that's strength. Having the ability to say 'No' when you don't want to do something: that's strength. Helping people without expectation: that's strength. Needing help for yourself and asking for it: that's strength. Being there for your family: that's strength.

Believing you're strong because you have power over others: that's weakness.

When the night at the boxing match with the old boys was a couple of hours in and they were a few drinks down, I noticed the bickering between us starting to wear thin and the hungry ego starting to look for heavier stimulation, so it wasn't long until the attention went to people outside the crew.

'Ya fuckin' dogs, what are you looking at?' one of our boys said, in a menacing tone. I looked over to the table of people they were talking to, a table filled with men chatting under their breath and possibly having a quiet word about how they were going to respond. As I sat there with that energy I started to think about what I'd do if the ego volcano exploded. *These are my old friends; I can't run away. Would I just break it up? I haven't hit someone in the street for 15 years: can I even still fight? I don't want to hurt anyone. Imagine getting locked up now. For what? Settle down lad,* I reasoned.

'Fuck 'em, Punchy, they've been staring at us all night.'

I sat for a little longer to give myself enough time to work out the best move.

'I'm off, lads. You gotta get up early if you wanna help save the world. Love you all.'

* * *

After this book was first released in late 2014 a schoolteacher read it and asked if I could come and speak to the students about my journey through addiction, mental-health issues and becoming successful. 'Successful?' I laughed inside. I was broke. The gym looked successful to the outside world but we were in debt. Jade and I were sharing a car, and there were nights after working 17 hours a day when we couldn't afford dinner. Successful?

I was a little hard on myself. Looking at where I had come from to what I was doing then, even though the money wasn't there the progress and changes I had made were out of this world. My measures of success then were all financial, but since being in and around money and having seemingly successful people around me I've witnessed a lot of their lifestyles and I don't believe that's success. It's great to have a truckload of money, but if you're stressed and miserable and finding your happiness in outside sources then what's the point? Success for me now is mental health, peace of mind, happiness and living true to my purpose . . . plus a heap of money, ha ha ha. The money did come when I started to focus on the other stuff.

After what I had been through, to be asked to speak at a school felt like success to me. I said I would do it and was given four weeks to prepare. I had come a long way, but the idea of speaking in front of a bunch of students about my story had me losing sleep. As I sat down to draft a cancellation email and tried to come up with an excuse I paused. *What would I talk about? There're heaps of bad guy gone good stories, why would mine be any different? What would have helped me at school? What will help them?*

Once I began to focus my attention away from how I was feeling and what it meant for me and started to feel into what it meant for the students listening and how it could benefit them, my nervousness started to drop . . . a little. It wasn't about me. *How could I help those who may be going through the same internal struggles I used to go through? Would they even listen?* I didn't want to come across as just another stooge trying to tell them what to do, so I wanted to use the heaviness of my stories to grab their attention and create a connection and then weave the messages throughout.

What messages, though? What had helped me? It was about becoming aware of the true self and false self. It was about how I realised most of my decisions had been governed by my worries about what other people thought about me. My resilience got me through it: how? What about the importance of my environment and how that impacted every aspect of my life, and also my body-image issues, mental-health practices, bullying, the impact of negative self-talk and beliefs. I needed to mention how important it is to focus on and take care of yourself first. How could I communicate all of that in an hour, plus my own story to keep them hooked?

I stepped up and pushed through my worries and nerves, and after a few weeks of rehearsing and designing my slides I was soon standing in front of Year 10 students at Georges River College in Hurstville. Halfway through the talk I noticed a couple of teachers had impressed looks on their faces and were nodding their heads at each other, and there wasn't a word coming out of the students as they stared at me. *Wow! I'm actually doing this and they're loving it!*

After the talk a bunch of students came up to speak to me and ask questions, and some teachers interrupted to thank me before they took off for their next class. One of the teachers asked if I could have a one on one chat to one of the students who was having some heavy thoughts and going through a heap of drama.

'Of course,' I said, although inside I felt pretty nervous. I had a great presentation, but I didn't know how to really listen to a young guy and help him. *What if I say something wrong? I'm not a psychologist: what do I do?* Thoughts were running through my head as we both entered the room. I sat with him for about 20 minutes, and I listened to him speaking about his journey more than anything. I gave him some advice, and he gave me a strong handshake and thanked me.

'We haven't seen him interact like that with someone before. You're great at this! How long have you been speaking with students for?'

'First time.'

From there my speaking career took off. I spoke at schools all across Australia, and pretty soon I was holding sessions for parents in the evening after speaking to their children during the day, and I'd also hold sessions for teachers and staff that focused on resilience, dealing with change, reducing stress and implementing self-care practices. The student/teacher/parent sessions worked incredibly well together, as not only were we all on the same page with language and topics after the talks but it showed the parents how their own self-talk and labels they'd placed on their kids and actions taken could dramatically impact their kids' mental health and confidence.

I now speak not only at schools but also at large corporate events and prisons. Initially, I didn't feel my talks were suitable for primary school students, and while I PG my story for them I still go in-depth regarding the masks we wear and negative self-talk. The angle I go with is around self-bullying, and how bullying in your own mind can result in anxiety, social awkwardness and reduced confidence. The young ones are so much more aware than we give them credit for. They're actually more aware than anyone else because they haven't been on this earth long enough to be fully conditioned by all the beliefs and social structures. They're in their purest state, and that's what I like to bring their attention to and ask them to hold on to – and it's working.

The corporate events have been hugely successful as well. I've spoken at some of Australia's biggest companies, entrepreneur forums, leadership events and even at Parliament House. After most of my talks or workshops I'm proud to say that the organisers and teachers tell me it's the best talk they've seen. Life's a trip.

I was due to speak in Sydney for Optus, one of Australia's biggest telecommunications companies, and when I arrived I parked in a back street and a load of memories vividly jumped into my mind. It was the same street where 12 years earlier I had been at a rave and stood side by side with my boys as we brawled with a rival crew. I sat in the car for a while reliving the memory. I laughed, but then I was overcome by an immense sadness. I don't see any of those boys any more. Many are dead and some are in gaol, while others are irreparably damaged. We were just kids.

How things have changed.

* * *

I tell Mum and Dad every day that I love them. What they did for me as I grew up – and never giving up on me – is something I can never repay. I try my best to, though. They're still happily married and living a simple life, and they absolutely adore their grandchildren.

My bro Ruben has recently had his first child, a little boy: Ruben Junior. The way Ruben has stepped up as a father is something I'm incredibly proud of him for. His whole world is his little boy, and it's been amazing to watch how much he's changed to become a strong and supportive dad.

My sister Sarah is living a happy life with two beautiful daughters, Allana and Mia. Sarah works hard to support her family, and the way she has raised her daughters blows my mind. My little sister is a beautiful woman who does anything for her children.

We're all still close. After everything we have been through as a family we Kennedys have a beautiful bond and we will always be there for each other.

* * *

For me life is great, and I love that I get to travel the country most weeks to speak and connect. However, I've been single for about seven years and I'm fully open and ready to have my own family.

Moving out of Sydney was something I never thought I wanted to do or would do, but when I finally made the move it was one of the best decisions of my life.

People often ask me why I'm so positive and happy. After being through what I've been through, how could I not be?

ACKNOWLEDGEMENTS

First I'd love to thank my amazing parents, Rube and Diane: throughout the years you've stood by my side and never stopped showing me love. If it wasn't for you I don't know where I'd be.

My brother Ruben and my sister Sarah: I'm super proud of you both. You've shown me what it means to lead a family of your own.

A massive thank you to a great man who dropped into my life recently and made the biggest impact on me: Dan Regan. The integrity and values this man upholds are something I haven't experienced before, and it has demanded my own huge levelling up. I thought I had a lot of things sorted, but the growth this solid brother has instilled in my life is something I'll be forever grateful for. Thanks, brother!

Lisa Hanrahan and the amazing team at Rockpool Publishing: the professionalism and speed with which you guys work really is something special. I'm honoured and excited to have been given the opportunity to work with you to get *Redemption Road* and *Sex, Drugs and a Buddhist Monk* out to the world.

Alex Smit is another great man I'm lucky to have in my life.

A huge thanks to the staff of the General Store at Byron Bay, who would let me sit in their spot and write the words you are now reading. Love the Genny!

All the amazing people who have followed and supported me throughout this journey: you know who you are.

Last, and certainly not least, I'd to thank God for all of it. Blessed.

ABOUT THE AUTHOR

Luke Kennedy, one of Australia's most sought-after public speakers, uses his personal story to inspire profound, lasting change and self-awareness for a wide range of audiences, from primary and high schools to businesses, special events and even prisons.

For eight years of his life Luke was an obese alcoholic and drug-addicted thug. He led a violent street-fighting crew and was stabbed on two separate occasions: once in his lung and the other time in his head. On the outside he looked strong and confident, even happy at times, but on the inside his thoughts haunted him. He was incredibly scared, depressed, anxious and paranoid and was obsessed with what others thought about him.

After losing 50 kilos Luke turned his life around through the disciplines of sport, as a state champion boxer, and business, and also through a constant desire to progress in every area of life: spiritually, emotionally, mentally and physically. Along with being a motivational speaker he is an author, mental-health advocate and mentor to troubled youth.

www.lukeskennedy.com

ALSO BY LUKE

SEX, DRUGS AND A BUDDHIST MONK

A stepping stone towards a silent mind

ISBN: 9781922579218

Sex, Drugs and a Buddhist Monk is a memoir that tells the story of a fateful (and nearly fatal) trip to Thailand that started in debauchery but ended in enlightenment.

A severely obese, depressed, anxious alcoholic and drug abuser, Luke Kennedy was trying to get his life together and reset his life when he ventured over to Thailand for one last hurrah. He partied hard and overdid it, and his path collided with prostitutes, drug dealers and violence. This is an action-packed story about a fight to escape violence and deal with a monk that forced Luke to confront his demons.